BLACK
PIONEERS

Henry Reynolds is the author of nine books, including *Why Weren't We Told?*, *Aborigines and Settlers*, *The Other Side of the Frontier*, *The Law of the Land*, *Fate of a Free People* and *This Whispering in Our Hearts*.

Born in Hobart, Tasmania, in 1938, Henry taught in secondary schools in Australia and England after receiving a Master of Arts from the University of Tasmania. On his appointment as lecturer at the Townsville University College, he was responsible for setting up the program in Australian history. He is currently Research Professor at the University of Tasmania and is the recipient of an Australian Research Council Senior Research Fellowship.

Henry Reynolds is married to Margaret Reynolds, a former senator for Queensland, and they have three children: John, Anna and Rebecca.

ALSO BY HENRY REYNOLDS

BLACK PIONEERS

HENRY REYNOLDS

PENGUIN BOOKS

Penguin Books Australia Ltd
487 Maroondah Highway, PO Box 257
Ringwood, Victoria 3134, Australia
Penguin Books Ltd
Harmondsworth, Middlesex, England
Penguin Putnam Inc.
375 Hudson Street, New York, New York 10014, USA
Penguin Books Canada Limited
10 Alcorn Avenue Toronto, Ontario, Canada M4V 3B2
Penguin Books (N.Z.) Ltd
Cnr Rosedale and Airborne Roads, Albany, Auckland, New Zealand
Penguin Books (South Africa) (Pty) Ltd
5 Watkins Street, Denver Ext 4, 2094, South Africa
Penguin Books India (P) Ltd
11, Community Centre, Panchsheel Park, New Delhi 110 017, India

First published as *With the White People* by Penguin Books Australia Ltd 1990
This revised edition published by Penguin Books Australia Ltd 2000

1 3 5 7 9 10 8 6 4 2

Designed by Erika Budiman, Penguin Design Studio
Front cover photograph *'Missus' and servants, Springsure District, c. 1912*
courtesy of John Oxley Library
Typeset in 12.5/16 pt Perpetua by Midland Typesetters, Maryborough, Victoria
Made and printed in Australia by Australian Print Group, Maryborough, Victoria

National Library of Australia Cataloguing-in-Publication data:
Reynolds, Henry, 1938– .
Black pioneers.
Bibliography.
Includes index.
ISBN 0 14 029820 7.
1. Aborigines, Australian. 2. Aborigines, Australian – Social conditions. 3. Indigenous
labor. 4. Employees – Australia. 5. Australia – History – 1788–1900.
I. Title.
994

www.penguin.com.au

CONTENTS

ACKNOWLEDGEMENTS

During the years of research that preceded the publication of *With the White People* in 1990 and in the ten years since that time, I have been assisted, encouraged, informed and inspired by a great number of people.

I owe much to the many elderly indigenous people, mainly around north Queensland, who trusted me with their stories, and to younger Aborigines and Islanders who talked about the lives of their parents and grandparents.

I have read the work of many fellow scholars, have heard their lectures and discussed and argued about issues of mutual interest. Among numerous colleagues I would like to acknowledge Bain Attwood, Jan Critchett, Heather Goodall, Geoff Grey, Anna Haebich, Ros Kidd, Marilyn Lake, Noel Loos, Anne McGrath, Russel McGregor, Dawn May, Peter Read and Debra Bird Rose. My friends at Penguin have been, as ever, helpful and professional. Jean Willoughby once again converted my longhand into a useable script.

INTRODUCTION

THE RECONCILIATION MOVEMENT of the 1990s has brought together thousands of Australians from all parts of the country and all walks of life – young and old, men and women, black and white. It is both like and unlike the earlier movement for amendment of the Constitution, which culminated in the referendum of 1967. This, too, was a broad coalition which embraced indigenous and non-indigenous people and which drew support from all over the Commonwealth. Reconciliation is both more ambitious in scope and less focused in purpose.

A further difference between the two movements is the relative importance given to history. The 1967 campaign sought to remedy the neglect and injustice enshrined in the two offending sections of the Constitution, but otherwise the past itself did not appear to be of much concern. The emphasis was on the future and the successful incorporation of Aborigines as equal citizens within the Commonwealth.

But the 1967 referendum was held just before the start of a dramatic rewriting of Australian history that can be conveniently dated from Professor W.E.H. Stanner's 1968 ABC Boyer Lectures entitled *After the Dreaming*. Reconciliation has been informed by the historical work of the last 25 years expressed in many genres – books, plays, films, paintings, songs. For their part, indigenous people have insisted that reconciliation must begin with a retelling of history to incorporate the Aboriginal and Islander experience. They expect white Australians to be honest about the past, to admit the truth about the devastation which followed in the wake of settlement. Many of the activists engaged in the reconciliation process relate their involvement to an engagement with history – to the discovery of the fact that white Australia has a black history and that they had never been taught about it as part of their formal education. In many parts of the country, reconciliation groups have addressed their own regional histories by conducting research, rewriting the local stories, and arranging for monuments and plaques to commemorate the events of an often troubled and turbulent past.

Reconciliation, then, has been propelled by a response to the past as much as by expectations for the future. The movement's critics have picked up on the historical emphasis and have often been as critical of interpretations of the past as they are of prescriptions for the future. In the process, history has been pushed into the centre of the political stage.

The prime minister, John Howard, has added his support to those who reject what has come to be called 'black-armband history', with its emphasis on the tragic story of European–Aboriginal relations. Such a focus, they argue, diverts attention from the achievements of the settlers, undermines national pride and threatens national cohesion.

The conflict is real and circles around some major points of disagreement. There is, for instance, the matter of violence. Traditionally Australia has been depicted as a peaceful place. It is a pleasing image – a continent without war and bloodshed, a land of peaceful settlement. The new history presented a profound challenge to this idyll. It emphasised the ubiquity of frontier conflict, which, while scattered and sporadic, lasted from 1788 until the 1920s. It was estimated that 20 000 and more Aborigines were killed, that massacres took place in which men, women and children were indiscriminately killed. The idea of settlement itself was called into question and replaced in many minds with the more uncompromising term 'invasion', although this is a description that others vehemently reject.

Land ownership has also sparked controversy. The long-held and comforting belief that Australia had been a *terra nullius* ran easily through both the community and the courts. It provided the agreeable assurance that when the British arrived at the end of the eighteenth century the continent had been there for the taking, that as nomads the Aborigines had no legal or moral claim on the land. The land had been

acquired by the British but not appropriated from the indigenous people. The British Crown, therefore, was not only the
legitimate, but also the first, owner of the land.

These ideas were dramatically up-ended when the High
Court recognised native title in the Mabo judgement in
1992, to the consternation of many people who felt a venerable legal tradition had been recklessly rejected by a court
bent on following politically fashionable discourse. The
judges' use of history was vehemently condemned by con-
servative commentators, who bristled when they read
references by Justices Deane and Gaudron to a legacy of
'unutterable shame'. The controversy surrounding the Mabo
case was overshadowed by the uproar which greeted the High
Court's 1996 decision in the Wik case, which found that the
ubiquitous pastoral leases did not necessarily extinguish
native title, suggesting that Aborigines retained vestigial
rights over much of Australia's vast and productive rangeland.

The launching of the Human Rights Commission's report
into the separation of Aboriginal and Torres Strait Islander
children from their families, *Bringing Them Home*, in April
1997 added further to the gathering storm of contention.
The report documented the state, territory and federal
government policies that had resulted in a large-scale process
of removing children from their families. It provided both
verbatim reports and summaries of testimony given by those
removed. It was widely read and much discussed. The sugges-
tion made by the authors of the report that Australian

governments had acted with genocidal intent in pursuing their policies whipped up another storm of controversy.

But the new historiography of settler–indigenous relations had other, more widely ramified, consequences for the country. The most significant one was that Aborigines were brought back into the national story from which they had been absent for most the twentieth century. Summing up the previous 30 years of historical work in an address to fellow academics in 1959, the professor of history at the Australian National University, John La Nauze, observed that in Australian history the Aborigines were only noticed in a melancholy anthropological footnote, in contrast with the much larger role accorded to indigenous people in comparable white-settler societies such as Canada, New Zealand and South Africa. But the challenge which emerged in the 1970s and 1980s was not simply a matter of making a little room for the Aborigines and then continuing on as usual. With indigenous people on board, the pace, direction and purpose of the journey had to be changed. It became increasingly hard to maintain the nation's commitment to the epic of peaceful pioneering, of settlement as a struggle with nature, of hard, clean, bloodless conquest of the land. The heroic tale became a tragic one – one of loss as well as gain, of destruction as well as development.

With the White People was first published in 1990. It was a typical product of the new historiography – of the project to incorporate the Aboriginal and Islander experience into the national story. But it related also to two earlier books: *The Other Side of the Frontier* (1981 and 1982) and *Frontier* (1987). As its title suggests, the first of the two focused on the Aboriginal experience of contact and conflict with European pioneers; the second concentrated on the same events as experienced by the settlers. Both dealt centrally with frontier conflict, with violence and hostility. *With the White People* was written to round out the story, to supply pieces of the jigsaw that had not up till then been used. It was about both black and white; it dealt with cooperation, or at least coexistence. It discussed accommodation and adaptation. Violence and brutality were an inescapable part of the story, but they did not overwhelm it. The book took for granted the background of frontier conflict and forced appropriation of land, but moved on from there to focus on the ways in which Aborigines 'came in' to European society, whether reluctantly or willingly, their curiosity about the new world made by the colonists and their adjustments and concessions to it.

But it was also about the pioneer settlers and the desire of many of them to bring frontier wars to a close and 'let in' their erstwhile enemies. The settlers' motives varied widely. Some wanted little more than an escape from the tension and anxiety which accompanied frontier skirmishing. Others sought access to Aboriginal knowledge of the country, to cheap labour or to women, either by force or negotiation, and in some cases by courtship of a kind.

Labour was by far the most important element of exchange between settlers and indigenes. With the end of convict transportation to mainland Australia in 1840, the outlying regions suffered from endemic labour shortages. Aboriginal and Islander men and women were absorbed into the economy in every industry and occupation – on sheep and cattle stations, in mining ventures, as fishermen, timber-getters, drovers, guides, trackers, police troopers, house-keepers, cooks, nursemaids, gardeners. European dependence on Aboriginal labour increased as settlement pushed up into tropical Australia, where life would have been much more difficult and uncomfortable without the indigenous input.

Aborigines and pioneer settlers lived and worked together in many different ways and often for much of their lives, but the relationships were never equal. The indigenous people came into white society at a profound disadvantage. They had to make dramatic cultural adjustments, had to adopt whitefella ways, learn the whitefella language and master innumerable new skills and novel customs. This represented a degree of adjustment and adaptation that over-shadowed anything required of the settlers in colonising the new world. And the Aborigines were virtually powerless, facing the steely solidarity of white society, its assumption of superiority, its racism and often invincible conviction that indigenous people were primitive, savage, childlike and inferior. The law, which theoretically treated all people alike, always favoured the whites. Aboriginal workers could be – and were – beaten, raped and even killed with impunity, often with social approval and certainly with settler unity to protect the perpetrator from interfering policemen or magistrates. Until governments intervened in the twentieth century, black employees were often pressed into service, held against their will, rarely paid and made to work as long and as hard as the white boss willed. Inattention, incompetence or negligence – or what was called 'cheekiness' – resulted in assault by fist, boot or stockwhip, or all three.

An example of Aboriginal powerlessness with particular contemporary resonance was the widespread taking of children, which began with settlement and continued throughout the colonial period with no intervention by government officials beyond the occasional expression of concern. As early as 1814, Tasmania's Governor Davey officially pronounced his indignation about and abhorrence of the kidnapping of Aboriginal children. But the practice went on in all parts of Australia for 100 years. How many children suffered this fate is impossible to determine. When governments took up and expanded the practice in the early twentieth century, they were adopting at an official level something that had been endemic in colonial society. Individuals often protested against the practice and observed that it invariably ended disastrously for the children, but it went on undisturbed. Black children could be treated as chattels, were exchanged between friends, relatives and neighbours and were occasionally sold for profit.

Settlers justified the custom with apparent ease. They believed that Aboriginal parents were not strongly attached to their children, would soon forget them and that, regardless of all other considerations, the children would be better off with Europeans, where they would be 'raised in civilisation' and taught about the saviour. Such justifications may seem flimsy and self-serving to a contemporary audience, but they were clearly cogent enough at the time to allow generations of settlers to participate in, or at least condone, the kidnapping of children and their permanent separation from their parents, kin and culture.

Perhaps the strongest reason for writing a book about black pioneers was the realisation that Aborigines and Torres Strait Islanders had made a significant contribution to the development of Australia, which had never been fairly or fully acknowledged. It seemed as if the legend of the explorer and the pioneer settler had been so central to the development of Australian nationalism that there was no discursive space left for black pioneers. If included, they would complicate the story, undermine white heroism, dim the glory. If Aborigines could be shown to have displayed the same skills and attributes as white frontier settlers – endurance, stoicism, resourcefulness, ability to live off the land – then the pioneers would be diminished and their distinctiveness called into question. Further investigation could lead to the conclusion that the Australian bushman owed much to the nameless 'black boy' who guided and tracked, hunted, foraged and

found water, showed him the finer points of bushcraft and
taught him about the country.

It is the pastoral industry which owes the greatest debt
to the Aborigines. Indigenous people were part of the
industry from the beginning. They often guided the exploring
parties, both public and private, into the bush and helped find
suitable land; they led bullock drays and flocks and herds
outward to take up chosen country. Black bushcraft and
knowledge were invaluable during the early years of settlement. Open-range grazing would have been impossible
without the Aborigines' skills. Aboriginal stockworkers
mastered all aspects of the industry, but above all they were
there – even in the most remote parts of Australia, where
they were the only viable workforce. Unlike itinerant white
workers, it was in their interest to stay put, to remain in their
own country. They could be drawn into the station workforce
at busy times of the year and released back into their traditional economy when work slackened. They worked long
hours for food, tobacco and scraps of clothing. Their contribution was large and various. Its monetary value has yet to
be quantified, but it must have been enormous.

My awareness of the role of Aboriginal and Islander
workers was sharpened by meeting and talking with old men
and women over many years in north Queensland. Many of
them had spent the whole of their working lives employed
as stockworkers, pearl or trochus divers, horsebreakers,
drovers, fencing contractors, shearers, farmhands and

domestic servants. They had often worked from their early childhood to old age, sometimes six or seven days a week from dawn to dusk, for meagre pay and rudimentary rations. Yet there was little sense of bitterness when they reminisced about their lives. They were usually proud of the skills they had acquired, of their capacity for hard work and of the contribution they thought they had made to national development. These old people, and thousands like them, were Australia's black pioneers.

At the same time as I was conversing with the indigenous people, I often heard students in seminars, or strangers in passing conversation or commentators in the media, argue that the Aborigines had done nothing to develop the country either before the Europeans arrived or subsequently. 'We were the people who developed this country, not the Abos': this was repeated with minor variations over and over again. It was one of the main arguments used to reject Aboriginal claims for land, or justice, or reparation.

But if the truth be known, most white Australians are not descendants of pioneers – of men and women who lived on the fringes of settlement and founded the great primary industries. Many trace their Australian origins back to more recent migrations, or to immigrants who arrived in the port cities and never moved beyond them except on holidays. In contrast, most Aborigines do have parents, grandparents and great-grandparents who were out there on the frontier working for the white people. Many of them are also descendants of white pioneers, carrying both their genetic inheritance and their names.

The great challenge which the reconciliation movement presents to Australia is not just to deal fairly with the past, to acknowledge the violence, brutality and bloodshed, but to tell a story which will be acceptable, and will do justice, to both black and white. It may be too hard a task. Both sides may want their own stories told in their own distinctive style, with their own heroes and martyrs. The two stories may never coalesce.

In New Zealand, part of the whole process of accommodation involves the writing of history. The Waitangi Tribunal requires that Maori and pakeha work together to find areas of common agreement about the various tribal histories. Australia has no process comparable with what happens under the aegis of Waitangi, but there is probably as much prospect here as in New Zealand to find at least the basis for accommodation. And it may come most readily by considering the history of the black pioneers and the land on which they worked. Aborigines' close relationship with their country assisted at the birth of the great outback industries. It may be just as valuable in repairing the damage to land done by European settlement. Land was always the major source of conflict in the past. It may become the site of lasting reconciliation in the future.

INTRODUCTION TO FIRST EDITION

In *THE OTHER SIDE OF THE FRONTIER* I dealt with the Aboriginal response to the invasion and settlement of Australia.[1] The main emphasis was on how the Aborigines had resisted the settlers and the consequences of that resistance. While researching and writing that book I was fully aware that resistance, for all its importance, was only part of the story, that for every tribesman and woman who defied the whites there were others who worked for the interlopers assisting in the process of colonisation, that collaboration was as common as confrontation. In the introduction to the first edition of the book I explained:

> Throughout the text there are ideas and themes which invite attention but which have been passed over with a brief mention. The important question of Aboriginal assistance to Europeans — as trackers, troopers and workers — has been held over for later consideration.[2]

That consideration was, in the event, later coming than

I would have expected in April 1981. My attention was re-directed to the question during the bicentenary celebrations in 1988. It was quite common at the time to hear white Australians say that the Aborigines had contributed nothing towards the creation of a prosperous modern society, that everything we now have rested on the sturdy foundations put down in the nineteenth century by the European pioneers. The emphasis given to resistance and confrontation by Aborigines during 1988 indirectly enhanced that argument. Neither black nor white seem willing to pay tribute to the labour and the skill of thousands of Aboriginal men, women and children who worked for the Europeans in all parts of the country and more particularly in the centre and north of the continent.

While discussing with students the question of who the pioneers actually were, I suggested an imaginary experiment involving six white Australians and six Aborigines chosen at random from anywhere in the country except the most remote black communities. If one were then to investigate the family histories of the dozen people so selected, it would be found that perhaps only two of the Europeans could lay any claim to pioneering ancestry – that is, to forebears who lived on the outer fringes of settlement and who were engaged in founding one or more of the great primary indus-tries. At least two of the group would be post-war immi-grants or their children, another two might trace their descent from late nineteenth- or early twentieth-century immigrants who had lived most of their lives in the large urban centres on the coast. With the six Aborigines the situation would probably be quite different. It is likely that all six would have parents, grandparents or great-grandparents who were stockworkers, shepherds, trackers, troopers, pearl-divers or servants at some time during their lives.

With the White People is about the black pioneers – those Aborigines who worked for the Europeans in a wide range of occupations in all corners of the continent from the earliest years of settlement. Like two earlier books, *Frontier*[3] and *The Other Side of the Frontier*, this one deals with Australia as a whole, with a slight emphasis on the north rather than the south of the country. It embraces the period from the early years in New South Wales to the First World War. There were good reasons for ending the story at that point. It is just beyond the reach of living memory and the book therefore avoids cutting into the increasing number of oral histories and autobiographies which deal with the 1920s, 1930s and 1940s. The early years of the twentieth century also saw the great expansion of government involvement in Aboriginal affairs, which continued to be of major importance until the 1960s. The period was also something of a watershed in white–Aboriginal affairs.

Part of this book will overlap with themes addressed in the two earlier volumes and some material used then has been redeployed. Some themes have already been aired in academic journals but most of the subject matter will be quite new to the general reader, to whom the book is addressed in the hope that as a nation we will at last pay tribute to the Aborigines who spent time with the white people, who were in a very real sense Australia's black pioneers.

one

CONQUERING THE
INTERIOR

WHEN THOMAS MITCHELL'S expedition returned to the settled districts late in 1836 after a nine-month-long journey along the rivers of the Murray–Darling system and into what was to become Victoria, he variously rewarded those who had accompanied him. The convict servants were given either pardons or tickets of leave, depending on their prior status. The Bathurst Aborigine, known to the Europeans as John Piper, received an old firelock gun, blankets, Mitchell's red coat, as well as a cocked hat and feather which had once belonged to Governor Darling. When offered a brass breastplate inscribed with the title 'King', he declared there were 'too many Kings already', and opted instead for the title 'Conqueror of the Interior'.[1] While Piper's material reward was slight, the preferred inscription gave clear recognition to the crucial role played by Aboriginal advisers and Aboriginal expertise in the exploration and settlement of Australia.

Those valiant heroes

Mitchell paid tribute to the contribution of his Aboriginal advisers, but their role has rarely been fully appreciated in the innumerable historical works that have celebrated the achievements of the explorers who 'discovered' inland Australia. It is not hard to see why. The explorers were seized on by writers in the late nineteenth and early twentieth centuries to provide colour and romance to what was thought to be a 'rather tame and uneventful story' singularly 'devoid of stirring incident'.[2] The bushman and writer Ernest Favenc believed that exploration was of consequence because it embraced 'so great a proportion of the romance of our past'.[3] In his *History of the Australian Colonies*, published in 1901, Joseph Finney predicted that when future generations of Australians 'set about making up [their] roll of illustrious heroes, founders and martyrs, there will be inscribed on it the immortal names of all the GREAT EXPLORERS'.[4] Before the First World War the explorers provided the heroism supplied in other nations by military prowess and success in battle. Indeed Australian history was illuminated by the heroism and fortitude of 'those who spent their lives in the service of discovery'.[5] The story appealed to the colonists 'as does the battle roll of nations'.[6] The explorers were engaged in 'warfare against the hostility of the wilderness'.[7] Theirs was a battle 'fought and won over great natural difficulties and obstacles'.[8] Such stirring deeds were ideal for the inculcation of national pride in the nation's youth. The explorers were paraded through the minds of several generations of Australian children to promote an 'honest and manly' pride in the nation.[9] In the preface to his *The Explorers of Australia,* Favenc expressed his hope

> that from these pages our youth . . . will form an adequate idea
> of the character of the men who helped to make Australia and
> some of the adverse conditions against which they struggled so
> nobly.[10]

In an earlier book with a similar title, Eliza Berry broke into verse addressing 'those valiant heroes' who ventured forth

> And brilliant record show
> Whose names but said, our children stand
> And noble deeds recall!
> Farewell! Ye heroes of our land,
> Ye brave explorers, all![11]

No one who reads the journals of the explorers can doubt their courage and determination. But the heroic image moulded so effectively by writers and artists before 1914 rested on many assumptions that are currently under siege. Of central importance is the belief that the explorers discovered a wilderness, that before the settlers arrived Australia was untouched, empty, pristine. Only then could the pathfinders play out their appointed role of discovery. Writing of his 1836 expedition, Mitchell argued that the territory travelled through was 'still for the most part in a state of nature' presenting 'a fair blank sheet' for the encroaching Europeans.[12] It was an idea readily taken up by the writers who celebrated the saga of exploration and the 'discovery' of

> The new abode for man
> The edge in light, within, a blank,
> A broad mysterious wild.[13]

USING LOCAL KNOWLEDGE
∫ Fire-stick farming

However, the explorers were not pushing out into a wilderness, they were trekking through country that had been in human occupation for hundreds of generations. It was land that had been skilfully managed and shaped by continuous and creative use of fire. The more perceptive settlers grasped the importance of this 'fire-stick farming'. The Royal Navy captain J. L. Stokes watched the local Aborigines burn the bush when his ship was at Albany in the 1840s. He described them 'kindling, moderating, and directing the destructive element', which under their care seemed almost 'to change its nature, acquiring, as it were, complete docility'.[14] At much the same time the German explorer Ludwig Leichhardt was making similar observations in the interior of Queensland. The natives, he noted,

> seemed to have burned the grass systematically along every watercourse, and round every waterhole, in order to have them

surrounded with young grass as soon as rain sets in . . . Long strips of lately burnt grass were frequently observed extending for many miles along the creeks. The banks of small isolated waterholes in the forest, were equally attended to . . . It is no doubt connected with a systematic management of their runs to attract game to particular spots, in the same way that stock-holders burn parts of theirs in proper seasons.[15]

Modern scholars have provided confirmation for the passing observations of Leichhardt and Stokes. Recent field-work in Arnhem Land has established the degree of delib-eration in the Aboriginal use of fire and their sophisticated understanding of such variables as seasonal conditions, time of day, dryness of vegetation, build-up of undergrowth and the relative degree of fire resistance among different plant communities.[16] Work in a range of disciplines has confirmed the argument of the distinguished anthropologist N. B. Tindale that the Aborigines 'had a significant hand in the moulding of the present configuration of parts of Australia. Indeed much of the grassland of Australia could have been brought into being as a result of this exploitation.'[17]

∫ Diversified pleasure grounds

The explorers sought out those areas of open, lightly wooded grassland where evidence of Aboriginal land management was most apparent. John Oxley was one of the first settlers to enthuse about the inland plains. During his expedition down the Lachlan Valley in 1817 he wrote:

> The timber standing at wide intervals, without any brush or undergrowth gave the country a fine park-like appearance. I never saw a country better adapted for the grazing of all kinds of stock than we passed over this day.

Oxley grasped the link between the presence of Aborigines and the availability of both water and land suitable for settlement. He thought the open country resembled 'diversified pleasure grounds irregularly laid out and planted'. The animation of the whole scene, he remarked,

> was greatly increased by the smoke of the native fires arising in every quarter distinctly marking that we were in a country which afforded them ample means of subsistence.[18]

The explorers were, then, not looking for empty land at all. They were seeking well-populated districts, the presence of resident clans indicating the availability of water, native fauna, grass, good country. Oxley assumed that any sign of Aboriginal presence was promising. Pathways, even axe-marked trees, were 'certain signs of approaching water'.[19] On their journey south from the settled districts of New South Wales in 1824, Hume and Hovell were on the lookout for Aboriginal camp fires 'as where they resort there is little doubt the country is passable and contains plenty of food'.[20] Stokes believed that in country where Aboriginal fires were constantly visible it was 'fair to infer that the inhabitants were numerous and the soil fertile'.[21] In the Maranoa, Mitchell concluded that open plains and columns of smoke 'indicated a good country'.[22] When Leichhardt's Aboriginal guide reported seeing fires all along a nearby range, the explorer wrote in his journal that 'this was welcome intelligence, for we knew that their presence indicated the existence of a good country'.[23] B. H. Babbage, the South Australian explorer, wrote that 'plenty of blacks, freshwater lakes, gum trees, and kangaroos' could be taken as 'tolerably certain indications of good country'.[24] Reflecting on the experience of a generation of inland exploration, Edward John Eyre wrote that

> the localities selected by Europeans, as best adapted for the purpose of cultivation or grazing, are those that would usually be equally valued above others, by the natives themselves, as places of resort, or districts in which they could most easily procure food.[25]

∫ Blackfellow's road

Explorers frequently used Aboriginal tracks, which criss-crossed many districts and which were often carefully maintained by fire and constant usage. Such paths were more common in mountain and forest country or in arid areas where water sources were scarce and widely separated. The explorer and later colonial governor George Grey discovered numerous beaten tracks in north-west Australia which were 'as completely path-ways as those we find in England leading from a village to a farm house'.[26] In Central Australia Charles Sturt travelled along trails which were 'as broad as a footpath in England, by a roadside, and were well trodden'.[27] A. C. Gregory, the colonial surveyor and explorer of north

Australia, came across a well-maintained path along which 'the loose stones had been cleared . . . and . . . piled in large heaps'.[28] Such tracks were not the meandering trails of aimless wanderers but linked wells, springs and other water sources, led to fords and mountain passes, and circumvented forests and other natural obstacles. On his so-called friendly mission to the Aborigines G. A. Robinson used well-maintained paths while travelling in western Tasmania. The track along the north-west coast avoided major topographical hazards and followed a more suitable route than the bridle path of the Van Diemen's Land Company.[29] In north Queensland half a century later, James Mulligan's exploring party struck 'a black fellows track or road' which led them around the rainforest and 'right between the range of hills'.[30] On the coast of Queensland the British geologist J. B. Jukes and his companions found tracks which took them through the mangroves.[31] Eyre discovered life-saving wells on a number of occasions by following paths along the Nullarbor.[32] While crossing dry country, Sturt found a track and followed it for six hours to a well full of rain water.[33] R. Austen, Western Australia's assistant surveyor, providentially struck a path in the Murchison district which led him to a

> beautiful well of water, in a bare limestone plain, that no-one could ever have expected to find water on. Had we missed this well, not a horse would have been saved.[34]

Burke and Wills learnt the value of Aboriginal tracks while on their journey back from Carpentaria. After floundering for miles through a bog, they came to a hard, well-trodden path that led them out of the swamp, on to drinking water and yam grounds where they feasted on what had been left behind after the local clans had harvested the crop.[35]

∫ Acquiring local knowledge

Local knowledge was more valuable to the explorers than paths and wells discovered by chance along the way. While writing of his experiences in Australia in the 1840s, Stokes observed that

> nothing could be more unwise than the hostility shown to the natives by the first settlers, as from them we must always calculate on learning much that is useful and valuable, with regard to the productions of the country; a knowledge which would otherwise consume much time to acquire.[36]

From the earliest years of settlement explorers and other travellers received valuable information from local Aborigines about fords, passes, short cuts, easy gradients.

When John Howe became bushed on his journey from Windsor to the Hunter River in 1819, he sent scouts out to find the local clans, for without their intimate knowledge of the locality he 'could proceed no further'.[37] While travelling beyond the Dividing Range in 1823, M. J. Currie abducted a local black, compelling him to direct the party, 'they being invariably well acquainted with the best passes in the hills'.[38] In 1836 J. S. Roe, the colony's surveyor general, recruited a local guide when on a journey from the Swan

River to Albany who 'commenced his intended avocation' by immediately leading the party 'towards the best crossing over soft ground'.[39] On an expedition north-east of York, the Western Australian settler J. H. Monger was assisted by local blacks who took the party over a difficult hill and then on firm tracks through salt lakes. The party would 'never have got through if it had not been for the natives'.[40] On his first expedition north of the settled districts Mitchell discovered the value of local guides, who examined the country on the line of march 'being anxious about the safe passage of our carts'. The reconnaissance was not in vain, for the clansmen led the party to 'an easy, open pass, through a range' that they had been told would present them with great difficulties. Mitchell noted in his journal: 'We crossed it with ease, however, guided by the natives.'[41] While travelling in northern New South Wales a few years later under the guidance of a local black, Mitchell again confirmed 'the advantage of having such guides':

> being now uncertain as to the further course of the Bogan, which had taken a great bend northward, we could thus make straight for each proposed waterhole, without following the bends of the river. The knowledge of the people was so exact as to location, that I could ascertain in setting out, the true bearing of those places by the direction in which they pointed; and in travelling on such a bearing, any obstacle in the way, was sure to be avoided by following the suggestions of the natives.[42]

$\int$ The search for water

Aboriginal knowledge of waterholes, soaks and wells was even more important for inland exploration than information about topography. Babbage was officially instructed on the eve of his 1858 expedition that he would probably 'fall in' with uncontacted blacks and 'receive valuable assistance from them, particularly in discovering freshwater springs'. It was good advice, for on his return from the parched inland local blacks gave him the 'names and positions of about 15 waters' along his line of march.[43] During R. H. Bland's 1848 expedition in Western Australia local blacks took the travellers to freshwater lakes and springs 'which at that dry season, we should have been unable to find without'.[44] A few years later Roe received similar assistance from a group of blacks who showed him the location of springs and wells along his intended route 'extending fifty miles to the boundary of their own immediate country'.[45]

During his journey into central Queensland, Mitchell was assisted by two local brothers who brought the party to waterholes 'where no stranger would have looked for water'. The waterholes were 'vitally important' to the expedition.[46] While recounting his experiences in South and Western Australia, Eyre explained that Aborigines met by chance had accompanied him for miles 'to point out where water was to be procured', and that he had been 'assisted by them in getting at it, if from the nature of the soil or my own inexperience, I had any difficulty in doing so myself.'[47]

Eyre appreciated the profound knowledge that underpinned
the Aboriginal mastery of their environment:

> Another very great advantage on the part of the natives is, the
> intimate knowledge they have of every nook and corner of the
> country they inhabit; does a shower of rain fall, they know
> the very rock where a little water is most likely to be collected,
> the very hole where it is the longest retained, and by repairing
> straight to the place they fill their skins, and thus obtain a supply
> that lasts them many days. Are there heavy dews at night, they
> know where the longest grass grows, from which they may
> collect the spangles, and water is sometimes procured thus in
> very great abundance.[48]

The search for water became all important as exploring
parties pushed out into the arid interior of the continent.
Contact with resident Aboriginal clans was essential for
survival. Parties scanned the horizon for any sign of smoke
and the ground for any tracks of the local inhabitants. While
trying to travel through dry country in Western Australia in
1864, the pioneer squatter Clarkson spent a week looking
for 'a local nigger' before attempting to advance into the
interior.[49] So crucial was the Aboriginal knowledge of the
country that it became customary for European parties to
'run down' resident Aborigines to force them to act as 'pilots
to water'.[50] While reporting on his expeditions into the
Gibson Desert in 1896–97, L. H. Wells admitted that
'without a guide in such country one is almost powerless'.[51]
While pushing out into the desert he was 'fortunate in

getting two natives . . . one of whom we chained up so that he would not escape before leading us to water'. Their prisoner took the party to several native wells which could have been 'passed close by without observation'.[52] During a similar expedition at much the same time, D. W. Carnegie was even more dependent on captured Aborigines. 'Throughout our journeys', he admitted, 'we never once found water by chance'.[53] He resorted to the practice of chaining captives up and refusing them any water until they were willing to lead the party to the nearest well. 'Thirst is a terrible thing', he wrote, but it was 'also a great quickener of the wits'. The result of 'this harsh treatment' was that before long the party was able to 'unload and make camp in one of the most charming little spots I have ever seen. A veritable oasis, though diminutive in size'.[54] On another occasion Carnegie captured a woman,

> as it had become clear to me for some time past that without the aid of the natives we could not hope to find water . . . I felt justified, therefore, in unceremoniously making captives from what wandering tribes we might fall in with. And in light of after events I say unhesitatingly that, without having done so, and without having to some extent used rough treatment to some natives we caught, we could not by any possibility have succeeded in crossing the desert.[55]

Explorers who used more diplomatic methods than Carnegie were often able to gain a complete inventory of resources in a given stretch of territory. Austen met a party of local blacks during an expedition in 1854 who gave him

> the names of the places we should pass on the way . . . and as
> far beyond it as their knowledge extended, which I took down
> in writing, and then inquired what kind of watering places,
> rocks, timber and food were to be found at each of them.[56]

When Sturt's expedition of 1844–45 was preparing to advance into the interior, a local black called Toonda drew in the sand

> a plan of the Darling for 300 miles, also of the Murray a good
> distance both above and below its junctions. He drew all the
> lagoons and gave the name of each; by comparing afterwards
> the bends he drew with Major Mitchell's chart, they both
> agreed.[57]

Black ambassadors

Local guides were also invaluable in negotiating with their neighbours to prepare for the peaceful reception of the travellers. Sturt found this service of enormous value in his journey along the Murray in 1830, as indicated in a number of entries in his journal. 'We fell in with another tribe of blacks', he noted, 'to who we were *literally consigned* by those who had been previously with us'. Later the party was taken to a meeting point by seven local clansmen, where they were introduced to two men 'belonging to the new tribe [who] went on ahead to prepare the neighbouring tribe to receive us'. While summing up his contact with local Aborigines Sturt observed that they had 'sent ambassadors forward regularly from one tribe to another, in order to prepare for our approach, a custom that not only saved us an infinity of time, but also great personal risk. Indeed I doubt very much whether we should ever have pushed so far down the river, had we not been assisted by the natives themselves'.[58] Mitchell was also aware of the advantages of local guides, writing in his journal:

> Another great advantage gained in the company of the natives was, our being perfectly safe from the danger of sudden colli-sion with a tribe. Their caution, in approaching water-holes was most remarkable; for they always cooyed from a great distance, and even on coming near a thick scrub, they sometimes request me to halt, until they could examine it.[59]

Sturt had further experience of the diplomatic skills of Aboriginal guides during his expedition into central Australia in 1844–45. Eyre, who was the protector of Aborigines on the Murray at the time, had recruited two influential local men, Camboli and Nadbuck, because he was 'quite aware of the importance of such attachées'.[60] Nadbuck proved his worth, Sturt observing that he was 'a perfect politician in his way and essential service to us'.[61] His ability to defuse dangerous situations was shown when the expedition approached a large Aboriginal party on the Darling. Sturt wrote:

> We here heard that there was a large encampment of natives about three miles above us, but none of them ventured to our camp . . . but our friend Nadbuck . . . was in a great bustle,

and showed infinite anxiety on the occasion. Neither were his apprehensions allayed on the following morning when we started. He went in advance to prepare the natives for our approach, and to ask permission for us to pass through their territory, but returned without having found them. Not long afterwards it was reported that the natives were in front.

On hearing this [Nadbuck] begged of me to stop the party, and away he went, full of bustle and importance, to satisfy himself. In a few minutes he returned and said we might go on. We had halted close to the brow of a gentle descent into a small creek junction at this particular spot, and on advancing a few paces came in view of the natives assembled on the bank of the river below . . . They looked with astonishment on the drays, which passed close to them; and I observed that several of them trembled greatly. At the time Nadbuck had walked to some little distance with two old men, holding each by the hand in the most affectionate manner, and he was apparently in deep and earnest conversation with them.[62]

The explorers did not discover 'a blank' or a 'broad mysterious wild' and in their day-to-day activities they were keenly aware of the presence of the resident Aborigines. They used the Aborigines' wells, tracks, shelters and camping grounds. They sought out those districts where indigenous population densities suggested open country, water and good soil. Expeditions were heavily dependent on information gathered from local people. In her brilliant study of Aboriginal usage and European usurpation in Western Australia entitled *Fire and*

Hearth, Sylvia Hallam examined the ways in which settlement was imposed on, and benefited from, the ancient society and economy. The Aborigines, she explained,

> had opened up a landscape in which it was possible for Euro-peans to move around, to pasture their flocks, to find good soils for agriculture, and water sources for themselves and their stock. The European communities inherited the possibilities of settle-ment and land use from the Aboriginal communities . . . So in south-western Australia, as elsewhere on the continent, European distributions and lines of communication followed Aboriginal distribution and lines of movement, and both owed much to the opening-up of the landscape by Aboriginal usage and particularly firing – both incidental to camping, gathering and travel and as part of the deliberate management of plant and animal resources.[63]

EMPLOYING EXPERT ADVISERS

The Aboriginal guide – the ubiquitous, albeit often anony-mous 'black boy' – played a vital role in the European explo-ration of the continent. Unlike casual advisers picked up temporarily along the line of march, the professional guides came from the 'settled' districts and were usually permanent members of the exploring parties in question. They provided many of the same services as local guides consulted briefly during the course of expeditions, but their contribution was distinctive enough to be considered separately, although some

overlap of material resulted. Their expertise derived both
from ancient Aboriginal traditions and from experience gained
in contact with the Europeans. These two aspects can be
considered in turn. The professional guides retained important
aspects of traditional bushcraft – they could track, hunt, find
water – but their skills had been generalised in such a way that
they could be utilised in any type of country, often very
different from their original homelands that had nurtured
the expertise in the first place. They were also linguists with
a number of dialects at their command and they were well
versed in the protocol of Aboriginal diplomacy. At the same
time they had overcome, often with enormous courage, their
traditional fear of culturally and linguistically alien Aborigines.
Added to these attributes were skills learnt from the Europeans – a working knowledge of English; the ability to handle
horses, sheep, cattle; familiarity with the white man's weapons,
which often developed into marksmanship of a high order.

The more generous-minded of the explorers paid tribute
to the many skills of their professional Aboriginal advisers.
While out on his expedition in the southern interior of New
South Wales, Mitchell noted in his journal:

> in most of our difficulties by flood and field, the intelligence and
> skill of our sable friends made the 'white fellows' appear rather
> stupid. They could read traces on the earth, climb trees, or dive
> into the water, better than the ablest of us. In tracing lost cattle,
> speaking to 'the wild natives', hunting, or diving, Piper was the
> most accomplished man in camp.[64]

Writing of his experience as a bushman and explorer, Eyre observed that in travelling about from one place to another he had

> always made it a point, if possible, to be accompanied by one or more natives, and I have often found great advantage from it. Attached to an exploring party they are frequently invaluable, as their perceptive powers are very great, and enable them both to see and hear anything at a much greater distance than a European. In tracking stray animals, and keeping on indistinct paths, they display a degree of perseverance and skill that is really wonderful. They are useful also in cutting bark canoes to cross a river, should such impede the progress of the party, and in diving for anything that may be lost in the water etc.[65]

∫ A tradition is born

The practice of taking guides from the 'settled' districts on exploring expeditions was initiated within the first few years of the establishment of Sydney. In 1791 marine captain Watkin Tench led a party inland accompanied by two guides, Bolanderee and Colbee, whom he hoped would provide 'much information relating to the country' and be able to illustrate 'their manner of living in the woods and the resources they rely upon in their journeys'.[66] In 1802 Barallier attempted to find a way over the Blue Mountains and engaged the Aborigine Gogy to accompany him, 'thinking he would be useful when [the party] advanced further inland'.[67] Maritime explorers followed suit. Matthew Flinders was accompanied by Bongaree from the Broken Bay tribe on his voyage to Moreton Bay in 1797 and during his circumnavigation of the continent in 1802. During his voyage along the south coast of the continent in 1800, Captain James Grant was accompanied by Euranabie, who was 'in many respects most useful'.[68]

The Aboriginal guides showed their prowess in the bush. Bolanderee and Colby were highly amused by the Europeans' clumsiness. 'The hindrances to walking . . . which plagued and entangled us so much', Tench explained, 'seemed not to be heeded by them, and they wound through them with ease.'[69] Grant found that Euranabie was particularly useful 'when penetrating a thicket, as he usually went first and cleared a passage'[70] for the Europeans to follow. At different times the guides built huts, made canoes, caught game or speared fish. By the 1820s the settlers had come to appreciate Aboriginal tracking skills. The surgeon Peter Cunningham explained that

> they possess amazing quickness of eye and ear, tracing a man's footstep with perfect ease through every description of country, provided it is sufficiently recent, and that no rain has fallen in the interval. They well guess, too, very correctly, *how long* the individual has passed, and tell whether it is the bare footstep of a white or a black man, by the nature of the impression.[71]

The guides' greatest value was in conducting diplomacy on behalf of the white man. Bongaree usually threw off his clothes and led the European party ashore endeavouring to open a dialogue with the local clans. Flinders paid tribute to his success 'in bringing about a friendly intercourse with the inhabitants of other parts of the coast'.[72] Barallier's guide Gogy negotiated with a 'mountaineer called Bungin' to allow for safe passage of the party. Gogy and Bungin introduced Barallier to a man who had never seen Europeans before and who was 'seized with great fright'. They attempted to reassure the newcomer, telling him that the white man would not do any harm but had come to 'gather some pebbles and plants'.[73]

Tench provided a more detailed account of a diplomatic exchange between his guides and members of inland clans:

About an hour after sunset, as we were chatting by the fireside, and preparing to go to rest, we heard voices at a little distance in the wood. Our natives catched the sound instantaneously, and bidding us be silent, listened attentively to the quarter whence it had proceeded. In a few minutes we heard the voices plainly; and wishing exceedingly to open a communication with this tribe, we begged our natives to call to them, and bid them to come to us, to assure them of good treatment, and that they should have something given them to eat. Colbee no longer hesitated, but gave them the signal of invitation, in a loud hollow cry. After some whooping, and shouting, on both sides, a man, with a lighted stick in his hand, advanced near enough to converse with us. The first words, which we could distinctly understand were 'I am Colbee, of the tribe of Càd-i-gal'. The stranger replied, 'I am Bèr-ee-wan, of the tribe of Boorooberongal'. Boladeree informed him also of his name, and that we were white men and friends, who would give him something to eat. Still he seemed irresolute. Colbee therefore advanced to him, took him by the hand, and led him to us. By the light of the moon, we were introduced to this gentleman, all our names being repeated in form by our two masters of the ceremonies, who said that we were Englishmen, and Bùd-yee-ree (good), that we came from the sea coast, and that we were travelling inland.[74]

The value of 'professional' guides, tested during the forays of the 1790s and early years of the nineteenth century, was fully borne out in the great expeditions which crossed the continent in the years between 1830 and 1900. Most parties were accompanied throughout their journeys by Aborigines from the 'settled' districts, many of whom had previously worked in the pastoral industry. One or two, like Tommy Windich, who accompanied the Forrest brothers on three of their expeditions into the interior of Western Australia, and Mitchell's guides John Piper and Yuranigh, achieved passing fame, while Eyre's Wylie and E. B. Kennedy's Jacky-Jacky were portrayed in the colonial press as the ideal type of humble and loyal servant. Rather than consider each expedition individually, it will be more convenient to examine the various ways in which the Aboriginal guides contributed to the success of the journeys that 'unlocked the inland'.

Tracking

Aboriginal tracking skills were of enormous value to the Europeans. They were employed almost every day in the bush and were essential for finding the horses, bullocks or camels that, during the night, frequently strayed away from the sleeping explorers. Until they were found and returned to camp all progress came to a halt. Sometimes they had to be tracked for many miles over difficult terrain. Without Aboriginal assistance many animals would have been lost altogether, jeopardising the whole venture. Mitchell mused over his dependence on the expertise of his guides while in northern New South Wales in 1846. Two bullocks lost by their drivers were found by Dicky, a ten-year-old Aboriginal boy. 'It must, indeed, appear strange to these people of the soil', he wrote, 'that the white man who brought such large animals as oxen with them into the country' was unable to find them 'without the assistance of a mere child of their own race'.[75] On his third expedition in the interior of South Australia in 1875, Ernest Giles wrote with admiration of the skill of old Jimmy, who

> was a splendid tracker; indeed, no human being in the world but an Australian aboriginal . . . could track a camel on some surfaces, for where there is any clayey soil, the creature leaves no more mark on the ground than an ant . . . and to follow such marks as they do leave, by firelight, was marvellous. Occasionally they would leave some marks that no one could mistake, where they passed over sandy ground – but for many hundreds of yards beyond, it would appear as though they must have flown over the ground, and had never put their feet to earth at all. By the time daylight appeared, old Jimmy had tracked them about three miles, then he went off, apparently quite regardless of any

tracks at all, walking at such a pace, that I would only keep up with him by occasionally running. We came upon the camels at length about six miles from the camp . . ."[76]

Aboriginal guides were also sent back on the tracks of expeditions to find articles lost or forgotten along the way. Leichhardt recorded how Charley had recovered every strap of a pack-saddle that had broken and been scattered in tall grass. George Grey sent his guide Kaiber back to find his pocket watch, which had fallen out while he galloped after a herd of wild cattle. Grey had doubts about the chances of finding the 'much valued' object because the ground was 'badly suited for the purposes of tracking, and the scrub was thick'. Nevertheless within half an hour the watch was restored to its grateful owner. 'This feat of Kaiber's', Grey wrote, 'surpassed anything of the sort I had previously seen performed by natives'.[77] But the ability to follow the tracks of lost expedition members was of even greater value. Yuranigh found Mitchell's shepherd when he was 'in full march' away from the expedition although his tracks circled 'in all directions'.[78] Murphy and Caleb, two members of Leichhardt's expedition of 1844–45, were missing for two days and 'had fairly lost themselves'. Although they were found 12 miles from the camp the search party had to ride 70 miles 'before they came up to them, and they would certainly have perished, had not Charley been able to track them'. Three months later Leichhardt himself was lost in the 'Bricklow' scrub of central Queensland and was saved when his guide Brown was able to recognise a place where the two had breakfasted two days earlier, enabling them to return to an anxious camp. Leichhardt referred in his journal to 'the wonderful quickness and accuracy' with which his Aboriginal guides were able to recognise localities seen previously. 'The impressions on their retina', he wrote,

> seem to be naturally more intense than on that of the European; and their recollections are remarkably exact, even to the most minute details. Trees peculiarly formed, broken branches, slight elevations of the ground – in fact, a hundred things, which we should remark only when paying great attention to a place – seem to form Daguerreotype [photographic] impression on their minds, every part of which is readily recollected.[79]

∫ Bushcraft

Other bush skills aided the explorers. Aboriginal guides were able to cut bark and prepare a shelter for the night within a few minutes of arrival at a camping spot. Bark canoes were crafted with equal expedition in order to ferry supplies – and people too if necessary – over stretches of deep water. The hunting ability of the 'blackboys' provided fresh food to augment everyday rations and at times of crisis saved parties from starvation. Many guides combined traditional skills with marksmanship. The Forrests' guide Tommy Windich was an excellent shot, providing the camp with kangaroo, emu, turkey, possum and ducks. 'Sugar bag', discovered and retrieved, provided the explorers with a welcome taste of honey. H. S. Russell, a pioneer squatter, found 'Jimmy's' bushcraft 'invaluable' during his Queensland expedition in 1842, referring to his guide's 'bee-hunting, sugar bag purveyance . . . to say nothing of his ever-watchful eye for . . . the tracks of kangaroo, on which we mostly fed, or a snake, iguana, or wallaby, invisible to our tame eyesight'.[80] When Leichhardt was bushed in the brigalow scrub Brown fed him by finding an edible root in an abandoned blacks' camp, shooting two pigeons and catching and cooking a lizard 'with a blunt tail and knobby scales'.[81] When Strzelecki's expedition ran out of food in Gippsland in 1840 they 'must have perished from starvation but for the exertions of Charlie the guide'.[82] While travelling in the north Queensland scrub William Hann's party lost their rations and 'had it not been that the black boy was a wonderful hunter they would probably have perished'.[83]

∫ Path-finding

Though travelling through strange country, the Aboriginal guides often had a greater appreciation of the lie of the land than the Europeans and selected the most desirable track through scrub or bog, over sandhills or across rivers. Daniel Bunce, who travelled with Leichhardt across the Darling Downs in 1850, was highly appreciative of his guide Wommai for his 'general knowledge of locale'.[84] While travelling in the north of the colony William Hodgkinson learnt from experience to depend on Larry's 'instinctive selection of the safest course'.[85] Mitchell found that Yuranigh was highly observant of features of the landscape 'to a degree that made his opinion of value in doubtful cases'. When uncertain himself, Mitchell's practice was to accept his guide's advice, and 'he was seldom wrong'.[86] When summing up his experience during his expedition into the interior of Queensland, Mitchell wrote of Yuranigh: 'his intelligence and his judgement rendered him so necessary to me, that he was ever at my elbow . . . confidence in him was never misplaced'.[87] It was common for Mitchell and other expedition leaders to take their Aboriginal guides with them on what Leichhardt called 'reconnoitring excursions' to examine the country ahead of the expedition and plan the easiest line of march. The guides frequently climbed tall trees to view the distant terrain and advise as to the best route to follow. Writing of his progress through Victoria's Western District, Mitchell outlined the role of his guides in determining the direction to be taken by the party:

> The whole management of the case now devolved on him [Piper] and the two boys . . . and this native party usually explored the woods with our dogs, for several miles in front of the column. The females kept nearer the party and often gave us notice of obstacles, in time to enable me to avoid them. My question on such occasions was, *dago nyollong yannagary*? (Which way shall we go?) to which one would reply, pointing in the proper direction, *yalyai nyollong – yannari*! (Go that way).[88]

∫ *The correct protocol*

The professional guides were also valuable as linguists and diplomats. While they were usually in foreign country and had a limited grasp of local dialects – or no knowledge at all – they were conversant with the protocol required in approaching Aboriginal camps and in gaining the confidence, or at least the tolerance, of resident clans. Mitchell's journals provide the most detailed descriptions, of the negotiations conducted by his guides Piper and Yuranigh. Both men were sent ahead to meet groups of Aborigines, many of whom had never seen white men before. 'I sent Piper forward', Mitchell explained on one occasion, 'to tell them who we were and thus, if possible, prevent any alarm at our appearance.'[89] Piper was also of great value when it looked as though there might be trouble. When surrounded by several camps of potentially hostile tribesmen, Mitchell 'did not interfere with them, relying chiefly on the sagacity and vigilance of Piper, who I directed to be particularly on the alert'.[90] He also appreciated the importance of Piper's knowledge of traditional protocol. Mitchell described how, while anxious to learn from local blacks the 'situation of the water', Piper realised that on his first meeting

> it was necessary, as usual on all such occasions, to continue for some time patient and silent. This formality was maintained very remarkably by the old man and Piper. In vain did I desire the latter to ask him a question; each stood silent for a full quarter of an hour about eight yards apart, neither looking at the other.

The female [Mitchell refers to her as 'Piper's gin'], however, became the intermediate channel of communication, for both spoke alternately in a low tone to her. At length Piper addressed the old man, raising his voice a little, but with his eyes averted; and the other answered him in the same way; until, at length, by slow degrees, they got into conversation. We were then informed that water was to be found a mile or two on, and the old man agreed to guide overseer Burnett and Piper to the place.[91]

The guides played an essential role in coaxing Aboriginal groups to meet the Europeans and to soothe their often acute anxieties. During Mitchell's 1846 expedition, Yuranigh sought a local black to guide the party to water. Eventually he brought a young man called Bilgawangara up to the camp. Despite Bilgawangara's fear of the Europeans and their animals Yuranigh was able to keep him with the expedition for ten days, during which time he took the white men to water and to feed for their animals and showed them the best route to pursue. Mitchell observed how Yuranigh 'endeavoured by every means to make [the stranger] at ease, and to induce him to remain with us'. A little later Yuranigh was

assiduously making to the stranger such explanations of our wants and purposes, as induced him to conduct us in the direction these required. He led us, thus admonished, over those parts of the country most favourable for the passage of wheels.[92]

Yuranigh was able to negotiate with local Aborigines even when he was unable to speak their language. As the expedition approached the Culgoa River, he met a local couple

and persuaded the man to guide the party although the
two 'scarcely understood a word of what each other said'.
Despite this difficulty Yuranigh had 'the address to overcome
the usual difficulties to intercourse between strange natives,
and their shyness to white men'[93] and to induce the young
man to guide the party to the river.

When they were able to communicate with resident
clans the guides elicited much valuable information. In April
1836, when Mitchell's party was poised to travel down the
valley of the Lachlan, Piper summarised the information he
had obtained from the local blacks, explaining

> that after eight of our daily journeys, according to his compre-
> hension, the bed of the Lachlan would contain no water, and that
> we must go right across 'the middle', as Piper understood,
> reaching in four days more a lagoon called 'Burrabidgin', or
> 'Burrabadimba': that there I must leave the carts, and go with
> the natives on horseback; and that in two days' travelling, at the
> rate we could then proceed, we should reach 'Oolawambiloa',
> a very great water. They also said that water could be found in
> the bush at the end of each of those four days' journey, by one
> of their tribe who would go with us, and who had twice been at
> the great water.[94]

∫ Pilots to water

Access to water was the single most important contribution
made by Aboriginal guides to European exploration. They

could find indistinct tracks of local clans – or of birds and animals – and follow them until they led to waterholes or wells. In 1848 J. S. Roe's guide, Bob, was able to 'walk direct to a small waterhole, entirety concealed from view by tufts of grass' although he was in an 'intricate' part of the country, almost totally unknown to him.[95] With a deep understanding of Aboriginal land-use the guides were often able to predict where water could be found even in the absence of fresh tracks. The South Australian explorer W. H. Tietkins's guide, Billy, found a small native well in central Australia in 1889 although there was 'not the slightest clue to guide anyone to it'.[96] Later in the expedition Billy pointed out to Tietkins, as they stood on a mountain, a particular patch of burnt grass 19 or so miles away and predicted that the party would find water there although it was not the only patch of grass that could be seen. In fact Tietkins reported that there were dozens. But the guide's judgement was sound. When the party reached the nominated spot they found an Aboriginal camp-site and nearby both a rock waterhole and a native well.[97]

In the desert Aboriginal guides looked for any sign of birds or animals to provide a clue to the presence of water. Peter Warburton's guide Charley noticed some diamond-sparrows rising from the ground and immediately ran to look for water, which he found in a small native well.[98] At a crucial moment during Forrest's third expedition, Tommy Windich found a spring after following emu tracks and then shooting a small marsupial which had recently drunk water. John

Forrest noted in his journal: 'Had we not found this spring our position would be very critical.'[99] At an equally desperate moment during Giles's fourth expedition, the guide Tommy found a lifesaving waterhole after the party had travelled 323 miles 'without having seen a drop of water'. He followed an emu track along a sandhill and saw 'a miniature lake lying in the sand, with plenty of that inestimable fluid'.[100]

Those dramatic moments when black guides saved explorers from death by starvation, thirst or hostile spears underlined the fact that successful expeditions were triply dependent on Aboriginal expertise. The Europeans made use of wells, waterholes, tracks and traditional camping grounds and sought out the land prepared by centuries of sophisticated land management. They solicited the advice of local clans and learnt about the districts they passed through and, when they behaved with reasonable decorum, were shepherded on peacefully from tribe to tribe along the line of march. They were heavily dependent on the bushcraft, linguistic skill and diplomatic poise of their professional guides. Any failure to exploit these sources of expertise and knowledge was likely to lead to disaster, as the fate of Burke and Wills illustrated.

∫ To live like the blacks

Though 'provided and equipped in the most ample and liberal manner',[101] the Burke and Wills expedition had less access to Aboriginal advice than any of the other large official parties that ventured into the interior of the continent. The nineteenth-century historian G.W. Rusden, who had himself travelled in the bush with black guides, observed that it was 'to be lamented that an expedition fitted out with so much expense was unaccompanied by an Australian native whose skill as a hunter would have spared the carried food for emergencies'.[102] On gaining command, Burke commenced 'severe pedestrian exercises' and began 'an active examination of the records of previous explorers so as to become thoroughly acquainted with the personal experiences of Australian pioneers of discovery'.[103] But he overlooked one of the most obvious features of his predecessors' experience – their utilisation of Aboriginal bushcraft.

Aboriginal guides were usefully employed as the various parties moved out on the first leg of the journey from the Darling to the Bulloo River, but they were not taken on to Cooper's Creek. From then on Burke and Wills did their best to avoid contact with Aborigines met along the way and reached for their guns when individuals attempted to come too close. 'Whenever the natives tried to bully or bounce us', Burke wrote, they 'were repulsed'.[104] On their journey north to Carpentaria and back to Cooper's Creek, the explorers came to appreciate the value of Aboriginal tracks and wells but were totally dependent on what they could find for themselves. Unlike their counterparts, who actively sought out the local people and coaxed them into communication, Burke and Wills drove them away. Just after leaving the depot at Cooper's Creek Wills wrote in his journal:

A large tribe of blacks came pestering us to go to their camp and have a dance, which we declined. They were very trouble-some, and nothing but the threat to shoot them will keep them away . . . from the little we have seen of them, they appear to be mean-spirited and contemptible in every respect.[105]

The attitudes towards the Aborigines adopted by other expe-dition members were clearly illustrated by the behaviour of the party left behind at Cooper's Creek. They lived within a stockade and did all they could to avoid contact with the resident clans. When questioned before the Royal Commis-sion into the expedition, the camp superintendent, William Brahe, was asked:

Did Mr. Burke give you any instructions about dealing with the natives in any way?

He answered:

Yes; at the time he left he seemed to think they would be very trouble-some, and he told me if they annoyed me at all to shoot them at once.

Not that Brahe and the party knew anything about the blacks, as several exchanges before the Commission showed:

Have you ever come across natives in any other part of the colony?

I have seen some in the Port Fairy district.

Had any of the men that were with you had any experience of natives before, do you know?

No.[106]

Given their inexperience and determination to avoid contact with the local clans, the Europeans were confined to their diet of rice, flour and salt pork and began to suffer from scurvy. They did little hunting, knew nothing of Aboriginal food plants and caught just one fish in four months.

When Burke, Wills and King returned to the deserted stockade their lack of bushcraft was equally apparent. They didn't know how to catch fish, track animals or gather wild food. They had no idea of the protocol needed to communicate with the blacks, who were increasingly seen as saviours rather than savages. Three entries in Wills's journal a month apart reflected the change:

> 30 April 1861: We are living the best way we can, like the blacks, but find it hard work.
>
> 6 May 1861: The present state of things is not calculated to raise our spirits much. The rations are rapidly diminishing; our clothes, especially the boots, are all going to pieces, and we have not the materials for repairing them properly . . . I suppose this will end in our having to live like the blacks for a few months.
>
> 4 June 1861: Started for the blacks' camp intending to test the practicability of living with them, and to see what I could learn as to their ways and manner.[107]

During the last weeks of their lives Burke and Wills were sleeping in gunyahs, harvesting nardoo and grinding it with stone tools scavenged from the blacks' camp. They had learnt, too late, one of the basic truths of Australian exploration.

∫ *Private assistants*

The failure of Burke and Wills to profit from Aboriginal expertise was all the more surprising given the widespread private use of black guides in all parts of the continent and from the earliest years of settlement. Anyone with colonial experience – and the prudent new chums without it – sought out an Aboriginal assistant before venturing into the bush. George Caley wrote to Joseph Banks in 1801 informing him that he intended to keep 'a bush native constant soon, as they can trace any thing so well in the bush'.[108] Twenty years later a visitor noted that when the colonist travelled 'through the woods' he was usually accompanied by 'a party of blacks as porters of his luggage and conductors of his route'.[109] Similar views were expressed in the other colonies, a South Australian pioneer observing that in the bush 'an active black is of much use, few whites can ever acquire the art of tracking as he can'.[110] The editor of the *Perth Gazette* believed that it was 'useless for any party of Europeans to go out without the assistance of a native as a guide'.[111] In the Port Phillip district at much the same time, the chief protector of Aborigines, G. A. Robinson, noted that black guides were 'found of infinite service to travellers' as a result of their 'knowledge of locality, quickness of perception, endurance of fatigue, their facility in procuring water and sustenance'.[112] Writing from Exmoor Station in central Queensland, Rachel Henning explained that 'people who are going for a long journey almost always take a black boy with them' because they were 'most useful servants in the bush'.[113] A fellow colonist observed at much the same time that the bullock-drivers 'always have a black man who serves them, and goes with them over the country on long journeys'.[114] The missionary Lancelot Threlkeld was just one of many travellers who 'engaged a blackfellow' to take him up the country. In their capacity as guides the Aborigines were, he explained, 'of most essential service' because while

> a map and a compass, are useful; . . . the local maps, which are obtained directly or indirectly from the Colonial Surveyors, have very few natural boundaries laid down, for the guidance of a stranger; and the compass, is a very uncertain benefit, when standing on the margin of an extensive morass, or when fixed in the dilemma of a thicket. But the blacks, with a perspicacity of vision which appears almost preternatural, track footsteps over bare rocks, and in the darkest or most infrequented parts of the forest. Our guide led us through what is here called, a *thick brush*; on entering which, he took off his shirt and trousers, to avoid their being torn. As we passed along, he trod down the long runners of the wild vine, lifted up the lianas which are as strong as pack-thread, sometimes went head first through a small opening, and sometimes feet first, but he was never at a loss which way to take, though we could not determine in which direction the sun laid; and around us it was an inextricable maze of matted ramifications.[115]

Aboriginal guides were particularly useful to parties which went out 'finding country', especially if the individuals in question lacked experience in the bush. G. A. Robinson observed that the settlers bore testimony to the 'efficiency and willingness of the natives in showing them runs and water'[116] and in guiding them 'through the intricacies of their forests', leading them to 'their Rivers, their springs, and rich pastures'.[117] Many of the tracks that travellers followed up country had been originally opened up by black guides. While discussing New South Wales roads in his 1826 survey of agriculture and grazing, James Atkinson explained that

> In the more recently settled parts of the country, the roads are in many places very bad, and the passage of the rivers and creeks is extremely difficult and dangerous: these roads are in fact nothing more than mere tracks, that have generally been formed by people who have settled themselves, or taken possession of a grazing run beyond the occupied part of the country. Having ascertained the most practical route to the spot they intend to occupy, the track is marked out by cutting pieces out of the bark of the trees along the line; this service is very frequently performed by black Natives, who have a most accurate local knowledge of the country, the track thus marked is followed by such as have occasion, and becomes a beaten path, and at length a road.[118]

∫ Appropriated bushcraft

The anthropologist N. B. Tindale argued some years ago that Aboriginal clans emphasised their ownership of land both by occupation 'time out of mind' and by their mastery of the food resources. They had, therefore, both a birthright to their land and a 'right over it by reason of knowledge'.[119] The encroaching Europeans not only occupied the land, they also appropriated both the local knowledge and much of the expert bushcraft. While discussing the way in which land-seeking settlers had made use of Aboriginal guides, G. A. Robinson explained that their 'knowledge of their country thus acquired, was turned to account' and eventually 'sold to speculators in runs'.[120] Many pioneers commented on the practical value of Aboriginal advice and assistance. 'In my own experience of work in the bush', a Western Australian pioneer recalled, 'progress would not have been half what it was if we had not had natives with us.'[121] A Victorian settler, commenting on the value of black guides on hunting and fishing expeditions, explained:

> they not only guided us accurately, but taught us many lessons in bushcraft, and in the mode of approaching game, which perhaps we should never have picked up otherwise.[122]

The noted nineteenth-century bushman John F. Mann, wishing to serve an apprenticeship in bushcraft, sought out an Aboriginal adviser. 'Being desirous of securing some knowledge of bush lore', he explained, 'before venturing on an exploring expedition into the interior, I was fortunate enough to fall in with a most intelligent blackfellow . . . who gave me much valuable information.'[123]

The Australian bushman owed much to the Aborigines. Many of their most characteristic skills – the ability to live

off the land, to travel light, to track and find water – derived
from the ancient indigenous bushcraft. Mitchell provided
a clear example of this debt. Camping with a party of blacks,
he found the water in a nearby pool hot and muddy. Fortunately his companions 'knew well how to obtain a cool and
clean draught'. They scratched a hole in the soft sand beside
the pool, in which the water rose cool but still muddy. They
then threw in tufts of long grass through which the water was
sucked free of sand and gravel. Mitchell was 'glad to follow
the example', finding the 'sweet fragrance of the grass an
agreeable addition to the luxury of drinking'.[124] Many other
bush customs were borrowed from Aboriginal guides.
Writing of New South Wales in the 1820s, surgeon Cunningham observed:

> In calling to each other at a distance, they make use of the word
> *Cooee* as we do the word *Hollo*, prolonging the sound of the *coo*,
> and closing that of the *ee* with a shrill jerk. This mode of call
> is found to be so infinitely preferable to the *Hollo*, both on
> account of its easier pronunciation and the great distance
> at which it can be heard, as to have become of general use
> throughout the colony; and a newcomer, in desiring an indi-
> vidual to call another back, soon learns to say '*Coo-ee* to him',
> instead of '*Hollow* to him'.[125]

The process of acculturation – of 'Australianisation' –
can be traced in the career of the early Western Australian
settler G. F. Moore. On his first expedition inland from the
infant colony he travelled heavily encumbered. His 'stock

was pretty large', he explained, and included four shirts, four pairs of stockings, two pairs of trousers, three pairs of shoes, two coats, a large pair of worsted stockings with leather soles, a straw hat for day and a blue cap for night, a hammock, blankets and a cloak.[126] On later expeditions he travelled with local Aborigines and came to admire their easy confidence in the bush. A few years later he travelled north of Perth accompanied by an Aboriginal guide called Weenat, who needed little persuasion and 'still less preparation' to accompany the party. 'A word of explanation of the object of the expedition, a piece of bread in one hand, a firestick in the other and he was ready.'[127] When camping for the night, Moore's conduct exposed him to the raillery of his guides, both male and female:

> Where shall we make a house, I said to my assistants? 'What for house make?' said she, pointing laughingly to the clear blue sky and bright moon. I felt ashamed of my effeminacy, so followed their example in laying myself down upon the ground, with my feet to the fire.[128]

∫ This treasured lore

In a paper on 'The Australian Aborigines' Water Quest' delivered to the Royal Geographical Society in Adelaide in 1895, A. T. Magarey emphasised how the Europeans had benefited from knowledge which had 'passed down from generation to generation'. The white man, he pointed out, 'inherited much of this treasured lore'.[129] But few of Magarey's contemporaries believed, as he did, that in developing their bushcraft and knowledge of the continent the settlers had availed themselves 'of the skill of the eminently intelligent aborigine'.[130] The common view at the time was that Aboriginal expertise was due to instinct rather than intellect, to biology rather than culture. Diverse and highly developed skills that had evolved over many centuries, and which could have been accepted as evidence to bolster arguments in favour of racial equality, were thrown into the balance to prove the reverse. Talents that were the product of long training were taken to be due to more acute senses, which in turn were attributed to a primitive and underdeveloped brain. The Queensland bushman E. B. Kennedy wrote disparagingly:

> And because these Blacks can track well, hunt well, and are exceedingly acute in all their senses, some bring forward these qualities as a proof of their intelligence, as if the fact of finding their daily food is any sign: What Dingo or other wild animal does not do the same?[131]

Aboriginal expertise was taken as convincing proof that they were less evolved and closer to the animals and, what is more, doomed to disappear from the face of the earth.

This was not a prospect that disturbed the population at large. By the turn of the century the colonists felt confident that they had made good their claim to Australia and that they had little to learn from the dispossessed Aborigines, the enthusiasm of amateur ethnographers notwithstanding. In February 1894 the Queensland newspapers reported the capture of the so-called Dora-Dora brothers by the local policemen Tom and Nat King. The brothers, originally from Queensland, had served in the Victorian police force. They eventually took to the bush, were involved in a number of crimes and travelled home, evading every attempt to capture them along the way until they reached central Queensland. The editor of the *Rockhampton Morning Bulletin* celebrated the event and commented that

> It was a difficult task, requiring the greatest patience and vigilance together with a knowledge of the bush and of native customs equal almost to the black they were after . . . The two constables have displayed much tenacity and skill, and deserve great credit for their capture. But beyond that, the arrest shows that even in his own field the blackfellow can be met, and conquered by the white man.[132]

The confidence of the Rockhampton editor that European bushmen could outwit the Aborigines was a very new phenomenon. Throughout the nineteenth century the settlers were keenly aware that the blacks were their masters in the bush. When faced with concerted resistance around the fringes of settlement, the Europeans responded by co-opting Aboriginal expertise in the cause of colonisation.

two

BLACK PIONEERS

PIONEER SQUATTERS FOLLOWED the tracks of the explorers into the interior. Like the explorers, they took Aboriginal guides and servants in their parties, with the result that young men and women from the settled districts of New South Wales were ubiquitous participants in the squatting rush of the 1830s and 1840s which spilled out over the whole of south-eastern Australia. A little later Swan Valley Aborigines participated in the occupation of the Murchison, Ashburton and Gascoyne districts in Western Australia. They were a valuable addition to the 'nomad tribe' of pastoral workers, combining bushcraft inherited from their ancient culture with new skills learnt from the Europeans and, as often as not, quickly mastered. Once the rush for new land consolidated, they lived and worked on sheep and cattle stations a long way from their tribal homelands, becoming part of a small skilled retinue isolated by race from the white workers and by culture and language from the tribespeople of the districts in question. While reminiscing about her childhood on a central Queensland station, Rosa Campbell Praed referred to 'several black boys' who were in regular employment, lived in a hut, wore clothes and 'had adopted, as far as possible, the customs of the white men'. She had little contact with the 'station blacks', who performed a range of unskilled tasks on a casual basis.

> They would not do menial work, but rode among the cattle, looked for lost sheep, and brought up the horses. Their mole-skins were always white. They wore Crimean shirts, with coloured handkerchiefs knotted above one shoulder and under the other, and sang songs in their own language set to oper-atic airs.[1]

Right-hand boys

Mary Durack paid tribute to Pumpkin, the Boontamurra man from Cooper's Creek who made such an important contribution to her family's pastoral enterprises. He was Patrick Durack's 'right-hand boy' and could master anything – horse-breaking, butchering, odd jobs, blacksmithing, gardening. With his many skills, Pumpkin was 'the mainstay' of Argyle Downs in the Kimberleys. Living among blacks who were initially hostile to his presence, he acted as a guardian to the whites, camping on the verandah when he suspected there might be a raid on the homestead. The local blacks were 'no countrymen of his and relentlessly he rode their tracks, reporting where they had chased and sometimes speared cattle and horses'. Having overcome his fear of hostile magic, he was able to travel at will over long distances and across assorted tribal territories. Like a white stockman, Pumpkin then 'reared up' his protégés Boxer and Ulysses to be invaluable members of the station workforce. He discouraged the 'careless pidgin form of English and taught his apprentices good manners and good stockmanship'. In later years Boxer was regarded as 'the best all round boy' in Western Australia.[2]

In her account of life on Mt Mulgrave Station on the Mitchell River, Evelyn Maunsell recalled the contribution of her 'boy' Albert. He had originally come from Wide Bay in southern Queensland but had been taken to Cooktown by a Dr Khorteum, who 'dressed him in a white suit and trained him to open the door, show patients in, and drive the buggy when the doctor went on his rounds'. After the doctor's death he was cast adrift and found his way to Maytown on the Palmer River goldfield. He was picked up there by the local police sergeant, who brought him to Mt Mulgrave and 'gave' him to the Maunsells. By then he was in his forties. Evelyn found him a 'blessing around the house'. He was 'always spotlessly clean' and continued to dress in an impeccable white suit. He 'looked after the washing and ironing and waited on the table inside as well as doing odd jobs about the homestead'. But as a 'foreigner', Albert was never accepted by the local clans and was often in fear of his life. When the whole station community travelled to the picnic race meeting at Palmerville he was acutely anxious about his security. While all the local Aborigines camped on the far side of the river, Albert stayed as close as he could to the Maunsells and slept in front of – and eventually in – their tent.[3]

The black workforce

There were many 'Pumpkins' and many 'Alberts' in colonial Australia, who lived in obscurity and whose lives and achievements were never recorded. But of even greater significance than their contribution to the European economy was the labour and the skill of thousands of Aboriginal men and women – and boys and girls – who were absorbed into the rural workforce on or near their own country following the arrival of the Europeans and their flocks and herds to take up 'their runs'. Squatters were more likely to employ Aboriginal labour if they had located themselves on the outer fringes of European settlement where white labour was scarce, unreliable and expensive. When the various gold-rushes drew off what white labour there was, the Aborigines became even more important. In 1852 the commissioner of crown lands for the Albert district abutting the Darling River reported that the local blacks were shepherding 50 000 sheep in the district. They were 'careful of the sheep committed to their charge', which were in better condition than they had been when Europeans were employed. They also washed and shore the sheep, the commissioner reporting that 'they clip much more closely and cleanly than it is possible to induce hired Europeans to do'.[4] Unlike the situation in south-eastern Australia, where labour was employed only in specific districts or at particular times, Aboriginal workers became the mainstay of the European economy in the northern half of the continent.

In her study of Aboriginal labour in the pastoral industry in north Queensland in the second half of the nineteenth century, Dawn May concluded that in 1886 there were over 1000 blacks permanently employed in the pastoral industry, representing about half the total workforce. On the more remote cattle stations the Aboriginal component of the workforce was much higher. Many more workers would have been temporarily drawn into the work for specific tasks or at those times of maximum demand for labour, especially at shearing and mustering.[5] In 1884 Robert J. Sholl, a former government resident in Western Australia's north district, estimated that between the Murchison and Fitzroy Rivers the Europeans employed 'some 1800' Aborigines, who constituted a highly significant section of the 'industrial population'.[6]

Official surveys in both Queensland and Western Australia in 1901 allow us to obtain a comprehensive picture of Aboriginal employment at the turn of the century. During that year Queensland's two protectors of Aborigines issued permits for the permanent employment of 2141 Aborigines. Many more would have been employed on a casual basis. These permits were for servants in the urban areas and for workers in the maritime industries, but the largest group would have been pastoral workers. The census of 1901 enumerated 1992 Aboriginal stockworkers and domestics in north Queensland.[7] Between September 1899 and June 1901 Western Australia's travelling inspector of Aborigines visited pastoral properties and mining camps in the sprawling Northern District. He counted the number of blacks employed on every pastoral property he visited. In all, over 2260 Aboriginal men and women worked in a wide range of occupations. In 1902 the inspector of police at Derby estimated that 1500 Aborigines were employed on stations in the Kimberleys.[8] It was officially estimated that 1000 Aborigines were employed by Europeans in the Northern Territory in 1912.[9] It may be impossible to arrive at any final assessment of the level of employment in northern Australia at the end of the nineteenth century, but it seems likely that there may have been as many as 10 000 permanent employees as well as others who worked casually on the sheep and cattle stations. Without that vital contribution it is hard to see how the northern pastoral and maritime industries could have survived.

∫ Very cheap and always on hand

One of the great advantages of black labour was simply that it was available in parts of the country where white workers were difficult to come by and expensive to employ. 'In the early days when white labour was scarce', a north Queensland pioneer recalled in 1896, 'they were always on hand.'[10] Aborigines who were living on their own land wanted to remain there. That was where they belonged, and they had no desire to head off for the nearest town, the latest diggings, or the big smoke. The arrival of a handful of whites and strange 'blackfellows' — no matter how hostile and threatening — could not change the determination to live on one's own land. The result was that there were no recruitment costs for 'station blacks' and when not needed they could be left to fend for themselves, to return to their traditional economy and hunt and forage in the bush. When there was a sudden demand for labour additional hands could be brought into the labour force and then dismissed when the situation eased. While visiting a station on the Ord River in 1896, a Western Australian official noted that there was a large camp of blacks on the far side of the creek on crown land. He explained that whenever the station required more hands 'they just send across for them and when they have too many they send them back again, so that they seldom have the same number on the station'.[11]

What was even more appealing to frontier squatters was that black labour was cheap. It was usually obtained in return for food, tobacco and clothing, and the quantities varied widely depending on the whim of the white boss. In addition, there was no need to provide housing. A few household servants could sleep on the verandah or under the house, but the station workforce could be left to its own devices as long as the camp was not so close as to be intrusive. Dawn May has estimated that at least four Aborigines could be engaged for the cost of one white person. A European stockman earned about £100 a year and a white domestic about £80, whereas food, clothing and tobacco for a black stockman was estimated to be worth £25.[12] This situation persisted in the Northern Territory and Western Australia until well into the twentieth century. In 1902 Queensland legislated to provide a minimum wage of 5s. a month – or £3 a year over and above rations and clothing. White employers deeply resented government interference 'between them and their black servants', whom they still regarded 'almost as slaves'. 'They miss the old days', the protector of Aborigines explained in 1902, 'when they could chain their blacks up and beat and abuse them how and when they liked.'[13] The situation was still much the same ten years later, the protector writing in his annual report for 1912:

> After working these blacks for years without any interference pastoralists have come to regard them as goods and chattels, and warmly resent the action of the Protector who dares to question such ownership.[14]

The growth and significance of the Aboriginal labour force can be gleaned from two Western Australian government reports, both dealing with sheep farming in the Murchison–Gascoyne District and written twenty years apart. In 1882 the government dispatched the magistrate R. Fairbairn to investigate the state of relations between the local Aborigines and the settlers. In doing so, Fairbairn built up a comprehensive picture of the existing situation. While examining the reasons for the frequently reported loss of sheep, he discovered that practically all the shepherding was done by Aboriginal women who were employed miles away from the head station and were very much left to their own devices. Even when white shepherds were employed they usually lived with Aboriginal women who actually did all the work. By various means the Aboriginal shepherdesses arranged for their kin to share in the abundant supply of meat. They either gave sheep away at night or allowed them to stray at an agreed locality where they could easily be dispatched and carried off into the bush. Despite the levying of this tribute on the squatters by the resident clans, the settlers told Fairbairn that they intended to continue in their use of black labour. He explained that

> the settlers take a business view of the position; they argue that unless the natives can be utilized as shepherds, sheep farming on the Gascoyne will not pay. A white man costs £50 per annum and his food, and it requires a cart, or at least a packhorse, to move him from one part of the run to another, a native will do the same work for his food, and a shirt occasionally, and he requires no assistance in moving with his sheep from one camp to another.[15]

Twenty years later the importance of black labour was even more marked. Of the ninety-odd stations between the De Grey and Ashburton Rivers visited by G. S. Olivey, Western Australia's travelling inspector of Aborigines, all but a handful employed Aboriginal men and women. On average there were about 25 Aborigines per station, but the numbers ranged from as few as four or five to as many as 60 or 70. Practically all the work was done by Aborigines – shepherding, mustering, housework, cooking, shearing, wool-scouring, carting, blacksmithing, pit-sawing, fencing. There were skilled 'half-caste' workers on a few stations, who earned modest wages, but the great majority of the 'station-blacks' received only rations and clothes. Rations consisted of flour, tea, sugar, tobacco and meat, which may often have been no more than bones and offal, for, as Olivey noted, 'when cattle are killed in a place there is always a lot of waste stuff that the natives get'. When concluding his short report on each station Olivey invariably remarked that the black workers were 'fat, sleek and contented'.[16] He had no idea if the 'station-blacks' ever got the proclaimed scale of rations, and as far as we know he never enquired of the recipients. Occasionally comments of the black stockmen were recorded, indicating that, at least on some stations, all was not well. In 1887 a police constable recorded a statement from Bobey and Sambo, two stockmen from the station of a prominent Northern District pastoral family. Speaking of his 'master', Mr McKay, Bobey said, 'he gives me only a small piece of damper 3 times a day no tea and no sugar no meat no cloth and no Bankit and he bets [belts] me sometimes'. Corroborating this claim, Sambo asserted that McKay 'does not give me ore my woman any flour all that he gives us to eat is a sheeps head every day and never flour ore tea ore sugar ore cloth ore blanket'.[17]

∫ *They can't be beat*

The advantages of Aboriginal labour were not confined to its cheapness. Black workers brought into the pastoral industry skills which were of enormous benefit to station owners and managers. They knew their country with an intimacy that no European could match. The profound understanding of the climate, topography, vegetation and water resources which a hunter–gatherer needed to prosper were equally useful to the pastoral industry once the stockmen and women had come to understand the needs and habits of the sheep and cattle and the objectives of the white boss. Aboriginal tracking abilities were also of great practical value on the pastoral properties, which remained unfenced in many places until well into the twentieth century. Without black stockmen and women it would have been almost impossible to keep the herds and flocks together. On the unfenced runs they 'proved themselves to be most trustworthy and efficient', and on account 'of their astonishing tracking and scrub riding abilities, no cattle could get away from them'.[18] In his reminiscences of the pastoral industry in central Queensland, A. C. Grant observed that:

> Day by day the cattle on the camps were gone through and absent ones noted and searched for until found. In this duty the blackboys were simply invaluable and their interest in the work and untiring skill in tracking contributed chiefly to the success which attended the pioneers in keeping their herds together.[19]

With experience, Aboriginal pastoral workers developed the new skills needed to handle horses, sheep and cattle. Most young people were avid horseriders and learnt to manage their mounts within a remarkably short time. Sophisticated knowledge of animal behaviour learnt in the bush was adapted to the demands of the European economy and many black stockworkers became skilled handlers of sheep and cattle and highly successful horsebreakers. A Gulf Country pioneer admitted in 1884: 'I don't know what we pioneers should have done without the blacks, for they can't be beat at looking after horses and cattle.'[20]

In many respects Aboriginal stockmen and women were better than their white counterparts and not just cheaper. They were as skilled in everyday tasks of the stock camp and had other talents that few European stockmen could match, including the ability at any time to live off the land and survive in the most difficult conditions. As noted in Chapter Three, W. E. Parry-Okeden, the Queensland police commissioner, was highly sceptical of his chances of recruiting white men to perform the functions of the native police, and those few who could, had learnt much of their bushcraft from the blacks in the first place. Walter Roth, the northern protector of Aborigines, discussed the problems he was having with north Queensland squatters while trying to encourage them to pay Aboriginal workers. He found their resistance difficult to understand because the employers 'both recognize and appreciate the value of Aboriginal labour' and when pressed on the question admitted that 'the blacks are better than the ordinary stockmen – they know the country better and are more reliable and obedient'.[21] The local protector at Normanton specifically asked leading Gulf Country squatters to compare white with Aboriginal labour. A few came down in favour of the Europeans, but most opted for the blacks. Their replies were published in *Parliamentary Papers* in 1904:

'As stock-riders, better than ordinary pick-up hand' (W. Ormsby Wiley, Milgarra); 'Better than the class walking about in the Gulf' (John Epworth, Delta Downs); 'They suit the purpose just as well as white labour' (W. Wright, Wallabadah); 'As good and, in a great many instances, better' (G. A. Bristow, Miranda Downs); 'Have proved more reliable than the general class of white stockmen in this district' (Thos. A. Simpson, late manager Carpentaria Downs, Forest Home, and Magowra stations); 'Better than the general run of pick-up white men. They know the country better, and are more biddable' (A. H. Underwood, Midlothian); 'Better than the average white' (Daniel Thorn, drover and station manager since 1872); 'As stock-riders and bushmen in many cases superior to the general station hands' (Reginald Hillcoat, Bonnarra); 'They are preferable and far more reliable than white labour among cattle, always sober, and more biddable' (John T. Roberts, Pastoral Inspector for the Bank of New South Wales); 'As good' (J. V. Milson, manager, Forest Home); 'Compare favourable with ordinary class of white stockman' (Ross Maclean, manager, Magowra); 'Compare better, with the ordinary run of white labour' (Robt. Currie, Marine Plains).[22]

∫ *Women's role*

Aboriginal women were frequently involved in stockwork.
They were the principal shepherds in the early years of settlement in Western Australia's Northern District and were
preferred to men for the same task in Queensland's central-
west.[23] On the northern cattle frontier – stretching from
Queensland through the Top End to the East Kimberleys –
women became accomplished stockworkers. The prominent
drover Matt Savage estimated that women made up 50 per
cent of all stockriders in the Kimberleys in the 1910s.[24] The
practice had taken root in north Queensland a generation
before. After visiting stations in the north-west of the colony
in 1883, a correspondent wrote to the *Queenslander* observing:

> what strikes one most forcibly is to see the gins, who are
> employed as stockmen nearly everywhere out here, strutting
> about in moleskins and flannel shirts, and with felt hats crammed
> . . . on their lovely heads and smoking short black pipes.[25]

Normanton's inspector of police informed his commissioner
in 1891 that it had been the practice to herd cattle with black
women 'for a great many years' owing to the fact that all the
males had been 'exterminated'.[26] A prospector travelling
south from Normanton to Camooweal in 1891 reported that
apart from a few white men most stations were run by 'gins
in trousers'.[27] The prominent cattleman Frank Hann was said
to have seven well-built women 'as a sort of bodyguard'.[28]
The inspector of police in the Northern Territory recalled
that in 1881:

a Queensland squatter arrived on our goldfields with a mob of
fat cattle; his only assistants were three or four so called boys but
were in reality, as the squatter himself informed me, young gins
dressed in men's clothing.[29]

Some women rose to be 'head-stockman' on their stations.
In the early 1880s the person in charge of stock at Beaudesert
was a woman named Kitty, and at Granada, Dinah, the best
stockrider on the station, held a similar position.[30]

These women's work-skills notwithstanding, white men
expected to have free access to female Aboriginal workers
regardless of the women's feelings or those of their tribal
husbands and other kin. Occasionally the white men were
frustrated by station owners or their spouses. The Durack
family tradition is that Patrick Durack imposed a strict
regime on Thylungra on the Cooper. 'There were no half-
castes born on Thylungra', Mary Durack reported, 'but there
were a few fellows who had the romance licked out of them
with [Patrick's] stock-whip just the same.'[31] In Queensland's
Gulf Country, Jane Bardsley took 'care of the gins' who
worked in the homestead, 'locking them up every night at
sunset, to look at their books, have their smoke and also be
free from molestation', but even her vigilance failed. The
Chinese cook got one of the women pregnant and she was
again 'molested' by a 'gentleman' passing through the station
on a hunting trip. 'I feel so angry with this man', she wrote,
'my blood is up. I would like to shoot some of these men.'[32]
Bardsley was at least aware of what was going on. Writing

of Byro Station in the north-west of Western Australia, a government official reported in 1898 that the white women on the station 'seem to be in the most blissful ignorance of what is going on down in the gully and just outside the garden wall'.[33]

On many stations there was no attempt to hide the extent of sexual relations between white station workers and black women. A pastoralist from the edge of the Nullarbor Plain told a South Australian Royal Commission in 1899 that he had known stations 'where every hand on the place had a gin, even down to boys of 15 years of age'.[34] Similar comments were made to a Western Australian Royal Commission six years later. On Fitzroy River stations, a witness observed, the 'Boss has his own fancy woman, and the overseer has from eight to ten to choose from'.[35] Reporting on his tour of western Queensland in 1900, southern protector Archibald Meston observed that on many stations 'there are no white women at all. On these the aboriginal women are usually at the mercy of anybody, from the proprietor or Manager, to the stockmen, cook, rouseabout and jackeroo.'[36]

When they were able to, the women endeavoured to exercise some control over who they accepted as sexual partners and on what terms. Their ability to extract money, food and tobacco from white men was often an important contribution to the comfort, and even the survival, of clan members and especially those who were too young or too old to work for the whites. The police constable at Boulia in far western Queensland reported in 1899 that on the local stations the women were

> as a rule . . . well supplied in food and cloth and some of the men working on the stations spend nearly all their wages on them buying them dresses, tobacco, pipes, matches, etc. [37]

Sometimes affection grew out of casual relations and attachments developed despite all the circumstances militating against them. An observer of outback life commented in 1898 that some of the men who lived with Aboriginal women had 'through constant association . . . learnt if not exactly to love them, to treat them with due consideration and kindness'. [38]

∫ Servants and companions

Women and girls made a significant contribution as workers in and around the station homestead both as *de facto* managers of all-male households and as the invaluable assistants and companions to the wives of owners and managers. They performed innumerable tasks around the homestead; they were 'maids of all work'. Few stations could have paid for white servants to perform the same tasks, which were frequently labour intensive. Like their male counterparts, the women were rarely paid. On his 1900 tour of western Queensland, Meston found only two stations where female servants were paid anything at all. 'And yet', he wrote in his report, 'several mistresses admitted to me that their aboriginal women did work for which they would have to pay a white woman 15s. or 20s. per week.' [39]

Women drew water from wells or from nearby rivers and waterholes and carried it to the homestead for gardens, washing and general household use. A visitor to Vena Park in north Queensland in 1886 was surprised to find an Aboriginal servant 'carrying water out of the lagoon to the vegetable garden at daydawn'.[40] In a letter to a friend Jane Bardsley explained that the women 'rise at dawn to water the flower and citrus gardens by carrying two kerosene tins of water arranged at the end of a stick'.[41] Washing was another station task requiring a significant contribution from Aboriginal women. Writing of her experiences in the Northern Territory in the 1880s, Mrs Dominic Daly recalled that her black assistants could not wash 'in the proper sense of the word', but they none the less rinsed the clothes, emptied the tubs, carried all the water and 'helped in the process of hanging out . . . and in many other ways'.[42] Women on Granada Station in the Cloncurry district washed, starched and ironed 'as well as any white laundress could do it'.[43]

Aboriginal women performed many of the routine household tasks – scrubbing, sweeping, dusting, scouring, chopping wood. Whenever possible the 'missus' would acquire a young girl or two, either from the local camp or from some more remote tribe, and 'train them up' to housework. Evelyn Maunsell, who lived on a remote Cape York cattle station, argued that they 'needed to be trained young if they were to be useful about the house'.[44] Katie Langloh Parker brought three young girls from the local camp into her house whom she found to be 'clever, willing and grateful'. As the 'taming process began', she taught them to be efficient servants and waitresses. To wait at table in summer she dressed them 'in little white frocks with red sashes' and gave them each 'a large palm leaf fan with which to fan us on the gaspingly still nights' as the 'boss' and 'missus' sat at dinner.[45] When Evelyn Maunsell sat down to read or sew, a three-year-old boy she called Robin squatted on the floor beside her. Her husband 'had fixed the switch of a cow's tail to a stick and with this Robin was supposed to keep the flies off [her]'. But before they had been sitting down for long 'the switch would stop, and there would be Robin, sound asleep, curled up on the cool cement like a puppy'.[46]

White women living on isolated stations were heavily dependent on their black servants during pregnancy, and when labour began unexpectedly the servants delivered the children as well. Evelyn Maunsell was called to the isolated Walsh River Telegraph Station when the manager's wife, Maud White, had gone into premature labour. When Evelyn arrived on the scene Fanny, the Aboriginal midwife, was already preparing for the delivery. Arthur White was beside himself and was 'reading up in a medical book what should be done'. Evelyn described how events unfolded:

> I remember I was in her bedroom with old Fanny, and Arthur White was outside the door with the medical book reading out what we should do. But what was actually happening seemed quite different from what he was reading, and while I was trying

to understand it all old Fanny just ignored us both and went ahead with whatever it was the black normally did. Arthur kept calling out, 'Don't take any notice of that old black fool; this is what the book says.'

The baby girl arrived in the middle of it all, and I remember calling to Arthur, 'How long does it say I've got to cut the cord?'

There was a pause while he looked for the place in the book, and then read it out, but it was nothing like what Fanny was doing. I tried to get him to describe it more clearly. He was nearly frantic with worry.

'Never mind old Fanny,' he yelled. 'Just do what the book says.'

I watched Fanny and I thought, 'She's brought more piccanninies into the world than Arthur White has ever seen.' So I let her go ahead without interfering and everything was all right.[47]

Aboriginal 'nurse-girls' often bore much of the burden of childcare while the 'missus' devoted herself to other pursuits. Colonial bureaucrat Charles Eden recalled that Kitty was an 'affectionate little thing' who was 'always in a good humour'. She spent hours amusing the Edens' child 'by beating a piece of tin, or affording some other entertainment'. On Hughenden Station the local women lay on a blanket and swung Norris Gray back and forth in his hammock to try and keep him cool in the fierce western heat. His mother, Eva Gray, hired an English nurse in Sydney and brought her to Hughenden, but on one 'melting hot' day of 108°F the nurse walked out 'after being very disagreeable'.

Fortunately for Eva, help was at hand. The wife of the local police magistrate 'kindly gave [her] one of her black gins "Jenny"', who became an indispensable part of the Gray household. She got up every morning at 5.30 a.m. to take the baby for a walk before breakfast. Within a few months Eva was so confident of Jenny's competence that she left her minding Norris all day while she rode off to neighbouring stations. He was carried on his nurse's shoulders and was even taken on hunting expeditions miles away from the homestead.[48] When Jane Bardsley went hunting or swimming on Midlothian Station her servant Kitty carried eighteen-month-old Fred 'in the native fashion'. 'He sits on her shoulders', she explained in a letter to her cousin,

> with his legs around her neck, holding onto her hair. Sometimes she pretends to be a bucking horse, and it looks as though Fred would be able to stick to anything. With his free hand he hits her to make her buck more.[49]

European station women were often uniquely isolated. They were usually miles away from the nearest white woman and in northern Australia travel was difficult for months on end during the wet season. Husbands and other stockmen were frequently out on the runs for days — and even weeks — on end. Battling loneliness and depression, they turned to the women from the camp for company and companionship. Evelyn Maunsell used to spend her afternoons with the women and children on the bank of the Mitchell River, where they swam and fished. About 5 p.m. the party would trail home and, as Evelyn admitted, 'the house always seemed particularly lonely then – and I would look at the plants I had put in and get my dinner, which I ate alone'.[50] Jane Bardsley went for Sunday picnics with the Aboriginal women and children, which usually began with a nude swim in a sandy-bottomed lagoon a few miles from the homestead. At first she 'felt shy at being naked', but everyone got used to the situation and so she 'did not mind'.[51]

Some women sought more than company from Aboriginal companions and were willing to learn as much as they could about the physical environment and the cultural traditions of the local clans. Maunsell and Bardsley in Queensland's Gulf Country, Katie Parker in western New South Wales and Ethel Hassell in the south-west of Western Australia all went on regular excursions with the Aboriginal women while they foraged for bush food. 'If I wanted to explore any distant part', Hassell wrote, 'I could always get some of the women to go with, the greatest difficulty being to put a limit on the number.'[52] Katie Parker declared that she would never forget her 'rambles through the bush with a retinue of natives'.[53] Both Hassell and Parker collected myths and legends and later wrote books on the subject. Parker's were bestsellers and went through many editions. Collecting the legends was both an entertaining and enriching experience. She wrote subsequently:

> I learnt that every distinctive bit of nature – say a heap of white
> stones, the red mistletoe, the gnarled dark excrescences on the

trees, and so on, each had its legend. How interesting the hearing
of them made my Bush life, and how it increased my sympathy
for the natives and widened my Bush horizons, for in those days
the coming of a Chinaman's melon-cart was an event, and a
visitor, a sensation.[54]

Like their male counterparts, station women learnt many
practical lessons while rambling in the bush. Hassell absorbed
'much about the habits and ways of the birds and animals'.
She studied tracking and other aspects of bushcraft which
she found 'more interesting than books'.[55] Bardsley learnt
that local fruits and yams made 'excellent food' and used them
to supplement a larder pinched in hard times.[56] Maunsell
was similarly instructed by the station women. Even the
four-year-old Robin could teach her about tracking. His
knowledge of nature 'was amazing', she recalled.

He would show me the tracks of different kinds of ants and tell
me where they were going and what sort of nest they had. He
showed me how to follow native bees to their nest.[57]

Bardsley spent so much time with her black companion that
she admitted that 'at times I feel black and I'm sure the
natives think that I am some dead relative who has jumped
up a white fellow'. The women wanted to initiate her. But
that was going much too far. Her husband told her that
'people who live in the Gulf for a long time become like
natives and that is one reason why we must get away'.[58]

Violent aftermath

Both Jane Bardsley and Evelyn Maunsell married and went
to live on outback cattle stations without any previous experience of life in the bush. Both quickly discovered the legacy
of violence which had accompanied European occupation of
Aboriginal land. When Maunsell went down to the river with
the Aboriginal women, she always walked at the rear of the
procession because the old hands had impressed on her that
the blacks could never be trusted. If they walked behind you
they might take the opportunity 'to belt you over the skull'.[59]
Bardsley's introduction took a different form. When she first
moved to Midlothian Station as a young bride she discovered
that her husband still suffered from the acute tensions of
frontier life. In order to wake him up from daytime siestas
she found it advisable 'to touch him with a long cane' kept
for the purpose. She explained in a letter that this procedure
was necessary because 'he jumps out of his bed very suddenly
and always strikes out'.[60]

Violence underlay all aspects of white–Aboriginal relations, even when not apparent on the surface. Practically all
districts in Australia – and more particularly in the north –
experienced periods of open conflict between incoming
settlers and resident clans. It varied in duration and inten-
sity; in Queensland it became institutionalised through the
agency of the native mounted police. An accommodation was
reached everywhere sooner or later and Aborigines 'came in'
to pastoral properties, where boys and girls and young men

and women were rapidly absorbed into a labour-hungry economy and sex-hungry male 'occupation force'. No matter how symbiotic relations became, even how amicable they were, the memory of the initial conflict lived on. Whites were always afraid of sudden, surreptitious revenge. A Cape York cattleman who managed a remote cattle station never trusted his Aboriginal stockmen despite shared experience, hardships and achievements. So concerned was he about their 'hidden nature' that a loaded revolver was his 'constant companion' night and day for six years.[61] For their part, the blacks were always aware of the Europeans' capacity for violence and the absence of any restraint on its exercise. Fear of sudden and often capricious brutality shadowed Aboriginal life for several generations. More than anything else, it determined their response to all Europeans, kind or cruel, friend or foe.

Black workers were at the mercy of their employers. They could be bashed and flogged at will. The law rarely provided any protection and in frontier districts public opinion was overwhelmingly in favour of 'keeping the blacks in their place'. White people openly spoke of 'chastising' their servants. Bosses who were 'hard on the blacks' were admired and respected. Cabinet ministers with frontier experience told their parliamentary colleagues that Aborigines had to be ruled 'by brute force', that the only way to deal with them was to give them 'a little stick'.[62] The Queensland officials who toured the colony (later state) at the turn of the century were soon made aware of the brutality which characterised white–Aboriginal relations. In the south-west, where settlement was at least a generation old, people made as light 'of knocking down a blackfellow with a sliprail or flogging him with a stockwhip as though it was having a drink'.[63] In his report to the home secretary on 'Aborigines West of the Warrego', Archibald Meston observed

> A few stations are remarkable for the fairness with which they treat their blacks and others have an unenviable notoriety for ill-usage of the men and disgraceful treatment of the women. Never before have I seen aboriginal men living under such extraordinary terrorism, many of them fine athletic fellows who could in case of a row have settled with their terrorisers in a very summary fashion. But many of them had long been treated as the dogs are treated and were scared into a belief that their employers wielded the power of life and death. They also knew that amongst most of the stations there was a mutual understanding that any run-away black would be hunted or brought back, and as they had no-one to whom they could appeal and no where to go they finally regarded their doom as inevitable and bore their wrongs in silence.[64]

Aboriginal men who attempted to 'settle with' any European were severely dealt with. The perception that any weakening of 'discipline' would disadvantage everyone, meant that white authority had to be constantly asserted. 'Cheeky' blacks were certain to get a severe beating and might even be killed as an example to their fellows. In 1880 an Aboriginal stockman on a western Queensland station wounded a white overseer who was assaulting his wife. It was an insult that could not be tolerated. Local whites decided that a black 'who raised his hand to a white man ought not to live'. He was tracked, caught, hamstrung and then handed over to the native police to be assassinated.[65] Murder was going out of fashion by the turn of the century in Queensland, although it continued in vogue in the more remote parts of the continent for another few decades. But 'cheeky' blacks still didn't get off lightly. In 1902 a Queensland government official visiting the small western settlement of Whitula investigated the beating of a stockman called Woonganeetha or Punch. He had returned to the house of Hackett, his employer, at 11 a.m. after working among the horses and asked for some breakfast.

'Don't ask me you black b ...', retorted this gentleman at the same time knocking Punch down with a clout on the head from a stick which old Hackett always carries. Punch got up, hit Hackett in the jaw and knocked him over. He only hit Hackett once, where as a white man would not have been satisfied until he had administered at least fifteen or twenty. Punch went without his breakfast. Then Brennan [Hackett's son-in-law] came home the worse for liquor and started on the boy but got beaten. Then Little of Tanbar [Station] and Hackett junior came home. Then the four of the them started on Punch with sticks and stockwhip and of course the boy got a bad whipping. These are common incidents in the west.[66]

∫ *Personal property*

Many station owners – and other people who had Aboriginal servants – clearly believed that they owned rather than employed the blacks who worked for them. In 1885 a correspondent wrote to the *Queenslander* from Thagomindah describing the situation of Aboriginal servants in the south-west of the colony. They were employed in all the towns and on every station. Indeed it was hard to see how the stations could 'be worked without their assistance'. They were 'bound by no agreements', but were talked about 'as my, or our niggers, and [were] not free to depart when they like[d]'. It was not considered etiquette to employ blacks 'belonging' to another station and when 'boys' or 'girls' ran away they were pursued, taken back and flogged.[67] In the following year and on the opposite side of the continent a police corporal observed similar conditions in the Pilbara. He was 'afraid the settlers look upon them [their black servants] a little too much as their slaves'. A child brought up on the station was considered to have no right to go away for 'if once their servant they consider him always their servant'.[68] In evidence given that year in a supreme court case in Perth, northern squatters outlined their view of the matter.[69] A Mr Rotton explained: 'In one sense I do think I can keep the natives as long as I like.' A fellow frontiersman discussed the circumstances at greater length, asserting that:

> I do know that, when a man takes up a run and finds a number
> of natives upon the country, as he finds work for those natives

that he has more right to their services than anyone else . . .
There are cases when an intending purchaser would give a
higher price for a run in consequence with it being well stocked
with natives. A purchaser . . . would properly come to the
conclusion that he might reckon on the perpetual services of
the natives.

In summing up, Chief Justice Onslow concluded that there
clearly was 'a very prevalent idea amongst the settlers that
they were entitled . . . for a very indefinite length of time
to the services of the natives in their employ'. His brother
judge Justice Stone appeared to be less perturbed about the
practice. He said he 'could see no more harm in giving
a higher price for a run well stocked with natives' than in
paying 'a higher price for land which had a good supply of
water'.[70]

Pearl divers

These same northern pastoralists who believed they 'owned'
the Aborigines whose land they were squatting on supple-
mented their incomes by participation in the pearling
industry that developed along the coast in the late 1860s and
early 1870s. From its inception until the mid-1880s the
industry was totally dependent on black labour, which was
ultimately replaced when diving suits were introduced.
Pearling began when coastal Aborigines showed local
pastoralists the beds of shell that were the source of their own
mother-of-pearl ornaments. With an appreciation of the

beds' commercial potential, the squatters with runs on the coast used the 'station blacks' to collect shell on the tidal flats and in shallow water, and then took them out in small boats to dive for more as the easily accessible beds were depleted. Once the shell was retrieved black labour was needed to open, clean, pack and transport it. The industry rapidly became a major contributor to the regional economy, the more so because the same workers could be employed in the pastoral industry for part of the year and then redeployed after the sheep had been yarded, culled and shorn.

During the period when pearling depended on Aboriginal divers, somewhere between 400 and 500 blacks were employed on the boats.[71] Without them the industry would not have survived. Any alternative labour force would have been hard to come by and would have absorbed most of the profits. As in the pastoral industry, the Aboriginal men and women were unpaid apart from the usual variable mix of food and tobacco. While describing the preparations necessary for a new season, a pearler wrote in 1869:

> you take the first of the ebb and glide away out of the creek . . . Then comes the most important part . . . the picking up of niggers . . . for pearling after all would never pay white labour.[72]

The cheapness of the labour was only part of the story, however. The Aboriginal divers had the endurance to cope with the often harsh conditions and the skills to retrieve the shell from the ocean floor. While discussing the industry in

1886, Edwin Streeter remarked that 'for finding shell' the black divers could not be beaten, 'whilst for powers of endurance' they were 'unequalled in the world'.[73] They were, an old north-western pioneer recalled, 'undoubtedly the finest swimmers in the world'.[74]

∫ Forced recruitment

As the demand for labour grew, the pearlers had to go further afield to satisfy the demand and engage in brutal and coercive methods to bring young men from the inland to dive for the shell. 'The method of obtaining this labour', A. C. Bligh wrote, 'is better imagined than described. It is sufficient to say that it was crude.'[75] Recruiting parties rode off into the bush, 'ran down' any likely recruits seen on the way, chained them together and force-marched them to the coast. While being 'tamed', and between voyages, the divers were often 'planted' on offshore islands until they were required. They were fed, and sometimes supplied with women, but if they swam to shore and ran away they were 'tracked, brought back and thrashed'.[76] There is strong evidence to suggest that good divers were bought and sold and were taken into consideration when luggers were put up for auction.[77] A witness told the supreme court in the Gribble case that when he left the north-west he sold his boat, worth £700 without 'the natives', for £1300.[78] In September 1883 Corporal Payne of the Derby police took down the statement of several young men who had been kidnapped by pearlers. It read in part:

Tabernabel alias Charley . . . states that the year before last he
was caught near the Yeeda River by M. N. Bryan, C. Wilson,
Hy Hunter and A. Mayall and chained by the neck with natives
Yannyre, Cockey and Jacky, who were also taken against their
will . . . also states he was again caught the following year (last
year) by the same men on the west side of King Sound and
chained up with a native named Liangnoora and both times taken
to Beagle Bay and from there to the Lacepede Islands and left
there for some time and then taken to Cossack to be signed [for
employment].[79]

Conditions on the small ships were unpleasant for all
who sailed in them. The treatment received by the divers
probably varied widely. Some captains sought to extract the
maximum effort from their divers by treating them fairly and
feeding them well. Others depended on rule by the gun, the
fist and the whip. The four young men who complained to
Corporal Payne explained to him that 'they do not like
pearling because the whites treat them so badly . . . when
diving get nothing to eat but damper, and water to drink'.[80]
While complaining about his treatment on a lugger a young
man told a colonial official that he was 'often sent up rigging,
get me hiding first and then sent up rigging, and no food and
no water for only five shells'.[81]

Sometimes the Europeans frankly admitted to their
violent methods and even boasted of them. A man named
Gould wrote to the government in 1878 describing how he
had dealt with a woman who tried to steal pearl shell. 'I made

a grab', he wrote, 'and caught her by the hair and flogged her till she pissed and shit herself Sir! Flogged her till she pissed and shit herself Sir!'[82]

∫ A scandalous state of affairs

Women were banned from diving in Western Australian waters as a result of legislation passed in 1872. Aboriginal men were phased out of the industry in the mid-1880s with the introduction of diving suits and indentured Asian crews. Blacks living in camps along the coast continued to service the industry, providing water, firewood and, more especially, company and sex in between voyages and during the lay-up season. Young women providing sexual pleasure were in a much stronger position with the lugger crews than they were on the sheep stations and benefited accordingly, although always under threat from sexually transmitted disease and the violence of husbands and lovers on the one hand and of clients on the other. The relative success of Aboriginal 'enterprise' in Broome enraged G. S. Olivey, who visited the town in 1901. He interviewed the leading residents who all told him that they couldn't get the local blacks to work for them. They believed the situation would remain the same while the women were 'allowed to live in the town and make a good living by prostitution'. Olivey cast his censorious gaze over the Asian quarter of the town, where it was:

impossible to walk along the main streets any time in the day
without seeing natives, men, women and children, lying and
loafing about . . . They rarely appeared to be doing any work;
at times a few might be seen carrying wood and water. The
majority of the loafers were women, for the most part under
thirty years of age. In no other town visited have I seen such a
scandalous state of affairs. The women are all well dressed, and
are to be seen at or about sundown carrying food away with
them to the camps.[83]

Olivey visited a number of Aboriginal women who were
married to Asians. They seemed to be 'very happy and contented'. Their surroundings were 'neat, clean and tidy' and
they had been 'raised above their ordinary level'. But for
all that, he insisted, 'the system of marrying Asiatics to
Aboriginal women should be stopped by law.' Such unions,
he urged 'often lead up to trouble, and are not desirable in
any way'.[84]

∫ A nasty stinking business

Aborigines and Torres Strait Islanders played a major role
in the maritime industries in Queensland. The *bêche-de-mer*
industry, in particular, was totally dependent on their labour.
During the 1880s and 1890s there were as many as 100 craft
engaged in the trade and somewhere between 500 and 1000
Aborigines employed at any one time. The ships sailed out of
Cooktown and Thursday Island and recruited their crews on
both sides of Cape York and from the larger Barrier Reef

islands. Initial recruitment involved force or fraud, but while they could initiate the local labour trade they could not sustain it. As the industry developed, and government regulation took hold, men and women chose to ship with the white men or were encouraged to do so by the elder men of authority. At times demand for labour greatly exceeded supply. In 1902 the recruiters were issued with permits by the government resident on Thursday Island to employ 990 blacks, but in the event they could only obtain 334. As a result Aboriginal coastal clans demanded – and received – 'bonuses' of flour, tobacco and other useful commodities in advance, payment often being made to the old men 'for their services in inducing the younger men to recruit'.[85]

Despite these conditions the industry never lost its bad reputation. 'It's not a nice business', John Douglas, the senior official on Thursday Island, wrote in 1893.

> Life on board one of these boats, or at the stations on the islands . . . is unspeakably squalid and dirty. For some men, however, it has an attraction, and there is often associated with it a good deal of illicit intercourse with native women. It is altogether a nasty stinking business.[86]

The collector of customs at Cooktown provided an insight into the way things often were. He wrote to the authorities in Brisbane in 1882 about the behaviour of two local captains who had sailed south to recruit 'boys' from Hinchinbrook and Dunk islands. They returned with eighteen individuals of both sexes, aged from nine to forty years. The captains cast lots for nine each of 'mixed sexes without reference to the inclinations or feelings' of the recruits. Before the ships sailed a young girl of nine or ten years old was paraded through the main street by one of the captains and taken to the local hotel to be 'busted'.[87]

The collection and processing of *bêche-de-mer* was highly labour intensive and could not have survived without unpaid Aboriginal labour. The going rate was from 5s to 10s a month paid in kind, normally clothes and tobacco supplied at highly inflated prices. Aborigines collected the *bêche-de-mer* at low tide on the exposed reefs or dived for them in shallow water. Once collected, they had to be quickly split open, washed, and then carried to a curing plant established on a nearby island, where they were sun-dried, smoked and bagged for transport to Cooktown and eventual export to Singapore and Hong Kong.

] *Black miners*

Aboriginal labour was far less important in the mining industry in north and central Australia than it was in sheep-farming and cattle-raising or pearl and *bêche-de-mer* collecting and processing. But there was some Aboriginal involvement from the start. Frontier prospectors were often accompanied by, and dependent upon, Aboriginal assistants in the same way as explorers and pioneer squatters had been before them. Their bushcraft, tracking ability and skill at finding water were all invaluable assets in the interior of the conti-

nent and could be directed at seeking evidence of minerali-
sation in the same way that they were used to find good
pastoral land and easy tracks across unknown country.

Once mineral fields developed, fringe camps sprang up,
providing cheap labour for innumerable domestic tasks in
communities where white servants either didn't exist or were
very expensive. On the smaller and more remote fields black
labour was even more significant.[88] The mining warden of the
Mulgrave goldfield wrote in 1891 that the local Aborigines
were 'very useful to the miners, who have so many difficulties to contend against, in a country so much broken and
covered with so dense a jungle'.[89] On the small and remote
Rocky goldfield on Cape York, the local clans provided the
labour to carry all the essential supplies for 18 miles over
mountainous country inaccessible to pack-horses. A visiting
royal commissioner who was investigating the mining industry
observed that

> the alleged ferocity and untrustworthiness of these blacks is
> utterly at variance with the experience of the two storekeepers
> who engaged them as carriers and have business relations with
> them. During that period they have never pilfered a single cake
> of tobacco, or any other item whatsoever of the multifarious
> necessaries of the miner which have been entrusted to their
> charge, although some of these commodities must have been of
> priceless value to the aboriginal mind.[90]

The companionship of Aboriginal women, either on a casual
or semi-permanent basis, greatly eased the hardship of life

on small and isolated mineral fields, where often only a handful of Europeans attempted to make a go of dubious claims. Miners' women often became adept at panning or dry blowing for gold and sorting samples of gold or tin ore. While visiting the Bangemall goldfield in 1900, the Western Australian travelling inspector of Aborigines observed that 'it appears to be looked upon as quite the correct thing to keep a woman on this field'. He didn't really approve, but supposed 'the absence of the influence of white women accounts for this to a certain extent'. Nevertheless he thought the women 'seemed contented with their lot, and were well dressed and fed'.[91] On some fields the miners imposed their own standards of conduct towards black women. On the struggling Starke River goldfield in north Queensland, the two dozen miners had 'adopted a firm code of honour', insisted upon by the two Webb brothers who were the 'lead-ing men' of the place. A visiting official noted in June 1898 that

> not so long ago, these two I am informed, gave a sound thrashing to one of the Europeans for attempting sexual connection with a gin against her consent: of course, where the woman is a consenting party, no interference is made.[92]

In central and northern Australia, the Aborigines were the mainstay of the European economy. Their labour was of crucial importance for sheep farmers in both Western

Australia and central Queensland and for cattle producers on the vast northern frontier, which sprawled 4000 kilometres across the continent. Aboriginal labour was also vitally important in the *bêche-de-mer* and pearling industries. In towns and mining camps black servants performed most of the domestic labour. Aboriginal women also provided the sexual pleasure and companionship which made harsh frontier lives bearable.

As many as 10 000 Aborigines were working for the Europeans at any one time at the turn of the century. If Dawn May's assessment of comparative labour costs is correct, then each full-time black worker saved the employer about £50 per year – in all, a massive 'subsidy' provided by the Aboriginal workforce and a critical ingredient in the economic survival of individuals and industries alike. But Aboriginal labour did more than provide white men and their families with financial security, or even in some cases with substantial fortunes. It ensured the viability of European settlement over at least one-third of the continent, allowing the colonists to sustain their claim to be in actual and effective occupation of the Australian land mass.

Did the Aborigines benefit from the occupation? In many ways they clearly didn't. Their land was usurped – usually with violence or the threat of violence – and their labour was ruthlessly exploited. The irony was that the blacks provided the muscle and the skill which allowed outback settlers to sustain themselves. However, the absence of European workers also meant that the blacks had an important role to play in the process of colonisation. They learnt new skills and were able to make a more gradual and secure adjustment to the European presence than their counterparts in the south. In the north and the centre the lack of a large resident European population and of agricultural development, and the sparsity of settlement, meant that the land remained unfenced and largely unchanged. What is more, many clans remained on or near their own land.

A number of recent studies have explained how a symbiotic relationship developed between Aboriginal society and the pastoral industry.[93] There clearly was a degree of compatibility between the life of the hunter–gatherer and that of the open-range stockworker or shepherd. At the same time there was also an overlap between traditional bush skills and those demanded by the new industries. Aborigines took pride in their achievement in the whites' world and realised that they were as good as or better than their European counterparts at many tasks and that their ancient bushcraft was of real, functional value.

As long as labour and sex were forthcoming, most frontier pastoralists tolerated the establishment of permanent camps on their runs and rarely bothered to interfere in Aboriginal cultural or ceremonial life. Indeed, ceremonial calendars were adjusted to accommodate the demands of the pastoral economy. Once mustering and shearing were over the 'station blacks' went walkabout for up to three months at a time. It was a mutually satisfactory arrangement. Aborigines could return to their own country, live off the land, camp with relatives from other stations – or, in the early days, with those who were still living traditionally out in the bush. The bush race meeting, the white people's annual festival, allowed clans from a wide area to meet and conduct important ceremonial business, arrange marriages, settle disputes and initiate the young.

Because Aboriginal culture survived and people continued to live on their own country, they never conceded that they had lost their land, and that viewpoint was not just wishful thinking. The European economy in much of outback Australia was precarious. White bosses came and went, beaten by distance, fickle markets, drought and bad management. Even when fortune smiled the characteristic thing to do was to sell up and move south or to the coast. Most sheep and cattle farmers remained all the while merely tenants on crown land. Clearly the whites had to be suffered, conciliated, appeased, managed, but they were almost certainly less important in Aboriginal eyes than the Europeans supposed.

The continuing strength of Aboriginal society and culture and the ever-present vulnerability of the white pioneers was to be of fundamental importance when the modern land rights movement emerged, allowing blacks in the Northern Territory to claim and gain title to their traditional lands. In many cases Aborigines were then able to use their land by combining traditional ways with sheep and cattle raising in a manner which they now determined. It is a development which is bound to follow sooner or later in both Western Australia and north Queensland.

three

BLACK TROOPERS

AS GUIDES, LINGUISTS AND diplomats, Aborigines assisted explorers and travellers throughout the continent. The rigours of travel were thereby eased, tensions reduced, conflict avoided. The proud boast of an explorer like Charles Sturt that he had never shed Aboriginal blood can be attributed as much to the influence of black guides and to lessons learnt from them as to the explorer's own temper and intentions. But the settlers found that those same skills which had been used principally for peaceful purposes could be turned to other, more aggressive and much more dubious ends.

The value of Aboriginal bushcraft for law enforcement was quickly apparent in the convict colonies. Clans living around the penal settlements were adept at tracking escapees and bringing them in from the bush. Those at Newcastle were of 'eminent service' to the commandant, Captain Allman, 'as bush constables in tracing and apprehending runaways'.[1] The visiting British official J. T. Bigge observed in 1819 that:

the native blacks that inhabit the neighbourhood of Port Hunter and Port Stephens have become very active in retaking the fugitive convicts. They accompany the soldiers who are sent in pursuit, and by extraordinary strength of sight that they possess . . . they can trace to a great distance, with great accuracy, the impressions of the human foot. Nor are they afraid of meeting the fugitive convicts in the woods, when sent in pursuit, without the soldiers; by their skill in throwing their long and pointed wooden darts they wound and disable them, strip them of their clothes, and bring them back as prisoners by unknown roads and paths . . .[2]

The penal authorities used the threat of black trackers and the concomitant certainty of capture to deter would-be escapees. On the eve of the convict era in Western Australia, the official guardian of Aborigines wrote to the colonial secretary assuring him that 'in the extraordinary aptitude of the Aborigines for tracking', the authorities had what would prove to be 'a powerful preventative of crime amongst the Convict population'.[3]

Dangerous and subtle enemies

While Aboriginal expertise was of great value to colonial governments when employed on their behalf, it was an enduring problem when those same bush skills were used to spearhead the resistance against the spread of settlement. The settlers quickly learnt that tribal Aborigines were 'dangerous and subtle enemies when at variance with the whites'.[4] The difficulty of catching fast-moving and elusive clans unawares was quickly apparent. George Caley informed his patron Sir Joseph Banks that, 'in some attempts to take them by surprise they completely duped us'.[5]

Later difficulties were foreshadowed when, in December 1790, Governor Phillip decided to 'strike a decisive blow' against the clans living around Botany Bay and dispatched the first punitive expedition in Australian history. At 4 a.m. the detachment of 40 private soldiers, three corporals, three sergeants, two surgeons, two lieutenants and two captains set off for Botany Bay with three days' provisions. By 9 a.m. the 'terrific procession' reached the head of the bay and walked in various directions until 4 p.m. without having seen blacks camped for the night. The new day was equally frustrating. When five 'Indians' were seen on the beach, the Europeans attempted to surround them. But as Watkin Tench, both leader and chronicler of the expedition, explained, they 'penetrated our design' and ran off, pursued ineffectively by panting soldiery. Ruefully Tench wrote: 'a contest between heavy-armed Europeans, fettered by ligatures, and naked unencumbered Indians, was too unequal to last long'.[6] The following day the soldiers marched towards a known campsite on the northern arm of the bay, but long before they reached their goal the residents took to their canoes. That evening the party camped near a freshwater swamp, passing a night of 'restless inquietude' caused by swarms of mosquitoes and sandflies that bit and stung 'without measure or intermission'.

Despite the failure of the expedition a second was soon under way. Marching forth at sunset, the troops proceeded to Botany Bay, waited for the tide to ebb and then attempted to cross a creek, where they were trapped in quicksand. Extricating themselves with great difficulty, the soldiers pushed on to the Aboriginal campsite, split up into three groups and crept from different directions up to the gunyahs (huts), only to find them empty. After another 24 hours of marching through the bush the expedition returned to Sydney to report their 'fruitless peregrination'.[7]

Our masters in the bush

The settlers' incompetence in the bush was obvious to the Aborigines, who entertained 'but a mean opinion of the white peoples' knowledge'.[8] Tom Petrie, an early Brisbane identity who had close contact with the local blacks, explained that when pursued they went into the scrub and poked fun 'at the whites who [were] unable to follow them'.[9] The missionary William Schmidt told members of a parliamentary select committee that on getting to know the Aborigines he found that they considered themselves superior to the Europeans because they were 'our masters in the bush'.[10] Perceptive white bushmen agreed with that assessment, Edward Eyre arguing that in the interior of the country the blacks had 'the advantage over the Europeans . . . that a swimmer has in the water over the man who cannot swim'.[11]

During the first generation of colonisation, the settlers were intimidated by Aboriginal expertise in the bush and rarely pursued their adversaries into the scrubland or forest. For their part, Aboriginal groups often taunted their pursuers by standing at the edge of sheltering vegetation shouting abuse and slapping their buttocks in derision. Reminiscing about 'battles' with the blacks in the early days, an old Queensland colonist recalled how a party of tribesmen had, before they disappeared among the trees, turned partly round and, with an 'insolent gesture, applied hearty smacks with their hands to that part of their persons which brave men never expose to the enemy'.[12] The settlers frequently expressed their reluctance to follow Aboriginal parties into rugged or forested country. A writer in the *Sydney Gazette* in 1814 commented on the difficulty of pursuing an enemy 'whose haunts are inaccessible, distant and unknown'.[13] Two years later a Lane Cove farmer wrote to the same paper detailing the depredations of local blacks, who had 'the advantage of security by the distance of their accustomed places of resort, whither they may retire without the possibility of being pursued'.[14] Similar problems confronted settlers in later years on frontiers remote from Sydney. In 1839 a squatter on the Gwydir River despaired at catching the blacks who were harassing his and neighbouring stations. He believed that the British army itself would have trouble coming up with the local blacks, 'so well acquainted are they with every thicket, reedy creek, morass, cave and hollow tree, in which they can secrete themselves'.[15]

∫ *A decided superiority over Europeans*

The problem of dealing with Aboriginal resistance in country which put the settlers at such a disadvantage was first fully confronted in Tasmania in the 1820s. The pioneer farmers and graziers took up pockets of open land amid rugged ranges of mountains and heavily forested hills. Surface water and food were widely available to Aboriginal parties in the high country, where horses were practically useless. Beleaguered colonists openly confessed their impotence in the face of coordinated attacks. 'They are seldom pursued by the settlers', a retired army captain told the government, 'from a despair of finding them in the almost inaccessible fastnesses.'[16] A fellow colonist, writing to the *Hobart Town Courier,* explained to the townspeople that 'they exercise such cunning, are so keen sighted, so well acquainted with the recesses of the woods, that our common means can never track them'.[17]

Similar views were heard on every hand. 'Coming up with them by day appears to me quite hopeless', a Derwent Valley farmer lamented.[18] 'To travel without scent of them', a colleague explained 'is of no use, they are so very subtile [sic].'[19] A police constable on the east coast referred to the 'utter impracticability of capturing by surprise or pursuit such a sagacious and wily race of people'.[20] 'I assure you', another anxious settler wrote, 'they are a most intricate set of people to capture. No one can conjecture how crafty and subtle they act in the bush.'[21] A settler in the Coal River valley, referring to a particularly hostile party that neither police nor soldiers could ever find, observed that the 'peculiar nature and habits' of the blacks gave them 'a decided superiority over Europeans'.[22]

The problems facing the Tasmanian settlers were dramatised by the failure of the so-called Black Line to push the surviving clans into the south-east corner of the island. The whole population was mobilised for six weeks while 2200 men, including 500 troops, walked across the country. The operation cost £30 000, equivalent to half of the colonial government's annual expenditure. In explaining the reasons for his massive campaign, Governor Arthur wrote home to his superiors:

> The mode which had for the last two years been adopted for expelling the Natives from the settled districts, or preventing their hostile incursions, by the establishment of military posts, or for capturing them by means of a few parties who were made to rove incessantly in the districts where they were liable to be found, has proved quite unavailing as a general security. The total want of information as to the situation of the tribes at any particular time; the facility and rapidity with which they move to some secret hiding place, after committing any atrocity . . . rendered pursuit on such occasions in most instances fruitless, for the rugged and woody nature of the country in which they always took refuge was sure to baffle any attempt to trace them in their course.[23]

Tracing guides

By the 1820s Aborigines were not just guiding explorers and travellers, they were being utilised to track down white miscreants in the bush. It was only a matter of time before the attempt would be made to employ black bushcraft in the struggle against Aboriginal resistance. The idea was promoted at much the same time in both New South Wales and Tasmania. Writing in the 1820s, the surgeon Cunningham observed that it was quite impossible to surprise blacks in the bush 'at any time except early in the morning, through the assistance of a native guide'.[24] An army captain dispatched with a party to 'disperse' Hunter River clans in 1826 was officially advised of 'the advantage, which [would] result from your Detachment being accompanied by some trusty intelligent Natives'.[25] Two years later a prominent Tasmanian settler wrote to Governor Arthur with suggestions about 'the means of checking the ravages' of island Aborigines, which included the idea of capture and exile. 'To attempt that capture', he argued,

> without the agency of one or more Individuals of that Race would be almost hopeless. On the other hand a Tribe might be pursued in any direction and quickly taken if the pursuing party were guided by the Natives. The peculiar tact of these as well as other savages in tracking is well known, and would – if employed – at once remove the obstacles which exist to the capture of the Tribes as long as Europeans alone direct the pursuit.[26]

The flamboyant convict Jorgen Jorgensen came to a similar conclusion after leading one of the roving parties in fruitless pursuit of the Aborigines. His experience convinced him of the 'superiority of the blacks, over us, in discovering the haunts of their countrymen'. Unless the settlers were 'taught by them', their frustrations would continue. What was more, black guides were 'otherwise useful' to European parties because they could 'discover water, where we would never think of looking for it, and in cases of emergency, might save a party from starvation, by procuring roots and other species of natural food for it'.[27] Anxious Tasmanian settlers proposed to bring Aborigines from Sydney to assist them in the bush. A retired military officer wrote to the government calling for their employment as 'tracing guides'.[28] The native-born pioneer of north-east Tasmania and subsequently founder of Melbourne, John Batman, took to the bush with two New South Wales blacks and planned to bring seven more across Bass Strait 'to be employed to communicate with the Aborigines of this island'.[29]

Batman's plans were frustrated by the contemporaneous success of George Augustus Robinson's so-called 'friendly mission' to the blacks in the bush. Between January 1830 and August 1834 Robinson led six expeditions through the island to negotiate with the tribes and persuade them to accept terms of settlement and especially resettlement on the islands of Bass Strait. Robinson's journeys were, then, of great significance in the history of Tasmania and earned him fame and fortune. But to an even greater extent than explorers on the mainland, he was highly dependent on the local Aborigines who accompanied him. Without them the 'friendly mission' would have been impossible. They looked after the Europeans in the bush, guided them, tracked and caught animals, and also sought out anxious and hostile clans, went forward to meet them and conducted negotiations on Robinson's behalf.

∫ *An active field police*

Tasmanian experience influenced the ideas of the penal reformer Alexander Maconochie, who arrived in the colony in 1836 as Governor Franklin's private secretary. In 1838 he drew up a detailed proposal for the creation of a native police force, which was favourably received in official circles. The plan deserves close attention. Like many humanitarians at the time, in both Britain and Australia, Maconochie was deeply concerned about the violence of Tasmania's Black War and hoped that new policies could be developed to avoid the same developments in the impending settlements on the mainland. With this in mind, he sought to devise a scheme 'founded on the peculiarity of [the Aboriginal] conditions and circumstances, calculated to preserve and improve them, while we also benefit ourselves'. Drawing on developments in Africa and India, and what he knew of the Roman Empire, Maconochie advocated the creation of an Aboriginal regiment to police the frontiers of settlement. It would, he argued, be more numerous, effective and economical than existing police forces. The black troopers would be employed in small parties 'much on the move in the field', dressed in a light, convenient 'somewhat ornamental dress'. Discipline would be firm but paternal. Between the troopers and their officers there would soon develop 'the strongest ties', which would provide the major means of discipline, for the 'silken cord would, as in every other case, be more effectual than the iron fetter'. Experience in the force would provide the optimum conditions for assimilation and general 'improvement':

> A knowledge of, and taste for European manners and civiliza-
> tion, would be thus extensively, yet silently implanted, and the
> habits of order, concert and decorum learnt and practiced in the
> field, would probably sooner pervade their huts, and family
> stations than is now thought possible.

As a result, 'the relative status of the black population would be raised in the estimation of the community; and a more universally civil and conciliating demeanor would consequently be maintained towards them'. With success would come amalgamation and equality, at least with the lower orders of Europeans.[30]

It was a persuasive document, judiciously combining a deft mixture of humanitarian sentiment, self-interest and practical advice, and was to have an important influence on the development of native police forces in Victoria, New South Wales and Queensland. In responding to Maconochie's proposal Governor Bourke wrote:

I have so far entered into your views respecting the aboriginal natives, as to authorise Captain Lonsdale [superintendent at Port Phillip] to employ them in the constabulary. I am inclined to think very well of the mode of management you propose.[31]

Formal Aboriginal participation in colonial police forces began in the 1840s and continued throughout the nineteenth century and on into the twentieth century. In many parts of Australia black trackers were attached to the established police forces and played a major role in the work of those bodies, especially in the more remote parts of the continent. Aboriginal forces, as envisaged by Maconochie, were established in Port Phillip in 1842 (after several earlier abortive attempts) and in the northern districts of New South Wales in 1848. The southern force, under the command of Henry Dana, operated in all parts of the colony until it was disbanded in 1852. It was established with a contingent of 23 troopers and gradually increased in size, reaching 65 for a short period in 1851. In all, 140 Aboriginal men served in the force.

The northern force had a much longer life. It passed into the hands of the new administration in New South Wales in 1856, then on to the Queensland government in 1859, continuing in operation until the first decade of the twentieth century. The force began on a small scale with 14 troopers in 1849, grew rapidly to an initial peak of 96 in 1852, then shrank during the 1850s only to grow again in the 1860s and 1870s, reaching a second and higher peak of 206 in 1878. Our knowledge of the force is inadequate. It appears that most of the records for the period after 1859 have disappeared and were probably deliberately destroyed at some time in the past. It is impossible to determine how many Aborigines served in the force during its long history, who they were, where they came from and what happened to them. Records kept by the New South Wales authorities for the period 1848 to 1858 provide a reasonable picture of operations during that time, and in the decade 175 blacks were recruited to serve in the force. If a similar rate of recruitment and attrition continued throughout the nineteenth century the total number of troopers must have reached or even exceeded 1000.[32]

Many features of Maconochie's plan for an 'active Field Police' were apparent in the operations of the two forces. They both had white officers and Aboriginal troopers, and both were used as a mobile force in troubled frontier districts with small mounted detachments patrolling regularly over large areas. Both forces were provided with 'somewhat ornamental' uniforms. The winter uniform of the Port Phillip force was made up of a dark green–black fabric, with a red stripe on the side of the pants, a jacket with a red collar and cuffs made of the same woollen fabric, and a cap of the same, also with a red stripe.[33] In his book *The Black Police*, A. J. Vogan described the uniform of a Queensland trooper 'in marching order'. It consisted of

a linen-covered shako [a round peaked cap], blue jacket garnished with red braid; and white duck trousers; brown leather gaiters [which] reach to the 'boys' knees, and he wears an old pair of . . . enormously long spurs on his 'Blucher' boots . . . a brass cartridge belt containing Snider cartridges, is slung, after the fashion of a sergeant's scarf, around his body.[34]

∫ Close up knock them down

If by chance Maconochie had remained interested in developments in the colonies after his return to England in 1840, he would have been deeply concerned with the way in which the native police forces diverged from his idea of a preventative force established to avoid the violence experienced in Tasmania and still keenly remembered while he lived there. Initially, at least, practice out in the field may have matched the official rhetoric, Marie Fels indeed asserting, in her study of the Port Phillip force, *Good Men and True*, that 'it cannot be too strongly emphasized that prevention of conflict was the main function of the force' and that it achieved that end not by violence but 'mainly by being there'. Frederick Walker, founder and first commandant of the northern force, was keenly aware of the problem of aligning principle with practice. In a letter to the colonial secretary in Sydney he outlined what he understood to be the principles that were meant to guide the activities of his troopers. He was, he explained, to take action for the 'maintenance of peace and order and not for the purpose of carrying war into an enemy country', to try and maintain peace and order 'by carrying the laws into effect both against white and black without distinction'. He considered the blacks 'as British subjects who like armed bushrangers were defying the law'. 'The object in sending out patrol parties', Walker explained, was principally 'that the hostile blacks from the frequent visits of the police, may be deterred from murder and felony'. This, he concluded, 'is the meaning of a Preventative Force'.[35] The colonial officials at the time attempted to control the activities of the force, insisting that inquiries be held whenever anyone was killed and that the police only take action when seeking to serve a warrant or when they had sworn evidence of criminal activity. While commenting on Walker's reports about clashes with the blacks, the New South Wales attorney-general, J. H. Plunkett, wrote that it could not be 'too strongly impressed' on the officers of the force 'that they should only fire in extreme cases where the necessity of it, is clear and obvious' and that even in all such cases 'a detailed investigation on oath should take place'.[36]

But exhortations from Sydney were one thing, life on the frontier quite another. The white officers were usually out on patrol alone with their troopers and were in effect a law unto themselves. They were supposed to record all incidents in duty books, but who was to know if they failed to do so? What is more, the action of riding into Aboriginal camps was certain to provoke a hostile reaction, which in turn could justify the taking of 'stern measures'. Walker outlined the situation in inimitable style in a speech to his troopers in August 1851:

What the Governor wants from you is to make charcoles quiet, he does not want them killed, and he *won't let* white fellows do so. If they won't be quiet, you must make them – that's all. But you will not shoot unless your Officer tells you. Mind if the charcoles begin to throw spears or nulla nullas at you *then* don't wait but close up knock them down.[37]

Dispersing depredators

Walker's stated intention of applying the law without distinction failed to take into account the conditions on the northern frontier. By the time he rode north there had already been ten years of bitter conflict. Much blood had been shed; racial hatred had taken deep root. The white frontiersmen considered that they were at war with the blacks, as Walker himself came to appreciate. Many settlers had told him that they believed the native police had been sent up to shoot the blacks. 'They still fancy that a system of warfare ought to be authorized by Government', he told his superiors in Sydney, 'and do not try to produce evidence upon which the Police can legally act, and in some cases have prevented the Officers from obtaining such evidence.'[38]

Control over the native police passed in 1856 from imperial officials ultimately answerable to the Colonial Office to the New South Wales government, and then onto the new administration in Brisbane three years later. Each step brought government closer to the frontier – geographically, intellectually, morally. At the same time a series of

Aboriginal attacks on frontier settlers, culminating in the killing of the Fraser family at Hornet Bank in 1857 and the Wills entourage at Cullinlaringoe four years later, deeply shocked and angered colonial opinion. In response the native police were unleashed. Revenge expeditions were not only sanctioned but encouraged; pre-emptive raids became commonplace. In January 1858 the commandant, E. V. Morisset, issued instructions to the officers of the force that reflected the harsh new outlook. 'It is the duty of the Officers', the tenth paragraph reads,

> at all times and opportunities to disperse any large assemblage of blacks; such meetings if not prevented, invariably lead to depredations or murder; and nothing but the mistaken kindness of the Officers in command inspired the blacks with sufficient confidence to commit the late fearful outrages on the Dawson River.[39]

The instruction to disperse large gatherings at all times and opportunities was not rescinded until 1896, thirty-eight years later. If there was ever any doubt about what 'to disperse' meant it was dispelled by the Queensland attorney-general, who told parliament in 1861 that it was 'idle to dispute' that the term 'meant nothing but firing at them'.[40] Clearly the need for warrants or affidavits or inquiries into the deaths of Aborigines had passed unless someone raised a complaint in public. The frontier settlers had the kind of force they had wanted all along. 'The natives', declared a prominent member of the 1861 Select Committee on the Native Police, 'must be regarded in the same light as inhabitants of a country under martial law'. He believed that 'from the natives knowing no law, entertaining any fears but those of the carbine, there were no other means of ruling them'.[41] The method of operation was made clear in evidence given by Lieutenant Frederick Wheeler to the committee. He was questioned by Mr Watts.

1. *You have said in your evidence that you never received any written or printed instructions from the Commandant?*
   Not in reference to the services peculiar to the Native Police. There are some general orders about the management of the men, and, to a certain degree in one clause you are instructed to disperse all assemblages of the blacks, because they always lead to cattle spearing or sheep stealing – they always lead to that.

2. *But you have no written or printed instructions?*
   No printed ones.

3. *In what way then do you act?*
   I act according to the letters I receive from squatters.

4. *Do you not think it is right that you should be cognizant of the facts before you take your measures?*
   If a man has been murdered or sheep or cattle have been stolen, I generally go to the station – go to the proprietor of the station – and ride about it, and pick up tracks.

5. *Do you take the precaution to go and see any cattle, or camps, that have been reported to have been rushed?*
   We could not track cattle far; where cattle have been killed, we

sometimes come upon a dead beast, that is very rare – but we can generally tell whether they have been rushed or not – whether the blacks have been through the run or not; besides, the proprietor of the station and the stock-keeper can tell us that.

6. *Do you think it right to pursue these blacks – say a month after their depredations?*
Well, yes, if you can be perfectly certain of the facts a month afterwards. I have always acted immediately – whenever I have been called upon, I have gone up to the station immediately.

7. *Do you not think that these depredators should be captured?*
You don't know who they are, it is the tribe you follow – you can't see the depredators.

8. *Do you not think there is any other way of dealing with them, except by shooting them?*
No, I don't think they can understand anything else except shooting them; at least, that is the case, so far as my experience goes.

9. *When you go to a camp, do you call, upon them in the Queen's name, in any way, to surrender?*
No, because directly they see you they run; you have to gallop to get on to them: if you were to call upon them to surrender, you would never be able to keep them in sight.[42]

∫ At open war

In 1848 the New South Wales government, and Frederick Walker as well, were anxious to stress that the native police force had not been created to carry war into 'an enemy country'. But talk of war was commonplace in Queensland in the second half of the century, many people agreeing with the local politician who told his parliamentary colleagues in 1861 that 'the people of this colony must be considered to be, as they always have been at open war with the Aborigines'.[43] Lieutenant J. O'C. Bligh was questioned on this issue by members of the 1861 Select Committee on the Native Police:

And they look upon us in the same light as the New Zealanders do, and make war upon us in the same way?
I think they do, and nothing but fear prevents them from carrying on a regular system of warfare.
And if we did not repel force by force they would drive us out of the country?
Yes, I think it is the most merciful way of dealing with them.
Then, on the occasion of an attack by the blacks, the Force is necessary as much for the assertion of our superiority, as for the purpose of punishing them for their depredations?
Yes.[44]

When answering queries about the activities of the force from the Colonial Office, Queensland ministers compared their situation with that of settlers in New Zealand and South Africa who had experienced war with the indigenous people. They pointed out,

that Queensland has always done, and intends always to do for itself, what has been hitherto done by the Imperial Government for the internal protection of the other Colonies – somewhat similarly circumstanced. The entire cost of the Native Police Corps is borne by the people of this Colony, who pay per head for protection more than the people of the United Kingdom pay per head for the same object, including the Army and Navy of the British Empire.[45]

∫ A cheap alternative

The arguments of the raw and assertive Queensland government may not have impressed experienced British officials, but the colonists did have a point. The native police force cost about £300 000 between 1860 and 1880. The £14 000 spent annually in that direction in the early 1860s represented about 5 per cent of the budget, almost equalling the cost of the ordinary police force and exceeding the money devoted to education and immigration. In 1863, for instance, the £14 500 spent on the force compared with £16 000 for the police, £8000 for education and £6000 for migration.[46] But even with expenditure of that order Queensland's native police force was very much cheaper than any possible alternative. When needled by imperial officials about dispersals around the outer fringe of settlement, the Queensland government suggested the pioneers could be protected as they had been in South Africa and New Zealand 'chiefly at the cost of the Mother Country, by means of Imperial Troops'. The memo in question continued:

If it is thought that the protection of the settlers in Queensland can be provided for by the imperial better than by the Colonial Government, it is, of course, open to the former to try here the experiment so long tried in New Zealand. The cost of such a policy to the British taxpayer should, however, be carefully calculated. At the lowest estimate, there are fifteen thousand (15 000) aborigines in Queensland; of whom it may be safely concluded that at least two thousand (2000) fighting men are hostile to the whites. It would seem to follow that ten thousand (10 000) soldiers and at least half a million sterling of British money yearly – would be necessary here as in New Zealand for the protection of the Colonists. It is true that the Australian Blacks are not nearly so formidable or so well armed as the Maoris. But then, on the other hand, it must be recollected that the northern island of New Zealand is only about the size of Ireland, and that its climate is peculiarly favourable to the health of the Europeans – whereas the Northern half of Queensland, in which the hostile natives are chiefly to be found is larger than the French Empire and is entirely within the tropics. The mortality among English troops in that climate would be nearly equal to what it is in India. The mere effort of marching under the burning sun, and of encamping in the open without protection from the nightly dews, would decimate English regiments annually and all experience shows English soldiers could not pursue the aborigines with effect when they retire into the almost impenetrable 'scrubs' and jungles of Northern Australia.[47]

Queenslanders may not have seriously considered the use of British troops on their vast frontier, but the alternative option of a force of white troopers was frequently canvassed during the second half of the nineteenth century. Such proposals ran into serious practical difficulties. Even at the end of the century it may have been difficult to find enough skilled bushmen, let alone recruit them into a frontier police force. What is more, the cost of a white force would have been prohibitive. There was a wide gap between acceptable European wages and what was paid to Aboriginal troopers throughout the life of the force. In 1848 Walker's troopers were paid 3d a day, compared to the 1s earned by white troopers in the border police. The troopers at Port Phillip received no regular wages. The disparity increased over time. By the late 1850s the troopers received 5d a day while white constables could expect about 3s 6d. In 1896 Police Commissioner Parry-Okeden estimated the cost of a mixed force of white policemen and black trackers. White constables were to earn £126 per annum, the trackers would only receive £8 2s 0d.[48] But the actual cost in wages was only part of the story. A white force would have required far more administrative support and back-up from non-combatants. The most detailed proposal for such a force envisaged an expensive regimental staff, a band and a hospital staffed by a qualified surgeon[49] – refinements which were never considered for the native police.

∫ Mainstays of the party

The advantages of Aboriginal police troopers went far beyond their cheapness. They brought with them into the two forces the expert bushcraft which had proved so useful to explorers and travellers. It was all the more essential because many of the white officers were recently arrived 'gentlemen' who could not have survived on their own up-country for more than a few days. The contrast between the young lieutenants and their troopers was emphasised by E. B. Kennedy in his reminiscences of service in the Queensland native police. As long as a man 'bore a good record, could ride and understand the use of firearms', he stood a good chance of being accepted and without any training sent to take control of a detachment of troopers.

'As for drill,' he wrote, 'beyond a few simple forms . . . I never saw it.' But he appreciated that 'the true drill' belonged to the troopers, who from the time 'they can walk are naturally drilled by members of their tribe to track, indulge in mimic warfare, and, above all, to scout'.[50]

While paying tribute to the value of Aboriginal expertise, Parry-Okeden observed that for bushcraft 'there is only one teacher – Nature – and only one school – the bush itself'. The only white men capable of performing the services of the troopers 'even in a very modified degree' were those who had 'gained experience by service in the Native Police, and by association with the native troopers, and observation of their methods and tactics'.[51]

The white officers were often dependent on their troopers for the most rudimentary survival skills – to guide them into the bush and to bring them out again. Lieutenant Bligh told the members of the 1861 Select Committee on the force that he always kept one of his men beside him 'in the scrub' for fear of getting lost. His colleague Lieutenant Carr thought that white troopers 'would be perfectly useless in the bush'. Indeed, if a party of European policemen were ever abandoned by their troopers 'in a strange country' it would 'take [them] weeks to get back – if, in fact [they] got back at all'.[52] The troopers came to know country regularly traversed and soon discovered the easiest paths through forests, swamps, mountain passes and over rivers and creeks. Their ability to quickly construct bark canoes was invaluable for crossing stretches of deep water. Kennedy recalled how his 'boys', the 'mainstays of the party', before crossing the Burdekin:

> cut a large sheet of bark from a gum tree, left it exposed for a few hours to the sun, with a stick here and there to prop it into shape, and behold a good canoe, then, filling this with carbines and ammunition, they swam over with it to the camp.[53]

The capacity of black troopers to live off the land for days at a time was apparent from the beginning. When Walker led his first contingent north along the Darling, the party was seriously delayed, ran out of rations, and lived off the land for seventeen days. Lieutenant Wheeler told the 1861 Select Committee that a detachment of the force could 'go for three weeks or a month together, remain out, and yet live without rations'.[54] His colleague Lieutenant Bligh explained that when he was out in the bush and ran short of rations, 'my men always find me sufficient to eat'.[55] While explaining why white troopers could not compare with black, Lieutenant Carr was questioned by the same committee:

Would whites be able to subsist in the bush, when their rations were consumed?

No.

Have you had any instance brought under your notice of the rations of the black troopers being consumed, and of their subsisting without them?

Yes, they are very frequently out of rations, when on duty.

For how long?

I can remember their being without rations for as many as nine days on one occasion.

How do you subsist generally?

By the troopers providing me with food.

You and your men fare alike?

Yes, on those occasions we live on roots, and a few odd possums. On one occasion we were very badly off, when after blacks who had committed a very serious outrage; we could not act, as on other occasions, and shoot game.

You do not think white troopers would be able to do that?

No, indeed, I do not.[56]

∫ *'Coming up' with the blacks*

The ability to forage and hunt while on patrol gave the native police detachments a remarkable degree of mobility, allowing them to travel light, leave pack horses behind if necessary and survive long periods without European rations. The troopers were also able to cope with the hardships necessarily asso-ciated with life in the bush, ones which few white men would or could cope with and certainly not without large financial incentives. The mobility of the detachments enabled them to track and find Aborigines out in the bush, something which white parties so often failed to do. The skill in being able to 'come up' with Aboriginal parties was at least as important as guns and horses in giving the Europeans a crucial advan-tage in frontier skirmishing. There are numerous cases on record in both Victoria and Queensland of troopers tracking fleeing parties for days on end over wild and rugged country despite the best efforts of their adversaries to throw them off the trail. In a report of December 1849, Walker described how his troopers had tracked a band of 'Fitzroy Downs blacks' for eight days,

> and at sundown, on the eighth day, I found that we were within one mile of their camp, but the Condamine much flooded between us; at 12 o'clock at night we swam the river, each man carrying his carbine and ammunition; the water was so cold that two of the settlers who accompanied us were nearly drowned; they were pulled out by my men. At day-break we approached the camp, when we were perceived by the blacks; they seized

their spears, and an engagement ensued; but they were soon compelled to fly . . .[57]

In evidence to select committees in 1856, 1858 and 1861 the pioneer squatters emphasised again and again that the troopers were essential to track the Aborigines in the bush and especially in the dense subtropical forests of southern and central Queensland. Even the best white troopers were thought to be unable to deal with Aboriginal resistance. Charles Archer, the pioneer of south and central Queensland, was examined on this question by the New South Wales Select Committee in 1856:

Do you consider that if a force of white men, such as the old Mounted Police, were substituted for the Native Police, they would be adapted to protect the outlying districts?

They would not be of any use whatever. I have had a good deal of experience of white men in dealing with the blacks, and they are not of the slightest use; they cannot track a black when a depredation has been committed, and if by good fortune they have found him he always manages to escape.[58]

The settlers were convinced that the native police gave them a decisive edge over their adversaries in the bush. Henry Dana wrote to the superintendent at Port Phillip after breaking Aboriginal resistance in the Portland Bay district, explaining that the fear 'with which the wild blacks regard the men, and their knowing that now they can be followed to any place they go to', would prevent them from thinking that they could 'commit depredations with impunity'.[59] The Queensland squatter–politician C. R. Haly was questioned about this issue by the 1861 Select Committee:

Is it from a feeling of dread at their skill among the blacks, that native troopers are more efficient than whites?
It is; because they know that Native Police can follow them – they often laugh at the efforts of the whites to follow them.[60]

A generation later, Parry-Okeden attributed the success of the native police to the exercise and exhibition of superior force by people whom the Aborigines in the bush recognised 'as capable of competing with them in their own tactics, tracking, bush cunning, lore or living, and by whom, in the fastnesses of their native mountains, scrubs, or mangrove swamps they know they can be followed and found'.[61] Davis, a convict escapee who lived with the Aborigines in the Brisbane Valley, confirmed the settlers' views when he gave evidence to the 1861 Select Committee. When asked his opinion of the force, he replied:

> As far as I have heard from the blacks, and from what I have seen, they are in great dread of the Native Police when tracking and following them.

The exchange continued:

They are in dread, you say, of the Native Police?
Yes.

More so than of the whites?
Yes, more so by a great deal.[62]

∫ Deflecting revenge

There were other, less obvious, and at the same time more sinister, reasons for preferring black troopers. The settlers believed, rightly or wrongly, that Aboriginal clans would be unaware of the connection between the police and the white frontiersmen and would therefore not seek to take revenge on the isolated stations. There possibly was something in that view. Groups attacked by the troopers may not even have seen the white officers, who were accustomed to lead from the rear, and even if they did, the authority of the lone European would not have been immediately apparent. Contemporary opinion on the question was asked before the 1861 Select Committee. J. K. Wilson was asked if the blacks would 'care much for a Police Force composed of white men'. In reply he said:

> The great fear I should have, if the Force were composed of white men, would be that the blacks would revenge themselves on the settlers for the acts of the Police. If any settler or stockman kills a blackfellow, they will kill a white man in return; and it would be the same if the White Police killed a blackfellow, they would be sure to have the life of a white man in lieu of him. They would take life for life in some shape or other, though it might be years afterwards . . . But with the Native Police Force the blacks do not seem to realize any connection with the settlers

at all, nor do they seek to revenge their deeds upon the white people – on the contrary, they frequently go to the white people for protection against the Police.[63]

∫ *The only force*

The native police were also an ideal vehicle for the execution of a policy that could never be openly admitted and that was always of doubtful legality. The operations of the forces along the frontiers were cloaked in secrecy. The officers received only the most perfunctory written instructions. Their reports were rarely made public. Successive governments resisted all attempts to set up a public inquiry into the operations of the force. Criticism was met variously by silence, subterfuge or scurrility. Officers were warned to be 'very particular in always avoiding indiscreet discussions'.[64] A senior police inspector admitted in 1880 that he was 'forbidden to publish any information which would give the public even the slightest glimpse of the doings of the Native Police'.[65] For their part, the troopers could have had little understanding of how their operations squared with the established legal principles or publicly espoused ideals of assorted govern-ments sitting hundreds of miles away in a town they had in all likelihood never seen. It had always been policy to keep the troopers away from other Europeans and out of the towns, where inquisitive ears might pick up stories of patient pursuit and sudden onslaught. Soon after the foundation of the force in northern New South Wales, Frederick Walker observed that 'one great advantage in employing aboriginal natives of this Colony as police is that it is impossible to tamper with them'.[66] Aborigines were unable to give sworn evidence in the Queensland courts until the 1880s. As long as the white officers followed their instructions prohibiting other Europeans from riding out with the force – and they were careful to dispose of the evidence – they were immune from legal action and shielded from the pressure of public opprobrium. During the debate in the Queensland parliament on the 1861 Select Committee report, Arthur (later Sir Arthur) Macalister remarked that 'if extermination were desired' and he thought, that 'appeared to be all that could be done – then the black police were the only force that could be employed'.[67]

∫ Appreciation on the frontier

The strong support afforded the native police by a substantial majority of frontier settlers was clear recognition of the role of the black troopers in breaking Aboriginal resistance over a large area of eastern Australia. The impact of police contingents was often dramatic and decisive when they swept into districts where resistance was most pronounced. This was certainly true of the Western District of Victoria in 1842 and in northern New South Wales and southern Queensland between 1849 and 1852, and subsequently in numerous localities in central and northern Queensland. Beleaguered settlers first came to appreciate Walker's force when it arrived on the Macintyre, Balonne and Condamine Rivers in the second half of 1849. Conflict with the Aborigines had already continued for most of the decade. Many stations had been abandoned in the face of effective and coordinated Aboriginal attacks. When Thomas Mitchell passed that way in 1846, en route to central Queensland, he observed that the 'advanced posts of an army are not better kept, and humiliating proofs that the white men had given way were visible in the remains of dairies burnt down, stockyards in ruins, untrodden roads'.[68] Settlers who stayed endured years of acute anxiety, during which

> not one of them could stir from his hut unarmed; when one milked or went for a bucket of water another fully armed stood over him; the horses in the paddocks were killed and the calves in the pens close to the huts where the men lived.[69]

Walker assessed the initial impact of his force. They arrived in the district in May 1849. By October the settlers 'laid aside their weapons' and the local clans were 'admitted everywhere at the Station'. A run worth less than £100 in May sold for £500 five months later, 'so much had property risen in value by the increased security'.[70] Confirmation of these claims was provided by the squatter–politician W. B. Tooth, who bought a station on the Condamine a short time before the native police arrived in the district. Mr Tooth recounted his experiences for the 1858 New South Wales Select Committee on the Aboriginal attacks on the Dawson River:

I bought a large cattle station there, from Mr. Larnach, just before the troopers came up. The blacks before that had been so very troublesome that he could not get a purchaser for it, and he had to sell it at a sacrifice in fact. You could scarcely get a man to go into that district for double the wages paid anywhere else, and no woman would go near it at all. The hutkeepers would not venture to go down to the waterhole without being armed with gun or pistol. But in less than three months after the Native Police came up, that district was so quiet that a man could walk about anywhere. Mr. Walker met the blacks killing cattle close to my camp, and they had a stand up fight for it. The blacks were so completely put down on that occasion, and terrified at the power of the police, that they never committed any more depredations near there. The place was quiet at once, and property became fifty per cent more valuable.'[71]

Many pioneer squatters believed that without the native police their situation would have been untenable. 'I think it is impossible to prosecute squatting pursuits out there without an efficient Native Police', a central Queensland pastoralist asserted in 1856, 'to extend them or even maintain the ground at present occupied.'[72] For Charles Eden, the establishment of the force was a 'question of absolute necessity, a choice between the protection of the pastoral industry of the country or the abandonment of that pursuit by the colonists'.[73] Robert Gray, the pioneer of the Hughenden district, found it difficult to see how 'the small and scattered population of white people' could have continued to occupy the country 'if an organized band of black police under European officers had not been available to protect them'.[74] A more measured view was taken by the prominent squatter–politician William Forster, who 'did not mean to say the country would not be taken up' without the force, because he did not think 'anything could stop the squatters; but the taking of new country would be accomplished less expeditiously, and would be attended with greater loss of life, if there were no Native Police'.[75] In retrospect this seems to have been a perceptive analysis of the situation. Pastoral expansion would almost certainly have proceeded with or without an organised native police. It would have been more costly in European lives but not necessarily so in Aboriginal ones. Frontier squatters may have pushed out more cautiously into new country and built more substantial and better-fortified huts in order to withstand sieges. In all likelihood they would have organised their own contingents of mounted vigilantes. A graphic illustration of frontier opinion was the motion passed by a public meeting in Rockhampton in 1865, which read

> That in the opinion of this meeting it should be made legal for any proprietor or manager, of a station, with the concurrence of one magistrate, to organize a force on any station threatened by aboriginals, or on which any outrage has been committed by them, to organize such force as may be necessary to disperse said blacks at once and that no one engaged in such dispersion shall be liable to any legal penalty.[76]

The prominent central Queensland pioneer Colin Archer was asked by a member of a parliamentary committee in 1860 if he thought 'it would be possible to do without the native police as long as we are extending our frontiers – under any other system?' Archer replied:

> I don't think it would be impossible, because we did without them before; but the squatters would have to depend upon themselves and turn out whenever there was occasion – always a very disagreeable duty.[77]

While the frontier settlers could probably have coped with the physical threat posed by Aboriginal resistance, they may have buckled under the increased financial burden of greater stock losses and much higher wages bills. On the other hand, more squatters may have adopted the alternative course of using diplomacy and peaceful negotiations to come to terms with neighbouring clans and find a solution to the problem of competing patterns of land use. Enough settlers did just that to suggest that it may have been a viable way of proceeding throughout the vast pastoral hinterland.

∫ *A new role*

The last native police contingent operated on Cape York Peninsula and was disbanded just before the First World War. As far back as the mid-1870s the Queensland authorities had begun to merge Aboriginal troopers with the ordinary police, attaching them as trackers to country police stations. But the overall situation did not change dramatically until the 1890s.

In 1896 the recently appointed Commissioner Parry-Okeden travelled with a party of troopers through remote parts of north Queensland and used them to establish contact with Aboriginal camps on the fringes of settlement. His troopers ventured into the camps, handed out tobacco, conducted negotiations and concluded meetings with corroborees. When reporting on his excursion Parry-Okeden advocated a radical reform of frontier policing policy. He pointed out that hitherto the force had 'apparently confined its operations to retaliatory action after the occurrence of outrages, and seems to have dropped all idea of employing merely deterrent or conciliatory methods'. The new man intended 'to change all that'.[78] He rescinded the instruction, first given to native police officers in 1858, that they were to disperse all large gatherings of Aborigines. In its place the detachments were to be accompanied by interpreters to communicate with blacks in the bush, and they were to 'abstain from any demonstrations of hostility'. The first objective of any scheme 'for bettering the blacks', the new commissioner wrote, was to 'establish friendly relations . . . thus begetting mutual confidence and trust'.[79]

In pursuing his policy of conciliation, Parry-Okeden believed that there was 'no such potent factor ready to hand, or indeed anywhere else, as native troopers properly officered, controlled and worked'. While they could be trained to be highly efficient soldiers and implicitly obey orders 'to shoot down whites or blacks', they were even more suited to implementing a policy of conciliation. By reason of their 'very light hearted genial nature', Parry-Okeden argued, 'they will, with much greater relish and celerity, join in a friendly "yabba", hunt or corrobboree with, or help, to feed their fellows'.[80]

The native police, the commissioner realised, could be used for good or ill, to crush or conciliate, for war or peace.

Parry-Okeden's comments contained a devastating, albeit implicit, condemnation of policies pursued by government throughout the second half of the century with disastrous consequences for Aboriginal tribes living across a quarter of the continent. He looked back to the way in which Aborigines had been employed as diplomats and linguists – as men of peace – by the explorers and by George Augustus Robinson sixty years before. Like the guides of exploring expeditions, troopers could have been given the task of recruiting local guides and interpreters in order to open communication with clans beyond the outer fringe of settlement. It may have been little more than a case of preparing them for the inevitability of European occupation and hegemony, but even that would have been preferable to indiscriminate onslaughts by troopers who were instructed for fifty years to have no 'communication whatever with the Aborigines of the district in which they may be stationed, or through which they may be passing'.[81]

∫ *Agents of dispossession*

Alexander Maconochie was a reformer who drew up plans for Aboriginal border regiments because, like many people at the time, he sought ways to avoid the violent conflict that had characterised the history of Tasmania in the late 1820s and early 1830s. At much the same time in both Britain and Australia, humanitarian critics of colonial practice argued that the fundamental reason for frontier conflict was that there had never been any recognition of Aboriginal land rights or compensation provided for property occupied by the settlers. Maconochie himself took this view, arguing that

> when a new territory is occupied, and the original rights of the natives ranging over it are consequently infringed, the *first* claim to a share of its increased value is surely *theirs?*[82]

Proposals for creating reserves and for giving statutory recognition to Aboriginal usufructuary rights on all pastoral land were conveyed to the Australian government by Earl Grey, the secretary of state for the colonies in 1848, and were received in Sydney a few weeks before money was voted to establish a native police force on the northern frontier. In his dispatch Grey referred to frontier conflict:

> The evil of occasional depredations or acts of violence between Settlers and natives in these outlying Districts is one which it is vain to expect can be wholly prevented. But a distinct understanding of the extent of their mutual rights is one step at least towards the maintenance of order and the mutual forebearance between the parties.[83]

The spirit of Grey's proposals lived on in clauses in
Queensland pastoral leases issued after 1859 that provided
for free access of Aboriginal clans to their land and the right
to continue to pursue their traditional lifestyle. But the
squatter-dominated governments in the new colony paid
little heed to rights enunciated on the other side of the
world. While writing a dispatch to the Colonial Office, Governor Bowen referred to Queensland as the 'State which now
possessed the Territory over which these few Aboriginal
tribes formerly wandered; for it would be incorrect to state
that they ever in any strict sense, occupied it'.[84]

A few voices spoke out against the orthodoxy. The liberal
Ipswich politician Dr Challinor argued that the Aborigines
should maintain their right to live on ancestral land or receive
compensation, but he had few influential supporters. The
articulate one-time squatter G. S. Lang published a pamphlet
in 1865 exposing the brutality of the Queensland frontier.
The prime cause of conflict he attributed to the failure to
recognise any Aboriginal right to land. He advocated government intervention spearheaded by an official curator
of Aborigines, who would negotiate an accommodation
between white and black and create large inviolate Aboriginal hunting reserves in every district. For months after the
lecture was published Lang was reviled and treated as a
traitor to his class; his proposals were vehemently rejected.[85]
In the following decade the radical Catholic priest Duncan
McNab advocated similar policies, suggesting that blacks

from the settled districts be used as linguists and diplomats to negotiate the terms of a settlement. But he found 'too generally prevailing a certain disposition to regard and treat as a fanatic, anyone who [showed] an inclination to advocate the cause of the aborigines'.[86] As far as the government or the squatters were concerned, the Aborigines had no rights at all and as a result there was nothing to negotiate about and no cause for compensation – or even consideration.

It is instructive to compare Queensland with Canada, where settlement of the western plains was taking place at exactly the same time as the native police were crushing Aboriginal resistance in central and north Queensland. Despite the many parallels between the two situations, the Canadian treatment of the plains Indians was strikingly different. Indian native title was recognised. A series of treaties was negotiated for the purchase of Indian land and compensation was arranged in the form of reserves, hunting rights, consumer goods and services. The mounted police oversaw the process of treaty making and protected the Indians against marauding frontiersmen. A celebrated Indian chief referred to the police as protecting the Indians as feathers protect the bird.[87] It was not a sentiment that would have been shared by Queensland Aborigines in the nineteenth century or even in the twentieth century.

Aboriginal troopers and trackers made a major contribution to the rapid spread of settlement in all parts of Australia. The Queensland native police played a decisive role

in crushing Aboriginal resistance and preparing the way
for untrammelled development of pastoralism, mining and
agriculture. The black troopers patrolled a frontier of great
size and diversity, tracking and dispersing resident clans in
cool southern valleys, parched western plains, dense wet
rainforests and tangled coastal mangroves. Although many
settlers 'did the necessary themselves', the native police,
combining Aboriginal bushcraft with European organisation
and technology, were the major instrument in the destruction of Aboriginal society. In Victoria the native police had a
much briefer career and were under both tighter institutional
control and more critical supervision. The southern force
probably killed fewer Aborigines than did the settlers themselves, although it played a decisive role in 'pacifying' Gippsland and parts of the Western District.

But the story doesn't end with the two forces created by
the New South Wales government in the 1840s. In South
Australia, the Northern Territory and Western Australia,
Aboriginal trackers, accompanying white police officers,
provided the bush skills needed to break black resistance
around the outer fringes of settlement. This was particularly
true of those rugged mountainous areas that both favoured
guerrilla warfare and disadvantaged the mounted police.
Trackers were of decisive importance in the police onslaught
in the Kimberleys in the 1890s. The two major black outlaws
of the north-west, Pigeon and Major, were both tracked and
shot by Aborigines.[88] And then there were the 'tame blacks'

who accompanied private punitive expeditions, providing the expertise needed to enable the settlers to track down their enemies and approach close enough to unsling their rifles.

∫ The decision to serve

Over the years many writers have referred to the activities of Aboriginal policemen, but few have attempted to examine the motivation of the trackers and troopers, preferring instead to see them as people without a will of their own who were bullied or tricked into working with the Europeans. In more recent times historians have been sensitive to the political overtones of the issue and have avoided asking embarrassing questions of their source material. Lack of evidence has further hampered discussion. Very few troopers recorded their side of the story. In many cases we don't even know who they were, where they came from or how long they served.

Marie Fels has provided us with an interesting and important interpretation of Aboriginal motivation for joining the Victorian force and has compiled detailed biographical details of many of the troopers.[89] Her comments focus closely on the particular situation in Port Phillip in the 1840s and need to be considerably augmented to provide an understanding of the role of troopers and trackers all over the country. The question of why young Aboriginal men became policemen cannot be answered until we ask why they 'came in' to European society in the first place, and having done so, why they worked for the settlers in a wide variety of occupations.

Aborigines both resisted and were attracted by European society. Curiosity drove them to experience the extra-ordinary sights and sounds and events that unfolded with settlement. Iron, glass and tobacco became highly desirable commodities. Horse-riding enchanted many young men and women once their initial fears had been overcome. Guns were objects of intense interest as well as of great fear.

Aborigines were also pushed into white society. Families and clans were broken up and scattered. Traditional economic activity became increasingly difficult; malnutrition and hun-ger haunted camps in the bush, while fear of punitive expe-ditions drove many to seek the protection of the local white boss or the nearest township. Having come in, their need for work was matched by the settlers' demands that the blacks 'make themselves useful'. Young people were quickly brought within the sway of the introduced economy – the men as casual unpaid labourers or stockmen, the women as domestic servants and concubines.

The native police forces were recruited from among the young men who were learning how to survive on the fringe of white society. Many of them probably had prior experi-ence of working for the Europeans and even those who hadn't would almost certainly have learnt from others what that entailed. A New South Wales squatter–politician told the 1858 Select Committee on Aboriginal resistance on the

Dawson River that 'it is not wild men we want for troopers, but men broken in by the squatters'.[90] In Queensland, the squatters frequently complained that their best 'boys' had either gone with or had been taken by the native police. And while many may have been pressed into the force, there were good reasons for choosing service as troopers rather than work as 'stockboys'. The Queensland native police pay of 5d a day was much less than white constables received, but it was rare for stockmen to be paid anything at all until the government forced the issue in the early twentieth century. The troopers were, then, better off than most of their contemporaries, who worked for food, tobacco, alcohol or opium. They could afford to buy themselves such small consumer items as pipes, looking glasses, marbles and 'regatta shirts, generally with very glaring patterns', which they gave to their women companions.[91] They were also better clothed than stockmen or fringe dwellers and better fed as well. The Queensland troopers received the same daily ration as immigrants on their journey to the colony. They could also hunt every day while on patrol, supplementing their rations with large quantities of bush food. Finally their equipment, arms and horses were probably better than those available to Aborigines working for pastoralists or farmers. Despite the disadvantages and dangers of the trooper's situation – and some of them are outlined below – it was probably a more predictable and secure way of life than that experienced by many others struggling to survive on the fringes of white society. The trooper might be away from kin for years on end (although this was not the case in Victoria), but so were countless young men and women who were taken away from their own districts and never returned.

∫ Sexual politics

One of the great difficulties facing young men who had come in was to gain access to women. The predictable ways of the past had broken down and in many frontier districts the whites had monopolised the young women, either by force or by negotiation with the older men. On pastoral stations Aboriginal women were preyed on by any and every white man whose whim it was to have a piece of 'black velvet' wherever and whenever he pleased. The troopers were encouraged to have their 'wives' with them in camp and were able to exploit their powerful position when on patrol to take local women or receive them as a tribute to their status and lethal reputation.

It seems that the white officers tolerated and even encouraged their troopers' sexual buccaneering and may have promoted it as one of the incentives for joining the force. In one of his addresses Walker told his troopers to 'Keep away from Gins when you are at a gunya [presumably at a station]. Do what you like when you are *in the bush*. I will not be angry with you then.'[92] The troopers may have had to 'lend' their own women to the white officers – indeed some of the worst cases of brutality in the force appear to have arisen from sexual jealousy – but that was where it stopped. They were not at the mercy of every passing white man.

〔 *The iron fist*

Numerous accounts of the native police have emphasised the violence used to maintain discipline and to prevent desertions, and indeed brutality runs like a dark thread through the history of the forces. From the beginning the idea was that the stern military discipline of the period should be imposed on the troopers, with the added consideration that 'savages' were thought to be as impulsive and wilful as children. Henry Dana believed that the relationship between black and white 'is as children to adults'. Taking into consideration, he argued, 'that these people are as children, they should be treated with lenity and proper indulgence'. But as policemen,

> they must be treated with firmness, to enforce implicit obser-
> vance and prompt obedience to the furtherance of discipline
> and order . . . and as they have certain refractory principles
> or features in their character which should be opposed to
> discipline and command, a wholesome rigour of punishment
> calculated to knock down the opposing principle, should be
> exercised.

With this objective in mind, Dana recommended 'rules and regulations as nearly approaching military law as due consideration of the character of these people would justify'. As for punishments, he suggested solitary confinement for minor offences:

but corporal punishment in cases of flagrant neglect, disobedi-
ence and insolence, would be wholesome and requisite to
restrain and prevent repetition; and anything approaching to
violence towards their officers should be punished by the lash
and imprisonment.[93]

Flogging was introduced into the northern force by Walker
and appears to have been employed throughout its history.
There are a number of recorded cases of great brutality
resulting in the death or serious injury of troopers, but how
often or how severely flogging was employed is impossible
to tell. For all that, the trooper only had to contend with his
officer; his contemporary on a station could be bashed by
anyone and everyone.

In Victoria, Dana attempted to prevent desertion by
telling the troopers that no matter where they went he could
come and find them. While writing to the superintendent of
the settlement he explained that

they all know that if they were to desert, I could take them again.
I am well acquainted with the place where each man was born,
and all their own haunts, their families and connexions, so that
if there was any inclination on their part to abscond, they are
perfectly well aware, that I could take them again.[94]

In Queensland deserters were shot. How often we cannot
determine, but many deserters may not have been caught –
or even pursued. Their fate may have depended on how much
start they got or how many broke ranks at any one time. If
enough troopers rode off into the bush, there was nothing

the white officer could do about it. He may not have even been able to report the desertion for days or weeks. Even when the remaining troopers were put on the trail of a deserter it was they, and not the officer, who determined if and when he was ever caught, simply by deciding whether or not to follow the delinquent's tracks. If there had been a prior understanding, the troopers would simply lose the trail.

∫ The silken cord

Despite the brutality and discipline, recruits continued to join the forces. Officers returned again and again to familiar districts, where knowledge of what service entailed must have been almost universal. Some recruits were probably running away from tribal justice, others from trouble with the whites. Once inducted into the force, many things kept them there apart from fear of discipline or death. The detachments clearly developed *esprit de corps*, sharing hardships and dangers. Troopers and officers came to depend on one another. Service provided a sort of social limbo where Aborigines were shielded from the worst results of powerlessness and servility. The work of the force depended on their expertise in the bush, a fact which was apparent on any and every day out on patrol. The troopers must have felt even more strongly the sentiments expressed by the black guides who told missionary Schmidt at Moreton Bay that, while they were servants on the stations, they were masters in the bush.[95] The obvious dependence of white officers must have undermined the image they sought to promote of authority and command. Service in the force also provided scope for the development of new skills that merged with and enhanced traditional bushcraft and that the troopers already took pride in. Many became splendid riders and talented marksmen. They were encouraged to display their talents to visiting dignitaries. Writing home to Britain, Governor Bowen praised the 'skilful riders and admirable marksmen' he had met while 'galloping over the prairies of the interior' on his official tours. 'I have more than once', he explained, 'seen a black trooper of my escort at the word of command unsling his carbine, and kill a bustard on the wing with a single bullet, at the distance of forty or fifty yards.'[96]

While outlining his plan for an Aboriginal 'Field Police', Maconochie observed that the silken cord would be more effective than the iron fetter in securing the commitment of black troopers. Clearly the more successful officers sought to exercise control by diplomacy and by building up mutual obligations. Walker and Dana both saw themselves as exercising a wise paternal authority over their respective forces while fully believing in their duty to impose 'corrective discipline' when required. A Queensland squatter told the 1858 Select Committee that Walker was 'extraordinarily familiar' with his troopers, more so than a 'gentleman' would be with his servants. The man's paternalism shows through in the surviving records of speeches he made to the force. 'Now boys', he said on one occasion, this is all I have to say to you except take care of yourself. Don't get sick any more for it breaks my heart. When you bogy [swim] don't stay long in the water.[97]

The more successful officers prided themselves on managing their troopers and binding them with silken cords of personal attachment and obligation. But it is very likely that the same process was working in the opposite direction. With all the skills of people nurtured in small kin-based communities, the troopers sought to influence their officers, to manage their managers. Paying respect, saluting, using deferential words and special terms like 'Marmy', adopting an appropriate demeanour – all were understandable and acceptable in terms of the wide variety of behavioural patterns which Aborigines traditionally adopted towards various kinsfolk. Such behaviour did not mean that the troopers were deferential to authority as such, to white men as a group, even to gentlemen as a class, but only to their own officer with whom quasi-kin relations had developed. Sexual relations between Aboriginal women and white officers may have been initiated as often by the troopers or by the women themselves as by the solitary white man. While entertaining the boss, the women were playing their time-honoured role of diplomats and negotiators and seeking to enmesh him in a web of obligation which could be subsequently activated to the blacks' advantage.

∫ *Why did they do it?*

However, the most contentious question remains. Why were Aboriginal troopers and trackers willing to become the instruments of the brutal frontier policies of colonial governments? Why did they kill other Aborigines? These are problems which require careful consideration.

The settlers quickly came to realise that Aborigines lived in relatively small groups in specific areas of land. Though they had some contact with other Aboriginal groups living in proximity and sharing common linguistic and cultural traditions, there was no concept of Australia as a whole or of Aboriginality. People related to their kin and to those who were near enough neighbours to be given that status. Aborigines who travelled long distances with the Europeans eventually came across people whose language was quite incomprehensible to them. The traditional view was that such distant people were dangerous or less than human or both. The settlers quickly became aware of the fear and suspicion evoked by strange blacks. The protector of Aborigines at Port Phillip, Edward S. Parker, was told that when tribesmen from distant regions appeared, 'they are foreign in speech, they are foreign in countenance, they are foreign altogether – they are no good'.[98] Foreigners were thought to be responsible for natural calamities and epidemic disease. It appears that the disastrous smallpox epidemic during the first generation of settlement was attributed to the powerful magic of distant tribes.

The Europeans were also aware that violence often

erupted between traditional enemies and indeed may have intensified as the spread of settlement brought them into much more frequent contact. Aborigines travelling with Europeans were particularly liable to attack and were, indeed, often killed or wounded by resident clans. The settlers used this danger to discourage their black servants from returning to their homelands. A Queensland trooper addressed a petition to the government in 1863 and, while outlining why he had deserted from the force, explained that he would have left his contingent in Rockhampton but was 'afraid of being turned into the Bush naked amongst Blacks who hated my people and so far from my own tribe'.[99] The explorer George Grey noted the fear of his guide Kaiber when forced to meet alien Aborigines:

> From his earliest infancy, he had been accustomed to dread these men; every storm that occurred he had been taught to consider as arising from their incantations: if one of his friends or relations died a natural death, he had attributed that death to the spells and unholy practices of these very people, with whom he was now directed to go and hold converse.[100]

Grey also noted that while blacks of his acquaintance strenuously tried to dissuade him from taking any action against neighbouring tribes, they took quite a different view of those in the distance. Because he had been speared on an earlier trip to the north, his acquaintances were convinced that a follow-up expedition would take revenge along the line of march. Grey explained how the local blacks:

kept continually requesting me, not to attempt to kill anybody, until I had passed a spot named Yal-gar-rin, about ten days journey to the north, and they then advised me indiscriminately to shoot everybody I saw.[101]

Clearly the attitude of troopers to the killing of Aborigines depended entirely on who the victims were. At Port Phillip, violence was contained in those regions where the troopers had links of culture or kinship but intensified in Gippsland, the home of traditional enemies. The northern force was traditionally recruited so far away from the scene of operations that any such prior contact – even of traditional enmity – was out of the question. Walker established the tradition by recruiting his first detachment a thousand miles away from the troubled northern frontier, and for a long time the troopers were brought from southern and central New South Wales. The importance of his recruitment policy was emphasised when, in the middle years of the 1850s, troopers were, for a short time, taken into the force in the region of operations with serious effects on operational efficiency. The force began to be absorbed into the kin politics of the district, as a perceptive local squatter realised, because the new recruits

carried on an intercourse with the tribes from which they were taken, and used their police authority to exercise a kind of tyranny over the tribes . . . Wherever they went they were always surrounded by a number of [local] women, who always act as emissaries between the wild tribes and those with whom they want to deal. The consequence of all these things was that the Native Police enforced their authority only at their own option. The officers hardly had any power over them and whatever good they did was greatly curtailed.[102]

As a result of the experience of these developments, the policy of recruiting in districts remote from the frontier was re-established, as was the determination to prevent contact between troopers and local clans.

The tribal structure of Aboriginal society was exploited in other ways as well. When Walker recruited his first contingent he deliberately selected the troopers from four different language groups, and this policy of mixing the members of each detachment was apparently persisted with throughout the history of the force. A native police officer explained the policy to a school inspector who visited the local barracks and noted that the troopers spoke to one another in English:

> You see . . . we have to mix the tribes in a troop. An officer of native police is entirely at their mercy if they concerted any united plan of attack on him [but because of] this confusion of tongues . . . they take no interest in one another, and herein lies our safety. If one man were to attack me the rest would come to my assistance, but if all belonged to the same tribe they would help one another, and the life of an officer would never be safe.[103]

Troopers and trackers killed Aborigines on the frontier, or helped Europeans to do so, because they were recruited and trained with that purpose in mind and deployed in districts where they were strangers with no particular sympathy for the local clans and where, indeed, they may have had a degree of hostility stemming from the deeply rooted traditional beliefs. We have no real idea of how the troopers viewed their military role. No doubt opinions varied widely according to personality and circumstances. But any initial antagonism towards the clans in the bush would have intensified in the course of conflict. The fighting was often desperate, albeit one-sided. The troopers were frequently in danger and both officers and men were killed and wounded in battle.

They were, however, much more than mindless instruments of European policy or of the will of their officers. The troopers were, after all, the masters in the bush. They and they alone could track Aboriginal groups desperate to escape from the pursuing police. Regardless of what the white officer wanted, it was ultimately the troopers' decision to 'come up' with parties fleeing or hiding in the bush. It was fully in their power to lead the detachment away from their quarry – and indeed that may have happened at times. Like mercenary forces the world over, the troopers probably rationed the number of confrontations they engaged in as much for their own safety and comfort as anything else. As in so many other cases, the Aborigines played up to the Europeans' belief that they were simple, childlike beings and used it with skill and subtlety to their own advantage and to make the best of the desperate situation in which they found themselves in the wake of the European invasion.

four

LIVING WITH THE
WHITE PEOPLE

FROM THE EARLIEST years of settlement Aboriginal
children lived for varying periods with European families,
often growing to adulthood with little contact with their
natural parents and other kin and in some cases having no
knowledge or recollection of them. The circumstances
surrounding the acquisition of Aboriginal children by Euro
pean families were rarely discussed in detail but no doubt they
varied widely. In some cases close kin had died from disease
or had been shot in punitive expeditions. Thus in July 1789
the young girl Abaroo was brought into a settlement suffering
from smallpox and on recovering was 'received as an inmate'
in the family of the clergyman Richard Johnson.[1] As described
in Chapter Six, James Bath was taken by the Europeans after
his parents were shot at Toongabbie, and adopted 'as a
foundling' by the convict George Bath.[2] The means by which
the Reverend Samuel Marsden acquired 'his boy' Tristan is
more difficult to determine. The child may have been stolen

from his parents. Marsden said little beyond explaining that the boy was 'taken from its mother's breast'.[3] And what was good enough for Samuel Marsden was good enough for many other settlers in all parts of the Australian colonies throughout the nineteenth century. Europeans kidnapped black children, or received them, with remarkably clear consciences. They were convinced that, almost regardless of circumstances, Aboriginal children were better off with white people, where they would be 'civilised' and 'trained-up' for useful tasks.

Catching them young

John Batman, the pioneer of settlement at Port Phillip, acquired two Tasmanian boys, Lurnerminner (or John Allen) and Rolepaner (or Ben Lomond), and refused to give them back to their parents, who complained to George Augustus Robinson. One of the mothers, Karnebunger (or Sally), 'frequently importuned and solicited' Robinson 'in the strongest terms to have her son restored'. He in turn informed the official Aborigines Committee that Batman refused to give up the boys and that this 'had been the cause of much grief both to the mother and to the natives generally'. When Robinson's son called on Batman to give up the boys, he refused, saying that they were 'as much his property as his farm and that he had as much right to keep them as the government'. It was recognised at the time that Batman would resist any attempt to take the boys away from him because 'they were too useful'. One minded the pigs, the other milked the cows. If they didn't work hard enough, Batman flogged them. He took the boys with him to Port Phillip and they didn't return to Tasmania until after his death in 1839.[4]

While driving stock overland from the settled districts to Port Phillip in 1837, Edward Eyre found 'two little black boys' aged about eight years old called Cootachah and Joshuing. They had been taken from the Murray by an earlier party and left on the banks of the Goulburn. Eyre 'attached them' to his own party, explaining in his autobiography that

> both were perfectly naked and seemed very hardy as well as full of life and spirits. They were allowed to occupy a corner of the tent at night but if it did not rain preferred always sleeping by the fires . . . They soon got reconciled to their new masters and were made very happy in such garments as we were able to supply them. Young as they were, too, we found them very active and useful, especially in tracking lost animals . . .[5]

Eyre took 'his boys' with him to Tasmania, where they were 'crowd pleasing trophies'. In Launceston they were 'objects of great curiosity': the locals crowded around and 'followed them in great numbers'. In Hobart, too, they were the centre of attention at the theatre and at a military parade where people gave them fruit, sweets and 'various little presents of one kind or another'.[6]

Cootachah and Joshuing accompanied Eyre on his next journey from New South Wales to South Australia. As they neared the Murray the party was met by the boys' kin. The parents were 'greatly delighted' to see the children again, the father of one 'especially showed a great deal of feeling and tenderness'. Eyre, determined to keep 'his boys', was unmoved. The tribe, he wrote,

> encamped around us for the night and when the next day we crossed the river and moved on for a mile or two they still followed and again encamped with us. It was only natural that they should, but I did not quite like it and I was moreover, afraid of losing the boys. By being very civil to the parents and making them sundry little presents they were however inclined to acquiesce in the children remaining with us.[7]

Three weeks later five members of the expedition deserted, taking Joshuing with them, but Eyre 'got another native boy' called Neramberein on his next expedition to South Australia.[8] Three years later Cootachah and Neramberein set out with Eyre and John Baxter to cross the Nullarbor. They shot Baxter and decamped rather than follow Eyre further into the wilderness.

∫ Sable valets

Men like Batman and Eyre wanted to hang on to 'their boys' because they were so useful. Young children of either sex had skills which were indispensable in the bush. As Thomas Mitchell discovered, even a six-year-old could track with greater confidence than many adult Europeans.[9] Children could be easily trained and disciplined, and once taken away from their own country were totally dependent on their

European patrons. They could be physically and sexually abused without fear of the law or public opinion. Colonial courts needed proof of age – which could rarely be provided – before action could be taken in cases of interracial paedophilia. Girls were 'tampered with' at an early age and, while there is little evidence one way or the other, boys were probably also dealt with in the same way by homosexual or bisexual 'bosses'. Even if not sexually exploited, young Aborigines were often employed as personal 'body servants', as Robert Dawson, manaager of the Australian Agricultural Company, termed them. An Aboriginal boy he called 'Wool Bill' became his 'sable valet', his 'faithful squire' who attended him on all occasions, helping him to dress and wash and shave. Writing of 'Wool Bill', Dawson explained that he

> encouraged his disposition to domesticate himself by every means in my power; and as I was always much amused and pleased with him, I made him my body servant during the journey. As soon as we had discovered a proper place, he untied my shoes, took off my stockings, and washed my feet, while I was seated at the edge of the river.[10]

The employment of 'sable valets' to enhance one's prestige probably dates back to the early years of settlement. At much the same time that Dawson was being pampered by his body servant in the bush, John Macarthur rode up to a ball at Government House in Sydney attended by a 'bodyguard of Aborigines' dressed in scarlet shirts, blue trousers and yellow handkerchiefs.[11] Well-presented black retainers became as desirable a part of a squatter's retinue as good horses and well-maintained plant. Writing of the gentlemen settlers of central Queensland, Rachel Henning explained that people going on long journeys always took 'black boys' with them because they were 'most useful servants in the bush'. When her brother Biddulph travelled from Exmoor to Port Denison in April 1865, he

> set off quite in style . . . driving the buggy and pair, with his big
> hairy dog 'Tiger' running after him, and Jimmy, one of the black
> boys, riding on horseback behind, the said Jimmy being gorgeous
> in new white trousers slightly too large for him, a scarlet
> Crimean shirt and scarlet cap. Biddulph bought scarlet for both
> the blackboys when he was last in Sydney. They are so fond of
> bright colours, and look best in them.[12]

Running them down

Far and away the greatest advantage of young Aboriginal servants was that they came cheap and were never paid beyond the provision of variable quantities of food and clothing. As a result, any European on or near the frontier, quite regardless of their own circumstances, could acquire and maintain a personal servant. The easiest way to obtain 'a young one' was to 'run one down' in the bush. People made no secret of the practice; indeed they spoke quite openly about it. In his *Memoirs of a Queensland Pioneer*, Wade-Broun explained that early in his pastoral career he had been 'anxious to get a young black boy' and was eventually able to obtain what he wanted. 'On one occasion', he recalled,

> while riding through the bush, I came upon the rear of the tribe of blacks . . . Among them was a lad about fourteen years . . . I rode quickly after him, stopped and caught him by a strap around his waist which was his only garment, pulled him on to my horse and rode away. Kindness, plenty of good food and clothes soon made him a happy little nigger and he remained with me for years.[13]

In her family saga *Kings in Grass Castles,* Mary Durack observed that within a few months of their arrival in the Kimberleys the overlanders had 'somehow acquired a few native boys between eight and fourteen years old'. McCaully had 'secured two likely youngsters named Tommy and Charlie', Kilfoyle had 'an inseparable named Sultan', while Michael Durack 'had three boys, Cherry, Davey and Billy'. It is not clear how the overlanders executed their kidnapping ventures. 'How they got hold of them', Mary explained, 'was nobody's business, but whether by fair means or foul they [the boys] were to stand a better chance of survival in the years to come than their bush tribespeople.'[14]

Those with a more tender conscience often convinced themselves, and others as well, that they had gained their captive children by a fair process of barter that was clearly understood and mutually acceptable. In her journal written at Glendower station in the Hughenden district in the late 1860s, Lucy Gray gave an account of how her husband Charles acquired 'a little black boy' while returning from a journey to a station 50 miles away. 'As he rode up in the dusk', she recorded:

> we could not imagine what it was he had behind him; it was the boy holding him tightly round the waist, & peering round his elbow, with a funny little grave face.
>
> At a word from C he slipped off, & stood waiting for him without taking notice of anyone else. C had bought him from an old gin for a couple of handkerchiefs, at least he asked her to give him the boy, which she did willingly, & he gave her his hand-kerchiefs as a present, with which she was delighted.
>
> Whereupon C had his hair cropped, & bought him a blue twill shirt, thus for the first time in his life he was clothed, & most completely, for the garment, made for a man, came down to his heels. He followed C silently, wherever he went, like a little dog who had found a master, standing close by him, & when C went into the house he sat by the doorstep watching for him to come out. At night he received a blanket in wh. [which] he curled himself up, as if he had been accustomed to it all his life. I thought it looked like making a slave of him, when C put hand-cuffs on his little slender black legs, to prevent him in a sudden fit of home-sickness, going back to his Mammy in the night. He did not seem at least affected by this want of confidence in him, but looked on with interest, & when it was over, put his head under his blanket & went to sleep.[15]

Aboriginal children were not safe from maurauding Europeans even when they were living in camps on the fringe of country towns. Soon after the local clans had been allowed to 'come in' to Bowen, the editor of the local paper over-heard a man say that he was going down to the camp at Queen's Beach 'to catch a young one'.[16] In January 1870 a party of six squatters who were staying in Townsville en route to their inland stations rode down to the fringe camp on the town common. William Hann 'got a little girl' for his wife, while Robert Gray 'got' both a boy and a girl. How the other four squatters fared was not recorded. Gray's two captives escaped that night but were retaken the next day and carried off into the interior.[17] The girl was given to his sister-in-law, Lucy. 'Mournful looking creatures they were, when first they came', Lucy noted in her journal. The girl, she wrote,

> who was about twelve, was for me to train to be a servant. Just
> then she did not look a hopeful subject. The journey must have
> been rather a trial to them, never having been on horseback
> before, to travel from forty to fifty miles a day. I do not think
> they knew for some days, that they had come to an end of their
> journeys. In their short experience of civilised life they had been
> accustomed to stop at a station to camp every night & go on
> again next day.[18]

Even after this ordeal the children, given the names Moggie and Billy, were not allowed to stay together. Robert Gray took Billy on to Hughenden, 28 miles further along the track. A week later Billy walked alone back to Glendower. Once he had recovered he was taken back to Hughenden, where he remained, hundreds of miles away from his home and separated from the only person who provided him with any links to his past.[19]

It was not necessary to catch one's own child – such things could be arranged through intermediaries. The protector of Aborigines at Normanton explained to his superiors that settlers in the more remote areas, where there were 'plenty of myalls about', were often importuned by towns-people 'to bring them in a boy or a girl'. 'In due time', he observed, 'the child arrives'. How they were separated from their parents was 'a subject of conjecture and surmise'.[20] Jane Bardsley was one such outside settler who sought to provide a young girl for her friends in town. She asked another station owner 'where the niggers [were] very savage – to catch a little Mary-mary' about ten years of age to 'break in for house-work'. She quickly explained in her letter that she did not mean her friend 'would use a rope as in breaking in a horse'. The child eventually arrived, but scratched and bit anyone who tried to touch her. Jane responded by tying her to her own servant, Kitty, for 'a few days, until she was quiet enough to take to town'. The child was delivered to her destination only with great difficulty and had to be locked up as soon as she arrived. Eventually she broke a window and escaped by swimming the Norman River, plunging into the mangroves and walking back to her country.[21]

Bardsley wanted to provide her friend with an Aboriginal child as a favour. Others sold or bartered children. Normanton's Protector Galbraith observed that 'a large number of individuals have an idea that they can trade an aboriginal as they would a horse or bullock'.[22] Mary Durack explained how her father and Pumpkin, his trusted Aboriginal servant, negotiated with a Queensland miner travelling to the Western Australian fields to exchange an eight-year-old boy for a mare and a tin of jam.[23] A Queensland squatter wrote to the police magistrate at Bowen in 1869 giving him an account of two men who had stolen a couple of Aboriginal boys and taken them to the goldfields to sell. He assumed the practice would continue because it 'paid so well'. In 1881 the Catholic priest Duncan McNab was informed by a reliable witness that he had seen a Queensland carrier 'run down a black boy', chain him to his dray and sell him two days later to another carrier for £2 10s 0.[24]

∫ From owner to owner

Children were handed on from person to person for all sorts of reasons with little concern for their feelings or preference. With the high degree of geographical mobility in the Australian colonies, people frequently moved on and usually left their Aboriginal servants to fend for themselves or simply 'gave' them to friends. One Normanton woman told the local protector of Aborigines that a black had been 'left to her by will'. The protector added wryly that the woman did not mention 'if probate had been granted'.[25] Settlers moving to other colonies or returning to Britain left their Aboriginal children behind, a practice apparent even in the most exalted circles. Thus Sir John and Lady Franklin decided not to take the eight-year-old Mathinna with them when they returned to Europe in 1843, although she had lived with them for the previous two years. 'But, strangely enough', a nineteenth-century writer observed,

> instead of being placed with a household of respectability and virtue, where at least her happiness would have been consulted, she was thrust into the Convict Orphan School, where some black children had been sent to be educated or to suffer and to die. Poor Mathinna was transferred sobbing and broken hearted, from . . . the luxury and grandeur of Government House, to a cold stretcher of the Queen's Asylum.[26]

More humble settlers behaved in a similar way to the Franklins and continued to do so throughout the nineteenth century. In 1902 the police in Brisbane took into custody a sixteen-year-old Aboriginal boy who was sleeping rough and begging for food. He was one of the boys who had 'belonged' to the prominent pastoralist Edward Palmer. After growing up on Canobie station, he was taken to Sydney by Palmer's widow where he 'passed beyond her control'. As a result she 'consigned him to a Mr. Hassall in Brisbane'. He ran away from his new 'owner' and lived as best he could until a concerned storekeeper reported him to the police.[27] A few years later, the Herberton Bench committed George Singleton to the Anglican Mission at Yarrabah for stealing a quantity of stream tin. It transpired that two months before his arrest his 'owner', who 'had reared him from infancy and

sent him to school', had left town leaving the boy behind
with no means of support.[28] In 1903 Queensland's northern
protector of Aborigines outlined the career of a young boy
called George who

> was taken away from Cooktown when a boy by a Mr. A–, and
> handed over to Dr. H–, in Townsville, who subsequently handed
> him over to a man named C–, a resident of Mackay. C–, left
> town two years ago for Brisbane and turned the boy adrift.[29]

The passage from 'owner' to 'owner' could be even more
rapid than in George's case. In his memoirs of life on the
northern goldfields, J. H. Binnie recalled that once, when his
family was on the road between Cooktown and the Palmer
River goldfield, the teamster's wife 'obtained a black girl,
about twelve years of age' from a passing bullock team. The
child could not speak or understand any English and
'moreover she was very nervous'. The drunken teamster
ordered the girl to go and collect water from a nearby lagoon
and when she failed to respond he flogged her with his horse-
whip. His wife spoke to the owner of a passing dray and
handed the girl over on the understanding that she would
be sent to live with friends of hers in Brisbane. As she once
again changed hands, 'the screams of the child were heart
rending'.[30] It seems unlikely that she ever reached Brisbane.
A concerned outback resident wrote to the Queensland
government in 1892 reporting that an acquaintance of his had
sent a young woman away with the mailman to be dispatched
to friends in the south. 'She went through Burketown while

I was there', he explained, 'consigned to a publican . . . she knew nothing of where she was going.'[31]

⌠ Cast adrift

Girls were regularly abandoned when they became pregnant, as invariably happened given their absolute vulnerability and the sexual rapacity of European men. Such matters were usually hidden from public view and remain so to modern historians. But once the various state governments began to exercise greater control over the Aborigines within their borders, such incidents were investigated and reported on. Queensland's northern protector of Aborigines observed that the majority of 'these female children [were] engaged mostly as nurse girls', but when they 'get into trouble are no longer wanted, but packed off to shift for themselves'.[32] He outlined the circumstances of Dolly, a thirteen-year-old part-Aboriginal girl, who had been employed 'for ten years past' by a Mrs M— who had applied for permission to send the girl to live on a cattle station. When permission was refused, the girl was handed over to the police. She was 'found to be seven months pregnant'. Mrs M— refused all requests to assist the girl, the Protector explaining:

> The girl having been with her mistress so many years with-out receiving any wages, and only possessing the two articles of clothing which she stood in, the Protector asked Mrs. M— what she was prepared to do for her, but could get no satisfaction.

Dolly had her child in Cooktown but it died soon after birth. She was subsequently sent to Yarrabah.[33]

The fate of Jane Bardsley's girl Pigeon was even more tragic. She was 'adopted' as a two-year-old and was a welcome addition to the then childless family. Bardsley wrote at the time:

> Since we have no child of our own we are treating her as our adopted one. She is such a tiny little mite and is grateful for our care. Tom has made her a wooden cot and she sleeps on the verandah near our door . . . I am much happier now that I have little Pigeon. She is a darling and will stretch out her frail little arms when either Tom or I go near her cot and whisper Missus or Boss with a loving light in her eyes.

When Bardsley had children of her own, Pigeon became their playmate and then their nursemaid, looking after seven of them when in her teens. Tiring of child-minding, she became the family's housemaid and waitress. 'She looks so smart in her navy uniform, white apron and cap', Bardsley explained, adding that she was 'a very valuable girl' who 'knew where everything was and absolutely spoiled the whole family'.

Eventually Pigeon rebelled. When the family retired to bed she would slip out of the house and gallop bareback into nearby Sarina. Eventually she became pregnant, but managed to keep it hidden and gave birth when Bardsley was away. The baby died and Pigeon was ordered to bed to be looked after by a nurse for nine days. Bardsley and her husband were adamant that Pigeon had to be sent away and she was dispatched to the Barambah Mission Station. How this was effected is best told in Bardsley's own words.

We had to wait until a female prisoner was being sent from Townsville to Brisbane, for then the warder in charge of the prisoner could take care of Pigeon.

We had to wait for six months before a chance came. Then we only had two days notice and Pigeon behaved very badly. She was so upset at the idea of being sent away that as fast as I packed her clothes she took them out of the port and began to tear them . . . At night, when she knew that the telephone service would be inoperable, she came into us with a gun and asked us for a cartridge as she wanted to shoot herself. Instead of giving her the cartridge we all hurried into one bedroom, and spent a dreadful night fearing that she would set the house on fire as she had threatened to do. She screamed hysterically, pleading not to be sent away as I was her mother.

In the morning she was calm but I was not. I had been crying all night so that my eyes were swollen and red. I had reared and nursed this girl almost from an infant and to have her going away was like losing another child.

I had to take her by coach to Mackay and when the time came for me to hand her over to the police, she screamed and flung her arms around my neck and cried, 'Don't let them take me away, I won't do it again. I love you Missus, you are my mother'.

Oh, dear! I shall not forget in a hurry her poor drawn little face as she pleaded for my help. I had had her for nineteen years.

I parted with her finally at the wharf and could hear her distressed goodbyes as the boat went out to sea.

In a subsequent letter, Bardsley wrote: 'We do miss our little Pigeon . . . I suppose it is just abo nature to stray as she did'.[34]

∫ Chastisement

Young girls were often placed in desperate situations – separated from family and kin, without friends and totally dependent on their 'owners'. They were expected to work for long hours at many household tasks and were left in charge of younger children, all for little or no pay, inadequate food and cast-off clothing. Beatings and abuse, while not universal, were certainly commonplace. Sometimes the 'missus' protected her charge from sexual exploitation and imposed authoritarian control over what little private life she had. Usually, however, molestation began at an early age. Young Aboriginal girls were universally considered to be fair fucking game by the 'boss', his sons, the Chinese cook or indeed anyone who had half a chance to 'bust a young gin'.

Flight was one possible remedy, but there was often nowhere to run to. The police or the boss would very likely track the fugitive down and flog her for her trouble. In 1900, Queensland's northern protector outlined the life experience of a young Aboriginal girl called N–, who was

working and living with Europeans, to who she had originally been given by the police. Ran away from her employer who forced her to come back — Satisfied myself she had been cruelly treated, sworn at, beaten, and kicked; she showed me a scar which she ascribed to her late employers boot; she apparently had no blanket, and certainly received no wages — the poor thing had proved a hard working and willing slave. I considered her about fifteen years old, if that, notwithstanding that she had had a baby (now dead) a good twelve months before.[35]

In 1900 a Mr and Mrs Boyce travelled from north-western Queensland to Toowoomba for a holiday. They were accompanied by their two young children and Gerribah, their ten-year-old Aboriginal 'nurse-girl'. They stayed at a boarding house overlooking the coastal plain. Several other guests became aware of the Boyces' brutal treatment of their servant and complained to the government. What was acceptable behaviour in the Gulf Country was, by the turn of the century, highly offensive in southern urban centres. The police and the protector of Aborigines investigated and took the girl away from her 'family', to the intense chagrin of the Boyces. Gerribah's statement to the Toowoomba police was corroborated by several boarding-house guests. It read:

Says she has been with Mrs. Boyce for a long time. Comes from Normanton. Used to do housework and mind the children. Mrs. Boyce never gave me any money.

Mrs. Boyce used to thrash me with riding whip, and hit me in the face. Sometimes I was thrashed because I forgot to do something Mrs. Boyce told me to do, and sometimes I did not know what the thrashing was for.

> Mr. Boyce used to kick me about the body. Sometimes I was
> sent without meals.[36]

Despite the incessant work and sporadic brutality, the 'missus' and the 'boss' were the nearest thing to parents many young Aboriginal servants had, and the children of the family the only approximation to siblings. They had lost contact with their own people and had forgotten – or never learnt – most aspects of traditional culture. At the same time, they had been taught to aspire to 'better things' without the means or the hope of achieving them. Writing with experience of such situations throughout north Queensland, the protector of Aborigines observed that 'while in such European employment' the young Aboriginal or part-Aboriginal girl 'develops that veneer of civilisation which teaches her to regard the full blood with contempt, and the half-caste male as her inferior'. The result was that 'she consequently falls an easy prey to the white man who, except in rare instances, she knows she can never marry'.[37] Even when conditions of living and employment were reasonable and where genuine bonds of affection had developed, the problems created by the young woman's maturing sexuality were often insuperable, as the case of Pigeon and Jane Bardsley showed.

Such complex situations had various outcomes. In 1901 Queensland's southern protector, Archibald Meston, sent an unnamed 26-year-old woman to the Aboriginal station at Durundur. In his official report on the incident he explained the attendant circumstances. She had been brought up from the age of five by a prominent police officer and his wife. They had no children of their own so they 'trained her exactly as if she had been their own daughter'. She was baptised and confirmed, 'slept in one of the best bedrooms, dined with her master and mistress at the table, and [was] treated in all respects as if they had been her father and mother'. While on a visit to Brisbane, the young woman was taken to Durundur and as a result asked Meston if she could stay there. To avoid 'paining the officer' he refused to accede to the request, but warned him 'that the woman wanted to be married'. The officer wouldn't hear of it, saying that she was 'too well guarded to land in any trouble'. Twenty months later she was found to be pregnant by a white man and the officer and his wife asked Meston to let her go to Durundur, where they would pay for her keep. Three months after the birth of the child she married an Aboriginal man who had originally come from Normanton.[38]

The conflicting pressures on Aboriginal boys were probably less intense than those which confronted adolescent girls who were 'with the white people' and which so often destroyed their lives. Like their female counterparts, however, they were totally dependent on the white boss and their treatment was determined by his moods and inclination. Among employers of Aboriginal labour it was widely accepted that violence was necessary to discipline and 'civilise' young black workers. No secret was made of it and 'chastisement' was openly advocated in the colonial press and parliaments. Those who promoted the need for a good flogging every now and then had a point. Seeing that Aboriginal servants were rarely paid and had little incentive to stay with demanding white bosses other than fear, such treatment was probably essential in many cases. 'Boys' who ran away were pursued, and if caught were severely punished. While giving evidence in 1884 in one of those rare cases where a white man was arraigned for flogging 'his' boys, the victim – a young boy known as Bushman – explained how his 'master', Guy Thomson, a Hamersley Range squatter, had beaten him for running away. Pointing to Thomson, he said:

> This fellow beat me. He tied me up by the legs and arms. He got a stockwhip and put a lash on. I fainted like dead . . . He hit me on the back . . . He hit me plenty of times. I had run away.[39]

Twenty years later, police in Ingham recorded the testimony of an Aboriginal boy found wandering about the town after he had run away from his boss, who was droving cattle from Cape York to Rockhampton:

> When the cattle was mustered at Lakefield Station, I no want to go long way from my country, and when he want me go, I run away. Mr. Donkin followed me, and catch me alonga paddock. He have em rope, and he beat me with it. Then he tie me alonga hands and body, then he drive me alonga horse to the station. Then he give me supper, and tell me go alonga cattle. When I come a long way alonga Palmer, I want to go back. Mr. Gleddon say, 'I can't let you go back, you must go alonga Rockhampton, and go back alonga boat'! Then I go alonga Tate and Dry River,

I think it. I run away alonga mountain, and I get frightened, and come back, alonga cattle again; too far strange blackfellow kill em me. Gleddon then beat me alonga whip.[40]

There was always a sharp discrepancy between the value of Aboriginal servants to the whites and the return accorded them for their labour. Most people who 'owned' boys and girls would not have been able to afford comparable white servants even if they had been available, and in most outback areas that was not the case. Though the Europeans constantly complained about 'unreliable', 'unfaithful', 'lazy' or 'stupid' servants, it is clear that in a wide range of pursuits – from nursing children to breaking horses – Aboriginal labour was both irreplaceable and indispensable. Occasionally the more independent-minded and self-confident servants were able to break away from white bosses and bargain for wages somewhat commensurate with their worth or to achieve a precarious independence. The squatter–aristocrat Harold Finch-Hatton discussed this situation in his book *Advance Australia*, published in 1885. He noted that

nearly every station in Queensland had one or two black boys employed on it as stock-riders, in which capacity they were very useful, as they soon learn to ride well, and are invaluable in tracking lost cattle and sheep. As a rule, however, they are not much use after they get about twenty years old. By that time they have begun to find out that they are useful; and as their idea of the value of their services seldom corresponds with that of their employer, they generally get sent away.[41]

∫ Experiments in civilisation

We will probably never know what happened to more than a small percentage of Aboriginal children who, for one reason or another, were taken to live with white people. What we do know suggests that the experiment – even when well intentioned – frequently ended in disaster. The results seem to have been much the same throughout the nineteenth century and in all parts of Australia.

Many of the children died before adulthood of introduced diseases to which they had no immunity – measles, whooping cough, influenza, tuberculosis. The result was that many of those children who were considered most promising, that is, who made steady progress in their European education, were struck down before or during adolescence, leading some observers to conclude that there were biological barriers to 'improvement', that regardless of intellectual capacity Aboriginal children could not cope with 'civilisation'. The careers of James Bath and Thomas Bungeleen, discussed in Chapter Six, closely conformed to the common pattern. John Helder Wedge's boy Mayday – who, as described in Chapter Six, was forbidden to mix with white servants – died prematurely while being 'brought under the influence of civilisation'. Wedge 'found' the boy while on a surveying expedition on the north-west coast of Tasmania. The lad 'attached himself' to the surveyor and accompanied him on all his expeditions and met with the 'greatest kindness from the settlers' visited on the way, being allowed to sit up to dinner with the adults, a privilege presumably not accorded to white children of a similar age. His conduct, Wedge recalled, was 'always correct and well behaved, and would compare favourably with most European boys of the same age'. He had acquired English 'tolerably well' and Wedge was on the point of teaching him to read when a 'severe inflammatory attack of the lungs carried him off'. But Wedge was confident that 'had his life been spared' he would never have 'returned to lead the uncivilised life from which he was rescued'.[42]

George Van Diemen was another Aboriginal boy 'found' in the Tasmanian bush. He was taken in by the prominent settler William Kermode, christened and taught his 'letters and his prayers'. He became 'obedient and tractable', was 'weaned from his wandering habits' and was 'even-tolerably cleanly'. Kermode took the boy on a return trip to England partly as an 'experiment of instructing and civilising a being of a race so little known'. Van Diemen was placed in the care of one George Greatbach, a dissenting minister at Southport in Lancashire. Here his behaviour was 'very favourable in every respect'. He was 'much loved' and 'conducted himself better than would have been expected'. His education was then taken over by a John Bradley of Liverpool. During nine months' schooling, Van Diemen not only impressed his tutor with his progress but confirmed the man's belief in racial equality. Bradley wrote to Kermode:

I feel much gratified in having had this boy with me, tho' but a little time, as it confirms me more in the opinion that I have long cherished: that man is on all parts of the globe the same; being a free agent he may mould himself to excellence, or debase himself below the brute, and that education, government, and established customs are the principal causes of the distinctions among nations. Let us place indiscriminately all the shades of colour in the human species, in the same climate, allow them the same means for the development of intellect; I apprehend the blacks will keep pace with the whites, for colour neither impairs the muscles nor enervates the mind.

Kermode and Van Diemen returned to Tasmania in February 1827. But the promise which so impressed his English tutor was never fulfilled; Van Diemen died later the same year.[43]

∫ Rebellion

Whether Van Diemen would have remained a model pupil is impossible to determine. But young people placed in similar situations showed a strong tendency to rebel violently in their early teens – to run away, steal, drink, engage in promiscuous sex and be generally destructive and disruptive. This pattern of resistance was apparent from the early years of settlement. In July 1805 the *Sydney Gazette* reported that an Aboriginal girl 'not exceeding 13 years' had burnt down several farm-houses on the Hawkesbury. She had been taken from the bush as a baby and 'raised from infancy' by a settler named Henry Lamb, 'in whose family she had remained'. She had never been known to 'intermingle with the Native Tribes, nor to hold any intercourse with them'. The girl burnt the Lambs' farmhouse and was caught attempting to do the same to a second family with whom the Lambs had taken refuge. The *Gazette* could suggest little reason for the behaviour of 'this juvenile desperado' beyond what was termed her 'unparalleled depravity, perfidy and ingratitude'.[44]

Samuel Marsden's 'boy' Tristan lived with the family for twelve years but in his teens began thieving and drinking and 'keeping low company'. He eventually ran away from Marsden while the family was in Rio en route to England. Marsden explained the failure of 'his experiment' by blaming not just the boy himself but the whole Aboriginal race, writing that the boy 'wanted that attachment to me and my family that we had just reason to look for'. He always 'seemed deficient in those feelings of social affection which are the very bonds of social life'.[45] In the decades that followed, many others sought to interpret the rebellion of Aboriginal children as manifestations of their savage nature.

In 1831 a Tasmanian government official prepared a list of 'incorrigible or abandoned' Aboriginal and part-Aboriginal girls who were 'about the town' in Launceston. Sixteen-year-old Margaret Thomas, for instance, had lived for some years with a Mrs Patten. She had been living a vagrant life for nine months before her arrest for theft. Mary Briggs was thirteen. She had been 'about the town a considerable time'. 'Several decent people' had taken her in but she would not remain with them. The surveyor J. H. Wedge had a 'half-caste' girl 'under his protection' between 1828 and 1834 when he wrote to the official Aboriginal committee about her:

> I took charge of her under an idea that she would be rescued from the dreadful state of depravity which prevail amongst that class of people [the sealers in Bass Strait], and that she would become a useful member of society. She has of late, however, notwithstanding the very great pains taken with her turned out so incorrigibly bad in *every* respect, as a drunkard, a thief and a prostitute.[46]

Wedge arranged for the girl to be sent to the Aboriginal settlement on Flinders Island. A similar fate awaited a girl brought up by Dr Temple Pearson, the assistant-surgeon at Campbell Town. She had been 'captured' in the bush on the east coast and was given to the Pearsons in 1827, when she was thought to be about seven or eight. Four years later the local police magistrate wrote to the colonial secretary asking that she be sent to Flinders Island, explaining that

> Mrs Pearson has paid great attention to her instruction, but it appears she has of late become so exceedingly obstinate and perverse that Mrs P finds it impossible to keep her under restraint. An inclination to pilfer trifling articles has of late shown itself and conscious of the impropriety of her conduct she endeavours to screen herself by falsehood.[47]

When, at the turn of the century, Queensland government officials began to assess the situation of Aborigines in the colony, they found that children brought up with

Europeans displayed remarkably similar patterns of behaviour to those noted in Tasmania two generations before. Protector Galbraith at Normanton commented on the many cases he had observed during his years living in the frontier towns of north Queensland. Most people, he wrote,

> will tell you that the child is better off with Europeans: in my opinion the contention is absurd. Most of the children will bolt (if old enough, and the distance not too great), and then they are termed ungrateful by *their owners*. This practice has been going on for years, and, with the exception of one or two cases personally known to me, without good results to the children: they change masters and mistresses, prostitution and disease follow, they can only speak pidgin English, and finally become pariahs amongst both whites and blacks.[48]

Galbraith's superior, Dr Walter Roth, reached a similar conclusion about the children who lived with whites. They were, he argued, brought up in an entirely false position as 'one of the family', which was always one of the reasons given for not paying Aboriginal servants. But the time arrived 'sooner or later' when the Aboriginal girl realised that she was a pariah 'amongst those very people with whom, probably ever since she [could] remember, she [had] associated with more or less as an equal'.[49]

Government reports of the period contain many examples of children and young people who for one reason or another ended up in Aboriginal reserves or missions, having run away from, been taken from or been abandoned by their 'owners'. Jack Baker was a 'half-caste' of twelve or thirteen who had been 'adopted' seven years earlier by the proprietor of a travelling circus. Having developed 'thieving propensities and getting beyond control', he was handed over by his 'owner' to the authorities, who sent him on to Yarrabah.[50] Two years earlier Tommy, a sixteen-year-old 'half-caste' girl, had preceded Jack Baker to the mission. For the previous eight years she had travelled over the country with a stockman called W. J. Smith. She admitted 'camping at night' with Smith, who was charged with harbouring.[51] At the same time 'Flora', an eight-year-old 'half-caste', was sent to the Mapoon Mission. She had been given to Mr W— about twelve months before by Mr M— of N— Station. She had 'become unmanageable by her employers'.[52] In a report to the Queensland government, the southern protector of Aborigines related the story of Katie Mackay, whom he had sent to Durundur. She was a native of the Mulgrave River, 'where nearly all her tribe were shot, her own father being shot while carrying her in his arms'. She was reared by a Mrs Mackay, a butcher's wife from Cairns, who brought her to Brisbane and passed her on to another family. The girl ran away with two white men who spent their time sailing in Moreton Bay, but when the boat capsized she came under the stern eye of the protector. Meston also reported how when at Springsure in the central-west, he was approached by one of the leading squatters of the district, who told him he would like him 'to take charge of his half-caste girl Dusty'. The girl was duly handed over to the local sergeant of police, who placed her temporarily in service in the town. When she was eventually brought down to the coast at Rockhampton, she was found to be suffering from 'recently contracted venereal' and ended up living in isolation on the Durundur reserve.[53]

The brutality and misery suffered by young Aborigines who lived with the white people in colonial Australia were never the whole story. There were many examples of black servants who remained with pioneer families throughout their lives, even when that meant living in exile from homeland and kin. In her family histories *Kings in Grass Castles* and *Sons in the Saddle*, Mary Durack makes many references to Pumpkin, the family's 'stalwart and capable retainer', who chose of his own free will to move with the Duracks from his country in Queensland to the East Kimberleys.[54] In such cases it is obvious that the family in question were regarded as kin and were accorded all the affection and protective concern appropriate to the relationship. On the other hand, the boss and his family were expected to reciprocate by providing European food, tobacco, access to horses and guns, and protection against both black and white enemies. Such traditional expectations were certainly commonplace among Aboriginal communities where at least some members worked for the Europeans, although they would have been far less common among children who had been removed from their tribes at an early age and who spent their whole lives in a social and cultural limbo.

For their part, white bosses often developed strong paternal affection for their 'boys' and decidedly non-paternal affection for the young women, although that could not be publicly displayed for fear of derision and social ostracism. The white bosses were proud of the bush skills and horsemanship of their boys, boasted of them to fellow squatters and saw that they were well turned out for occasional trips to town or to the local bush race meeting. Enlightened self-interest often meant that black workers were adequately fed, clothed and equipped. Shared experience, common dangers and hardships on the frontier cemented relations between boys and bosses and between house servants and station women. Along with stark inequality of status and power, there was also mutual interdependence in an often harsh and dangerous environment.

The fact that servants were frequently chastised did not necessarily mean that the whites in question were without feeling for the targets of their whips and boots and fists, although many bosses were callous and some brutal beyond the boundaries of sadism. The universal frontier practice of calling black men 'boys' regardless of their age certainly demeaned and belittled the bearers of the epithet. However, it also reflected the firm conviction that Aborigines were very much like children who, it was thought at the time, needed constant correction and would be spoiled if spared the rod. The brutal Mrs Boyce, who shocked the residents of the Toowoomba guest house by thrashing her 'nurse-girl', told investigating officials that she only chastised her 'to the extent as she would chastise her own'[55] and that may, indeed, have been true.

For a minority of settlers, close association with black servants provided the opportunity to learn about Aboriginal languages and culture, and out of that grew an appreciation and respect that were unusual at the time. The Darling River pioneer David Bonney found on investigation that the Aborigines were 'better, nobler, and more intellectual than [they were] generally believed to be by those who have not lived among any of the tribes'. All who had done so 'and taken the trouble to learn something of their language, so as to better understand them, must have formed a good opinion of them'.[56] But most frontier settlers did not see their association with black guides and workers as an opportunity for cultural exploration and enrichment. They had a more mundane end in view. A few practical lessons in bushcraft were acceptable, but that was as far as it went. Their interest was economic rather than intellectual. Black workers were a desirable adjunct to European pioneering in all parts of Australia. In the northern half of the country they were an essential condition of success.

five

FRINGE DWELLERS

WILLIAM THOMAS ARRIVED in the infant colony of Victoria when the squatting rush was under way, and by the early 1850s he had been involved with Victorian Aborigines for fifteen years. He watched the dispossession, deplored the violence and documented the accompanying social disruption. He saw a whole generation destroyed by disease and deprivation, and by conflict both with the whites and within the black community. While writing a six-monthly report for the government in 1853, he concluded that all Aboriginal resistance was at an end and that the 'weapons of opposition' had been 'laid aside'. Armed police were no longer necessary 'to keep Aborigines in awe' and loopholes in huts were 'no more needed'. At the same time, the blacks had taken up the reaping hook and their 'erratic habits' had 'at length given way to European Employment'. Indeed, they were, Thomas argued, 'as hirelings working for their support and know well the value of money and receive not as formerly merely a good feed and tobacco for payment but hard cash'. He appreciated that the diversity of skills required in the bush had 'added in no small degree to their advancement and general usefulness'. Local blacks were engaged in 'breaking in horses, mustering cattle, shepherding, sheep washing (at which they excel Europeans *in care*), reaping even to tying up'.

Thomas realised that although many Aborigines had been absorbed into the rural economy, they had not become Europeanised. Work and industry had not provided the means to assimilate the indigenous people, as many colonists had hoped. He appreciated that their 'nationality' had been weakened but 'not totally broken up'. They hadn't forgotten bush tucker, and got it when and where they could. What is more, they continued to move across the country as they had always done, although their travelling was now due to their 'shifting from one locality to another' in search of work. But beyond a minimum of adaptation necessary for survival, all further efforts 'so far to improve their condition [had] been without avail'. Thomas explained the situation to his superiors:

> I have pressed, the farmers and others have urged they become as us not merely in work and diet but stop in house . . . comfortably clad and stretched [sic] . . . is what they'll hear nought of, the hook, axe or bridle down and all further of civil-isation for the day is over, off goes apparel and they bask under the canopy of heaven as in their primitive [sic] wildness evidently enjoying their freedom from encumbrance . . . nor have they any desire to be meddled with further, such is their wandering

propensities, that all kindness, entreaty or persuasion can not secure them one day beyond their determination and latterly they have been particularly cautious how they make bargains for labour on this account.[1]

Thomas was writing during the gold-rushes, at a time of maximum demand for Aboriginal labour due to the 'dearthly supply' of white workers. However, his observations about the Aboriginal response to participation in the European workforce were relevant to many other parts of Australia during the nineteenth century. Clans who had come through the violence, disruption and disease of the first years of the invasion lived as best they could on the fringes of towns and villages or camped when they were able to in favoured spots in the countryside. While working fitfully for the whites, they sought a stable and satisfactory synthesis between the old ways and the new.

∫ Coming to town

The colonial towns attracted Aborigines from the hinterland, who came in to see the whites and experience the cornucopia of novel and exciting possessions brought from the other side of the world. The commissioner of crown lands at Geelong observed in 1841 that the town 'attracts them greatly, partly from curiosity' and partly by the ease with which they could obtain meat, rice, flour and sugar in exchange for birds and skins and by 'occasionally carrying out parcels from the stores, or chopping wood'.[2] One of William

Thomas's most thankless tasks was to try and keep the blacks out of Melbourne and encourage them to leave when they were living in what quickly became almost permanent urban camps. Adelaide attracted clans from as far away as 200 to 350 kilometres. In the 1840s the average Aboriginal population in the town was 300, but on occasions as many as 800 were in residence. Edward Eyre explained that

> the facility of obtaining scraps by begging, small rewards for trifling jobs of work, donations from the charitable, and a variety of broken victuals, offal etc, enable them to collect in large numbers, and indulge to the uttermost their curiosity in observing the novelties around them, in meeting strange tribes, and joining them either in war or festivity, in procuring tools, clothes etc. to carry back and barter in their own districts.[3]

The attraction of the towns was, then, real enough; but it was only half the story. Many family groups were driven in from the countryside by the violence of the frontier, the difficulty of finding enough to eat in their own country, or because they were literally forced off their land by the squatters and police. A Cooktown resident met a small party of local blacks who were in camp eating meat and loaves of bread acquired in the nearby town, and asked them why they didn't live in the bush from the proceeds of hunting and gathering. They replied, 'White fellow along a yarraman [horse], too much break him spear, burn yams, cut him old man with whip, white man too much kill him kangaroo.'[4] At much the same time a colonial official visiting a town camp near the

Queensland–New South Wales border was told that the indigenous animals had practically disappeared from the district,

> and that they cannot get a living if they go on a hunting excursion as in their days of old, also that their dogs are poisoned off, leaving themselves almost useless after game.[5]

The plight of the 'town blacks' was outlined by a police magistrate in Rockhampton in 1871 when responding to agitation to expel the local camps:

> They are driven from many stations in the bush, and their dogs which they use for hunting the scrubs are poisoned almost everywhere so that the use of their own country is literally taken away from them, and if they are able to be driven out of town their only course will be to roll themselves up in their annual shoddy donative called a blanket, and die.[6]

A sympathetic local resident wrote to the paper, arguing that it was 'only to save their lives' that the Aborigines remained about the town. When they ventured into the interior they were 'hunted back again by the native police'. Signing himself 'A Lover of Justice', he concluded with several rhetorical questions:

> Let those who are so bitter against the blacks look at a map of the country and see the division lines of the runs and the towns and they say where can we send the blacks to? for the whole country is taken up, the people won't allow them in the town, and the squatters won't have them on the runs. Where, Mr Editor, can they go?[7]

∫ First meeting

For some clans it was not so much a matter of being attracted towards, or thrust into, the burgeoning colonial towns as of the towns coming to them, suddenly appearing and then mushrooming on their own traditional territory. Such unexpected and unprecedented developments must have been a source of anguish and astonishment. One such meeting between local clans and pioneer townspeople was described by Abijou Good, who was staying in Mackay in 1863 prior to travelling into the interior. His diary entry for 24 September is worth quoting in full, his eccentric punctuation and spelling notwithstanding.

> i am still at the Royal Hotel & to day i have witnessed a sight that i have long wished to behold it was the meeting for the first time on one side at least of the two races of the human family. i stated before that the settlement was situated on the bank of the pioneer river which at this place is about half a mile wide. the opposite side is covered with a very dense wood it is known to be filled with blacks but no white man has ever landed for they are reported to be very feirce armed with spears & clubs as wild as thier native forests. this being sunday the most of the people were at the settlement when some one gave the alarm that the blacks were to be seen on other side the river. the report soon spread & in a place where there are but eighteen dwellings it dos not take long to get the most of the people together however we were soon on the bank of the river & sure enough there stood

six or seven stalward fellows armed with spears & clubs thier
bushy hair standing out on all sides making thier heads appear
many times larger than they really were. the whites shouted to
them & invited them to come across the river to our side, for
which invitation they treated us to some of thier most hideous
yells. at lenth two of the most corageous threw down thier spears
& holding up thier hands high above thier head to show us that
they were with out arms of any kind they dashed in to the water
which at this time would not take a man higher than his waist
(the tide being out) when they had got some little distance from
the shore yells thier black bretheren seemed to remind them that
they were running into danger & i beleive they would have gone
back had not the whites gone into the water to meet them. after
a great deal of caution the two partys met about the middle of
the river on meeting the whites held out both thier hands which
the blacks seemed to understand as a sign of freindship for they
seised the hands & commenced a very curious dance this dance
would have been very amusing on shore but in the water it was
doubly so, the whites danced too as well as they were able &
being english of course they shouted hurra as loud as thier lungs
would allow them while the blacks laughed and grined & shouted
a great many things which it would puzzle me discribe. meat
bread & rum was given to them, the blacks on the opposite shore
had by this time augmented to the number of about fify no
sooner did they see thier brethern kindly treated than they
rushed into the water & came across pell mell to our side no
sooner did they set thier feet on shore than they commenced

to dance & to yell beautifully they were all men & they were all intirely naked a great many of them made signs to be allowed to go into the settlement but this could [not] be allowed unless they had some clothes on after a little delay a pair of trousers was found for one a shirt for another a coat for another & soon about a dosen of them was lead into the settlement where everything they saw created a long consultation amonst them selves everything was new to them but their wonderment reached its highist pitch when they saw a cart moving they could not make out the wheels. the wheels going round was a mystery they could not solve they remained in the settlement till near dark & by this time they loaded themselves with all triffles they could find, one picked up an old red powder flask another an old horse shoe some one thing & some another, by this time the people of the place had become tired of thier company & some had been opposed to thier coming at all three or four of these now came out of their tents & discharged thier guns in the iar this had the desired effect for in a few minets about a hundred of them was to be seen rushing across the river as if for very life & we saw no more of them for that night.[8]

There were further developments before Good left town. Four days after the first meeting, he got up before sunrise just in time to see a large party of blacks hurrying along the riverbank carrying large bundles of booty taken from the settlement during the night. Running to the hotel, he grabbed a revolver. Dashing back to the river he 'discharged six shots in quick succession in the air'. The blacks rushed into the river; the townspeople spilled out of their dwellings grabbing clothes and guns on the way and assembled at the water's edge. They began firing 'so rapid that one would have thought that a battle was being fought'. But the shots were 'fired in the iar it were only to hasten the flight of the blacks', who could be seen scrambling up the beach on the other side of the river 'in greatest confussion'.

A week later a party of Aboriginal women came into town 'as naked as they were born'. They treated the wide-eyed spectators to 'a very rude kind of dance & by signs & gestures tried thier very best [to] excite a certain desire in the white males of the settlement'. Good concluded that the women had been sent by their 'black husbands' to 'lessen if possible the breach which they made by the attempt to rob the settlement'.[9] He is silent on what happened when the dancing stopped.

∫ On the fringe

While Europeans squatted on Aboriginal land and founded hundreds of towns and villages, the Aborigines in turn established just as many fringe camps on the outskirts of the new settlements. Many towns in colonial Australia had attendant fringe camps at some time or another. The bigger towns had two or three. Very little information about these camps has survived, but as far as we can tell they varied considerably in size from one or two families to communities of a hundred or so. No doubt all camps waxed and waned according to the seasons, the availability of food and work and the continuing compulsions of local ceremonial calendars.

Campsites changed over time, but the underlying relationship with the European town remained the same, characterised throughout by social distance and gross structural inequality. The location of the camps said it all. They were invariably out of town and often a kilometre or two away from the nearest houses — out of earshot, out of sight and usually out of mind. Other than that, sites varied according to local geography. They could be over the river, down in the dry creek bed, out beyond the graveyard, the Chinese gardens, the slaughterhouse or the rubbish-dump, invariably on land that no one else wanted and well away from the town's water supply.

The architecture varied, as surviving photographs from all parts of Australia indicate. Traditional techniques survived in many areas, as did the use of local building materials such as thatch, bark, reeds or leaves laid onto a framework of saplings. European materials such as iron sheeting, tin plate, bags and blankets were widely adopted. With growing knowledge of European bush carpentry, Aborigines began to build structures that looked increasingly like the slab huts of miners and selectors. Camp dwellers used both European and traditional artifacts. Spears and boomerangs continued to be used for hunting, but contemporary photos indicate that tins, buckets, bottles and axes were readily available for a wide variety of tasks.

Among the few available descriptions of nineteenth-century fringe camps are those provided by Queensland government officials who, in the late 1890s, surveyed Aboriginal communities all over the colony. Particular attention was paid to the town camps at Mitchell, Roma and Charleville. The Mitchell camp was a kilometre from town on a bare, exposed bank of the Maranoa River. Thirty-two blacks were living in the camp when the officials visited, but individuals came and went depending on when work was available on local stations. Sickness was rife, many residents were addicted to opium, and malnutrition was evident. The camp dwellers explained that they were 'often two or three days without food'. When they were given rations, 'there was no mistaking their signs of hunger'. The mortality rate was catastrophic. There had been 20 deaths in the six months prior to the visitation.

Conditions were no better at Charleville, where 64 people were living in 'miserable ricketty structures of tin and rags, neither proof against wind nor rain'. Several of the town's leading citizens accompanied the visiting official and confessed they had no idea of conditions in the camp, 'though living so near them'. Opium addiction was apparent, and while the majority of residents were 'fairly healthy', they showed the effects of 'continued defective nutrition'. The Roma camp was on a creek 2 kilometres or so from town adjacent to the Chinese gardens. The 28 men, 22 women and 12 children were living in conditions similar to those in the

Mitchell and Charleville camps. Residents were 'nearly all dirty and ragged, and spiritless and miserable'. The camp provided 'no protection against rain or cold'. Their clothing was 'certainly not the kind required to keep them warm in a Roma winter' and they suffered from 'periods of enforced starvation'. When given government rations, they 'proceeded to cooking and eating as if food was a scarce necessity'.[10]

The desperate poverty observed in the three small pastoral towns was apparent in other places as well. In 1887 the warden of the Etheridge goldfield reported that most blacks from the large local camp were emaciated and 'in great stress to the point of starvation'. They could be seen every day 'watching the hotels for scraps of food being thrown out'.[11] At much the same time, the secretary of Townsville's Aborigines Protection Association observed that 'very frequently' the local 'town blacks' were 'simply starving'. The local sergeant of police concurred, noting that 'enough food [was] the exception'.[12] In 1890 the 25 old people in a town camp at Maryborough were described as a 'little mob of blear eyed maimed creatures'.[13] Farther south at Mungindi, the 30 local blacks were in 'a starving and destitute condition'.[14] Twenty-two Aborigines who lived in the Springsure camp in 1902 were 'in a very destitute condition'.[15]

Poverty and destitution were, then, only too obvious in many town camps. But that was never the whole story. Conditions varied widely over time and from place to place. By their very nature the camps may have become refuges for those, who through age, illness or addiction, were unable to find or keep work in the rural economy or to support themselves by hunting and gathering. The specific situations in the camps outside Roma, Mitchell and Charleville were due, in part, to particular local circumstances. The three towns offered only a limited amount of work and the government survey was carried out in the middle of a prolonged drought that had crippled the local economy, impoverishing both black and white. Opium addiction was certainly widespread in many parts of north Australia at the time, but it was by no means universal. The drought-stricken countryside provided little bush food, while in more favoured districts the European presence had scarcely affected the ability of local blacks to live by hunting and gathering.

The most fortunate camps were those with easy access to the sea or a major river system. Port Douglas blacks lived on the beach, and while both men and women worked in the town, their 'old hunting and fishing sources of food [were] also available, being little affected by the small and scattered suburban settlement'.[16] A Western Australian government official visiting Broome in 1903 reported that the camps near the town 'had a plentiful supply of fish and native food'. There could, he believed, be no doubt that 'the majority of these natives get all the food they require'. Locals told him that anywhere along the bay the blacks could 'obtain quantities of food in the way of fish of all kinds'.[17]

∫ *An admirable auxiliary*

Work was the major nexus between town and camp. Indeed, the labour of thousands of men and women played an important, and generally overlooked, part in the economy of colonial Australian towns. In the absence of large numbers of white servants, they performed a range of indispensable tasks – the dirty, boring, onerous jobs – often for little or no money. The town blacks carried water, gathered and chopped wood, stripped bark, washed clothes, scrubbed floors, scoured pots, buried garbage and nightsoil, and cared for children and domestic animals. The protector of Aborigines at Normanton reported in 1904 that the local blacks came into town about nine and left at six in the evening. They had 'their regular employer', were 'orderly, biddable and very honest' and were employed as 'house-boys, fire-wood cutters, yard cleaners, nurse-girls, washerwomen, charwomen etc'.[18] A German missionary observed the arrival of the town blacks in Cooktown one morning in 1896 after they had crossed the Endeavour River:

> The blacks have left the camp and are preparing to come across the water. They come over in groups, mostly family groups, using canoes, which mostly leave only when they are fully occupied. Once they reach the town they seem to be audible and visible everywhere: dirty and very scantily clad, they shout and chatter, but they know where they are heading for. Many of them are being expected . . . The wife of the Clerk of the Court is calling one black girl.

'Come on, Annie, quickly, it's Saturday, I have a lot of work for you today, you have to sweep all through the house for me.'

'Tobacco, missy, just a little bit!'

'Afterwards, Annie, as much as you like, afterwards; but now get on with it!'

And elsewhere: Long Ah Kong, the jovial plump Chinese is beckoning to a black lad, while carefully tucking up his long plait: 'Billy, lad, come and sweep my store for me. I'll give you a lovely watermelon!'

There is a third, Tommy, who does not need to be told what to do. He has some wood to split every morning for C., the publican, and he doesn't mind doing it because the reward is well and truly worth it . . . beer![19]

Townspeople were loud in their complaints about the local blacks, but the occasional observer gave recognition to their important contribution to the community. A pioneer Gladstone resident remarked that the town would 'suffer much from want of labour' if the blacks were 'not to be found . . . ever willing to render any service required of them'.[20] 'Far from being a curse,' a second townsman wrote, 'they prove an admirable, and in our present position, an almost necessary social auxiliary – ministering to our wants and necessities in fifty different ways.'[21]

It is impossible to determine how many Aborigines worked in the colonial towns, but judging by the estimates of Normanton's protector of Aborigines the number, at least in north Australia, may have been quite large. In 1903, when the total population of the town was only about 500, he estimated that 150 Aborigines were employed on a daily basis.[22] If the protector's estimate was even approximately correct, it clearly meant that almost every household engaged Aboriginal servants and many must have employed more than one. Some confirmation of this level of employment is provided by Jane Bardsley, who arrived in Normanton in 1895 after leaving her Brisbane boarding school. She found that she had 'nothing to do' but practise music and singing because 'we have black labour for all jobs'.[23] Clearly if the Normanton estimate was even close to the truth and the same situation was apparent in comparable towns in other parts of northern Australia, then Aboriginal labour was a major and greatly underestimated factor in the urban economies.

As far as the Europeans were concerned, the great advantage of Aboriginal labour was that it was cheap and could, at least initially, be obtained in return for tobacco, food scraps or old clothes. That situation persisted where the Aboriginal bargaining position remained weak either because supply exceeded demand or the alternatives of rural work or living on bush food were not available. But black camp dwellers found ways to respond to exploitative or brutal employers. Normanton workers never returned to employers who treated them unfairly.[24] 'At first they work fairly well', a Palmer goldfield resident wrote, but 'scheming, pilfering, shamming sickness and other devices soon become manifest.'[25] Eventually black workers came to appreciate

the value of their labour and demanded payment in cash.
A Cooktown pioneer noted in 1875 that the local Aborigines, who had once given a good day's work for tobacco, flour
and sugar, were now bargaining 'with all the shrewdness of
a white man'.[26]

∫ 'Indecent exposure'

The 'town blacks' had their own agenda and sought to use
the town for their own advantage and in their own way. They
showed no particular desire to adopt European clothing – or
any clothing at all, for that matter; more particularly so in
subtropical and tropical Australia. For their part, the townspeople were often gravely concerned about Aboriginal
nakedness. 'It is really too bad that this sort of thing should
be permitted by the police', thundered an outraged Townsville resident on seeing the first large party of blacks walk
through town. His demand that they be 'sufficiently clothed
to prevent indecent exposure' was echoed in countless other
pioneer townships in all parts of the continent.[27] Men took
their stand in defence of the sensibilities of women and
children. A Bowen resident complained that 'henceforth no
female with a sense of decency' could venture into the
suburbs, 'for in all directions the naked savages [were] now
to be met with'. Even children were 'becoming familiarised
with the undisguised appearance of open, shameless, unre-
buked vice'.[28] The same concerns were voiced in Brisbane,
the editor of the *Queensland Guardian* complaining that 'every

kind of riot and indecency' was taking place within sight
of Queen Street, which made it impossible for respectable
women to walk that way – although he admitted that a
'number of young lads [had been] feeding their prurient
curiosity by gazing on the scene'.[29]

It is clear that 'town blacks' tried to come to terms with
what initially must have seemed a strange ritual, the purpose
of which may not have been immediately apparent. Various
attempts were made to conform with European customs by
wearing assorted scraps of clothing, by using body paint or
by carrying branches of shrubs in front of what they had
come to understand were the offending parts of the anatomy.
But an accommodation was reached everywhere sooner or
later. When Bardsley arrived in Normanton she found the
local black children were allowed to walk about naked, but
at the age of nine or ten they were forced to don European
clothes – men's shirts for the girls, moleskin pants and shirts
for the boys. It was all rather shocking for the convent-
educated girl. 'At first I would feel my cheeks burn with
shame and quickly look the other way,' she explained, 'but
now I am sophisticated and do not even shut an eye.'[30] The
editor of the *Port Denison Times* described the process of
accommodation in Bowen:

> They on the one hand accommodate themselves to our prejudices
> by, as a general rule putting on some clothing, or such apology for
> it as they can get, when they come into town; we, on our part,
> seem to be learning that the ideas of scantiness of clothing, or even

nudity, and immodesty are not inseparably associated, and at any rate, if we meet an unfortunate devil who has been unable to procure as much clothing as we should like to see upon him, have found out that it is possible to avoid any very serious shock by outraged feelings by simply looking the other way.[31]

∫ Noise and riot

European anger and insecurity intensified whenever the local Aborigines moved too close to town. The constant activity in three camps on the outskirts of Darwin in February 1874 provoked an irate townsman to write to the local paper complaining that there was 'always some occasion for noise and riot . . . one night there is a marriage, another a death, and another a pitched battle about gins'.[32] A few days later the camps were moved farther away from town. Anxiety about what the blacks might be doing intensified at night. Strange nocturnal noises fed latent fears of violence and revenge. The editor of the *Rockhampton Bulletin* referred to the 'feeling of apprehension when savage howls and shrieks are heard in the streets after night fall'.[33] In Ravenswood, 'night was rendered hideous by their yells . . . and chatter'.[34] There was an outcry in Barcaldine in 1887 when the local blacks established a large camp on an allotment surrounded by houses, where they made a huge fire and danced naked before it. As in all such cases, the camp was soon moved to a safe distance out of town.[35] Useful industry by day was one thing, uninhibited relaxation at night quite another.

Until they were prevented from doing so, Aboriginal clans carried out revenge killings on other Aborigines within the towns because that was where the chosen victim tended to flee in an attempt to escape the avengers. Both men and women were killed in or near European settlements, often in broad daylight. Charles Symmons, Perth's protector of Aborigines, noted in 1842 that 'native fights were constantly occurring; our town sites, nay Perth itself, were theatres of their strife'. Armed blacks murdered their victims 'at noonday on the very threshold of our doors'.[36] It was a complaint that could be heard in towns and villages all over Australia.

Even more alarming for townspeople were the pitched battles between rival tribal groups which often erupted within the towns themselves. They were chosen as the sites for trials of strength and redressing of wrongs either because the Europeans had unwittingly co-opted traditional meeting places for their settlements or because food available in the town itself enabled large parties to gather together for long enough to complete their business – something they could no longer do in the countryside. In both 1843 and 1844 there were large battles in Adelaide between the local blacks and those from the Murray River.[37]

In reminiscences recorded in the early years of this century, old pioneers recalled seeing Aboriginal battles in their childhood. Charles Dudley heard a major fight in the streets of Gympie one night and saw a dead body the next day.[38] Thomas Welsby remembered a similar battle in Ipswich.

While it raged three families crowded into his parents' house, the adult men with their guns loaded and ready.[39] J. S. Hassall had a similar recollection of early Bathurst, but in his case local blacks came and hid from their pursuers in his house.[40] In the late 1880s and early 1890s there were a series of battles in Cooktown's streets. In July 1888 a fight broke out near the hospital. The 'opposing forces went in real good slogging at each other, spears flying about in all directions, and the air being thick with the yells of savage warriors'. The Europeans took refuge in the hospital. The combatants were 'dispersed with difficulty' when the town police fired over their heads.[41] There were further battles in 1891, 1893 and 1894.

∫ Innocent appropriation

Constant begging was a greater annoyance to Europeans than occasional tribal battles or intermittent executions. What is more, the Aborigines appear to have excelled at it. 'As beggars,' the surgeon Peter Cunningham wrote in the 1820s, 'the whole world will not produce their match. They do not attempt to *coax* you, but rely on incessant importunity, following you, side by side, from street to street, as constant as your shadow.'[42] For their part, blacks saw no reason at all why the Europeans should not be constantly encouraged to share their abundant possessions either by persuasion, persistence, veiled threats of violence or appeal to latent guilt about dispossession. Begging as whites knew it carried no moral opprobrium whereas the Europeans' manifest selfishness did.

The traditional esteem given to sharing merged with the post-settlement conviction that the Europeans owed blacks a very large debt indeed and needed to be constantly reminded of the fact. What is more, begging became a grim necessity for many communities as they strove to find enough to eat to stay alive.

When they first walked into the towns, parties of Aborigines picked up the Europeans' possessions at every opportunity, probably not appreciating the strength of the white passion for private property. When the first party entered Townsville,

> many ludicrous scenes occurred during the exertions of the blacks to thieve and the whites to prevent them; and in the majority of cases the former were the victors. Nothing seemed to be too hot or too heavy for them; a crinoline and a pillow case were stolen from one house, a breakfast at the next, and blankets and axes at the next. Not even the precincts of the Courthouse were held sacred by these marauders. One of them made ingenious use of a spear to fish the cloth from the magisterial table through the bars of the window, and was successful in carrying it away in triumph. They were with some trouble induced to leave the town.[43]

Such innocent appropriation of property did not last long, however. The Europeans saw to that. It was not that the Aborigines accepted the European version of things; they just became more skilful, subtle and surreptitious in their raids on European property. Complaints about pilfering were almost universal. In the 1840s, for instance, there were almost identical complaints from townspeople in such widely scattered communities as Maitland, Portland and Port Lincoln.[44] Town blacks often became skilful burglars, mastering the details of European houses, their doors, windows and locks. Writing of the truly massive robberies undertaken by Maryborough clans, the local commissioner of crown lands told his superiors in Sydney in 1855 that he had great trouble curbing their exuberant expropriation of property. Their movements, he explained, 'are so stealthy, and they are such adepts in the Commission of robberies which they perpetrate during the night, that it is impossible to detect them'.[45] Things were much the same fourteen years later, the local paper writing with grudging admiration of the black burglars, who acted 'as though they had served an apprenticeship in London or New York'.[46]

∫ Corrective violence

Violence was a common European response to what was considered unacceptable behaviour by their Aboriginal neighbours. A Bowen resident observed in 1884 that every man seemed to consider himself justified in personally 'carrying out the utmost rigour of the law' towards the blacks around town, 'often for some trivial and insignificant offence'.[47] In Maryborough, likewise, private individuals took the liberty of administering 'a sound thrashing for offences against the decency and peace of the neighbourhood'.[48] In Townsville in

1870 the editor of the local paper remarked that it was a pity
that the blacks had been let into town because 'their pilfering
propensities and impudence [were] becoming rapidly developed'. The problem was that they had minds and objectives
of their own, and 'simply ordering them away from the
vicinity of a dwelling house, even when in a state of nudity
[was] absurd'. He concluded rather plaintively that they 'will
not obey the orders of the dominant race in this particular'.
The answer was clear. The orders had to be 'enforced by the
application of a stick or some other offensive weapon to their
backs, and then the chances are the blow will be returned'.[49]
The danger of such retaliation led to the organisation of vigi-
lante groups like the armed and mounted party which drove
the blacks' camp away from North Rockhampton in August
1867.[50] In Taroom in 1892 a 'large and influential meeting'
met on a Saturday night to discuss the presence of the blacks
in town. On Sunday morning all the male adults 'turned out
en masse' and removed the local camps to what was considered an appropriate distance.[51]

∫ The curfew

Two means of control were adopted in all parts of Australia:
Aboriginal camps were kept well away from town, and all
blacks were to be out of town between sunset and sunrise
regardless of the legal niceties of the situation. In 1853 the
subguardian of Aborigines at Albany directed that 'all natives
except indentured servants' were to sleep 'at an appointed

distance from the town, and not to be seen prowling about after dark'.[52] At Bourke the police ordered all local blacks to camp on the far side of the Darling, 'with a supplementary order that although they might visit the village at day time, none should remain after six'.[53] G. S. Olivey, Western Australia's travelling inspector of Aborigines, reported in 1900 that at Carnarvon the police had 'a good hold of the natives, keeping all except those working some two miles from the town'.[54] At a public meeting held in Townsville's Theatre Royal in 1871 it was resolved that

> the daily visits of the aboriginals within the boundaries of the town cause many annoyances and loss of property through their pilfering habits, and that it is highly necessary that proper means should be at once taken to prevent them frequenting the streets at night.[55]

Visitors often watched the blacks being driven out of town and reacted with amusement or horror depending on their view of such things. The visiting naturalist J. W. Gray discovered in 1875 that the local Aborigines were not allowed in Brisbane after sundown or on Sundays, and that 'at either of these times they [were] used very roughly by the police, sometimes being whipped out'.[56] At Bourke, 'most of the poor devils' crossed the river at the appropriate time but the 'few stragglers who loitered were horsewhipped through the streets' by the local police sergeant. He began his rounds every day after sunset 'and on the first crack of the lash, shirt-tails could be seen flying towards the river, which the blacks used to take in their stride, whether it was a "banker" or otherwise'.[57] When she was staying in Townsville Lucy Gray discovered that there was a large blacks' camp on the far side of the creek. Townspeople employed the residents 'cutting wood, drawing water etc & gave them old clothes, food, tobacco . . . or money', but all the workers were 'obliged to decamp at sundown'. She noted in her diary:

> In the evening & morning we used to watch them from the hotel, trooping across: old & young even the gins with their picanninies, though the place abounded in sharks. White people would not venture to bathe there. The blacks did not seem afraid – though they had to swim (unless it was low water) carrying their clothes on their heads & in the evening, whatever spoil they had gotten or earned in the day.[58]

Two Sydney sisters visiting Maryborough in 1885 were shocked at the way things were done in Queensland. They had met an Aboriginal woman in the morning while out for an early walk, and in the evening

> saw the same sable lady . . . being driven out of the town across the river by the mounted police, and our feelings were deeply outraged at the way they were driven down the street, like so many sheep or dogs, to the water's edge, when they plunged in and swam to the opposite side to their camps.[59]

Ongoing discussion about imposing curfews on 'town blacks' reflected both the sharp division of opinion on the question and the doubtful legality of the actions required to enforce them. Shifting official and popular attitudes were reflected in Queensland in the twenty years between 1876 and 1895. In 1876 controversy flared in Gympie when a correspondent adopting the nom de plume 'Humanity' wrote to the local paper drawing attention to 'an act of great cruelty and injustice'. He (or was it she?) described how he had seen the police 'clearing them out', as it was called locally, and in the process stockwhipping an old man known to the European as Croppy. The offending constable was 'an excellent hand with the stockwhip and [used] it in the best style at one blow fairly felling the poor fellow to the ground'.

Following the publication of the letter the local police magistrate was instructed to hold an inquiry into the incident. In his evidence the constable explained that it had always been the custom in the town to 'clear all out when any became troublesome', and while it was normal for the officer in question to carry a stockwhip he had merely cracked the whip without actually striking anyone. It seemed an unlikely story. But in his report to the authorities in Brisbane, the police magistrate explained that it appeared to be a common practice 'to drive the blacks out of the place in this and other townships when they become troublesome'. While the practice was 'doubtless illegal in itself', local conditions made it necessary because if the blacks were 'unchecked in any way they would proceed to outrage'.[60] The response of the commissioner of police was to insist that 'such practices be discontinued' under pain of instant dismissal.[61] But 'such practices' undoubtedly did continue and were eventually

sanctioned by the government, the colonial secretary Horace
Tozer writing in 1896 that 'Aborigines are, or should be
removed after the sun goes down and no law is necessary
to justify this save the law of necessity'.[62]

∫ Brutal ambivalence

The fluctuating legal view of 'clearing them out' reflected
the deep ambivalence of townspeople. Some wanted the
blacks in, others wanted them out. Some were tolerant,
many were not. Town meetings frequently passed motions
calling for the local Aborigines to be kept out of town, but
one convened by the police in Cooktown in 1889 gave strong
support to their continuing participation in the life of the
community. A local resident wrote to the *Endeavour Times* in
1891 claiming that there were many householders who
declared that the blacks were 'most industrious, useful and
honest helps'. Drawing on seventeen years' experience in the
district, he declared that they were less trouble than the Europeans or the Chinese.[63] The editor of the *Port Denison Times*
argued in 1877 that a projected Aboriginal reserve should
certainly be out of town, but not 'too far from town as the
blacks [were] very useful for certain kinds of rough work'.
What was more, the townspeople had 'as much right to their
services as country residents'.[64] People who were shocked
by promiscuous interracial sex wanted the camps as far away
as possible. The large number of men who sought sexual
adventure there wanted them close enough to be accessible

when they swaggered away from the pubs at night, but not so close that moralists and gossips could see who was joining the nocturnal procession. As it was, word got round that even men 'holding positions that would entitle one to think better things of them' were known to 'resort to the native camps for no other purpose than debauching the gins'.[65]

Officials who responded to demands to 'keep the blacks out' were subsequently importuned to let them back in again. The sub-guardian of Aborigines at Albany explained in 1852 that while he often gave orders to drive the local blacks away, there were 'parties who [found] it inconvenient having them driven out of town'.[66] A particularly gross case of self-interest was that of a Mr Gilder, who acted as the doctor in the small central Queensland community of St Lawrence. After the local blacks were driven out of town he complained bitterly to the local native police officer and made a formal statement before the local Justices of the Peace to the effect

> that by their being kept out he was a loser of between £3 and £4 a week as he made that amount treating white people for venereal disease caught from the gins and also that he got his wood and water for nothing [the officer] presumed by treating the Blacks and if it were not for the Blacks he would have to shut up.[67]

But perhaps the best illustration of the brutal ambivalence of many townspeople was the procession into and out of town forced upon the Aborigines of Coen at the whim of the Europeans. The local protector of Aborigines wrote with a weary cynicism in 1908 that:

if there are any complaints made to me about the blacks stealing jam tins, looking over fences where sweet potatoes are growing, dirtying the river water etc, I listen to the complaints, then remove all the aborigines out of the town, and keep them out for about a week. By that time all the housewives are very pleased to see them return again; so that things jog along smoothly until some poor old gin happens to steal another sardine tin, when out they go again.[68]

The location of town camps said much about the relationship between black and white in Australian towns in the nineteenth century and early twentieth century. Conditions varied from place to place, but even the best camps were without clean water, sewage collection or any of the other municipal services that were increasingly available to Europeans. Many of them provided inadequate protection against the weather. Disease, malnutrition and death crouched among the humpies along with addiction to opium and alcohol and violence that accompanied and furthered social breakdown. Camp dwellers were also prey to the random brutality of the Europeans and raids by drunken louts bent on sexual pillage.

The distance between town and camp probably suited the blacks as well as the whites. There is certainly no reason to suppose that the camp dwellers wanted to be any closer to the Europeans than they had to be, the various inconveniences of distance notwithstanding. They probably had as little to do with the whites as they could and above all wanted to avoid their prying eyes, censorious glances and niggling interference even when it was well meaning. The short journey between black and white communities provided a cultural buffer zone allowing the Aborigines to preserve many aspects of their culture – initiation, mortuary rituals, corroborees – that would have been disrupted if the whites were more often on hand.

During the early years of the twentieth century, Australian governments assumed tighter controls over Aboriginal communities. Increasingly, town camps were broken up and the residents sent away to reserves like Palm Island in Queensland and Moore River in Western Australia. After the First World War dozens of Queensland camps were swept away. The sort of controls which the blacks had avoided in the town camps were rigidly imposed on reserves and missions, even though housing and nutrition were often little better than before. Where town camps survived, the segregation, squalor and inequality common in the nineteenth century continued until the 1940s and 1950s and can still be found today in some parts of the country.[69]

∫ *By fits and starts*

Aborigines who worked in rural industry often visited town camps between jobs to see friends and relatives and to have a holiday. But in many parts of southern Australia camps were more commonly in the countryside than on the outskirts of town and the residents combined employment on farms and

stations with hunting and gathering on or near traditional
territories. Indeed, the combination of casual work and the
traditional quest for food had evolved in the old settled
districts in the early years of the nineteenth century. Writing
of the farming districts near Sydney in the 1820s, Cunningham noted that many of the local blacks would 'work at
harvest, and attend to other matters about the farm, having
been brought up from infancy among the farming whites'.
In 1826 a settler had employed an Aboriginal team to reap
30 acres of wheat. The job was completed in fourteen days
'as well as by whites'. They were 'always out before the
whites in the morning, and were fed and paid a regular price
for their labour'.[70] Within a few years of the first settlement
of South Australia the local blacks were assisting with the
harvest, Edward Eyre observing that at Encounter Bay during
1843, '70 to 100 acres of wheat or barley, were reaped by
them; at Adelaide from 50 to 60 acres, and at Lyndoch Valley
they aided in cutting and getting in 200 acres'.[71] The
clergyman at Encounter Bay wrote to the Adelaide papers
in 1841 explaining that the local blacks were 'now as good
reapers as ordinary English men of the same class, and two
of them will reap more than most'.[72] But while Aboriginal
skills were apparent from early on, they were only willing to
work 'by fits and starts'[73] and at other times pleased themselves and lived in the bush. They needed to participate in the
European economy in order to survive and afford luxuries
like tobacco and flour and sugar, but as William Thomas

observed in Victoria, their 'nationality' was 'not totally broken up'. They worked when they pleased and on their own terms.

∫ Aptitude for employment

We will never be able to recreate a comprehensive picture of the Aboriginal contribution to the early colonial economy, but a particularly useful survey was conducted by the 1845 Select Committee of the New South Wales Legislative Council. The Council sent a questionnaire – or circular letter as it was then called – to magistrates, commissioners of crown lands, Justices of the Peace and clergy all over the colony, which at the time comprised the whole of south-eastern Australia from southern Queensland to Bass Strait. In all, seventy notables responded to twenty-three questions about the Aborigines in their own districts. The questions included three concerned with employment:

> What proportion of them are either regularly or occasionally employed by the settlers, and in what way?
>
> In what manner are they remunerated?
>
> What habits have they bearing upon their aptitude for employment?[74]

The answers provided much interesting information. Aborigines worked for the Europeans in all parts of New South Wales in 1845, with the exception of the troubled frontier districts of southern Queensland. G. A. Robinson provided the most comprehensive list of occupations, reporting that blacks had been employed as shepherds, bullock drivers, stock and hut keepers, messengers, domestics, sheep washers, whalers, collectors of skins, and guides.[75] Large numbers were employed at those times of maximum demand for labour – the wheat, corn and potato harvests or sheep washing and shearing. In the long-settled districts young men had become competent horsemen and travelled with European parties into the new districts of Port Phillip, South Australia and Moreton Bay. On the lower Hawkesbury, Bill Falconer and Bill Ferris had not only adopted European first and family names but were successful professional horsebreakers as well. Ferris was also cultivating 3 acres of land for himself.[76] Most Aborigines still worked for food, clothing and tobacco, but those with more experience of the Europeans were demanding to be paid in cash. 'They have commonly been remunerated in provisions, clothes, tea, sugar, tobacco etc', observed Francis Flanagan, JP, at Broulee, 'but many of them now insist on being paid in money'.[77] The Reverend Bolton of Hexham similarly noted that 'they know the value of money and prefer receiving it to any other kind of payment'.[78]

Numerous respondents commented on Aboriginal abilities. They were 'apt enough at all occupations of a farm',[79] they had the 'ability and skill to do almost all kinds of work'[80] and the 'ability and aptitude for almost every employment'.[81] Their skill as reapers was also recognised, the magistrates at Bungonia observing that they were 'invariably the best reapers in the field',[82] while at Port Phillip their skills as shepherds, stock-keepers and bullock drivers had been found 'equal and in many instances superior to Europeans'.[83]

Despite these observations, the overwhelming conclusion of the Europeans was that most Aborigines only worked occasionally and would never stay long in any one employ. Historians have assumed that this pattern of irregular and intermittent work was due to the presence of a convict work-force or because the blacks had not sufficiently mastered the skills required in the rural economy. However, neither of these reasons was mentioned by contemporaries. Overwhelmingly they referred to the nature of the Aboriginal response to the demands of European employment, to their 'erratic and capri-cious disposition', which did not permit them to 'continue in any employ for a given time'.[84] Their 'love of change' inter-fered with 'any systematic or regular employment';[85] no inducements would 'keep them from the bush';[86] no depen-dence could be 'placed upon their remaining any fixed time, and no wages could induce them to remain from their tribes'.[87] What was more, when they were tired of a job they would 'not work for any consideration'.[88]

The most important reason for the irregular pattern of work was not that the Aborigines weren't wanted or couldn't perform the tasks at hand, but rather that they worked when and where they wanted and only as often as absolutely neces-sary. The Reverend Rogers from Gosford observed that 'none of them [were] regularly employed by the settlers, for they

will not engage themselves'.[89] His colleague at Patterson
explained that very few blacks were employed 'because they
will not work; the settlers would willingly employ them in
various ways if they would only work'.[90] The Bungonia
magistrates noted that on their occasional visits the blacks
were employed 'by the settlers very constantly', but only
'when they [could] be got to work – which [was] not often.
Indeed it was very seldom they [could] be induced to work,
and then but few at a time, and for a very short period.'[91]
James Gunther, the Anglican clergyman at Mudgee, believed
that 'the most ample remuneration does not prove a sufficient stimulus to them for regular work, or an encouragement to prefer our way of living as a continuance'.[92]

That was the nub of the matter. As far as possible the
majority of Aborigines sought to continue to follow their
own way of life while making the minimum necessary adaptations for survival in the new world. They moved across
their traditional territories (the Europeans called this their
'beat') in much the same-sized bands as in the past and worked
when they wanted tobacco or when they were unable to win
enough from the bush. Even then they only worked till they
had 'procured a sufficiency of food'.[93] The balance of the time
was spent in what the Europeans chose to call 'a state of
wandering beggary, with a little hunting and fishing, and the
contribution of several farm houses'.[94] The Reverend
Hamilton at Goulburn observed that the local blacks had 'no
certain means of subsistence', but he believed that 'they never

want, obtaining always necessary food freely, or for work, or finding it for themselves in the bush'.[95] His colleague at Morpeth remarked that in his parish,

> their condition is one neither of independence nor of dependence. The rivers, lagoons and forests continue to afford a portion of what is necessary to their support; the settlers supply, in remuneration for occasional trifling services, the deficiency.[96]

∫ Bush workers

A series of government reports in New South Wales, Victoria and Western Australia enable us to examine the circumstances of Aborigines in rural areas in the late nineteenth century.[97] Over the years since 1845 there had been an ever-increasing involvement in the work of farms and stations, although this varied widely according to the nature of particular local economies. In 1881, for instance, the New South Wales Protection Board reported that there was a high level of Aboriginal employment all over the colony. In the Clarence and Richmond valleys the local blacks were 'fairly well employed in such work as maize-pulling, binding and stripping sugar cane, clearing and burning off scrub, ring barking etc'. South coast families were 'employed in farm pursuits, at saw mills, and on wharves loading and unloading cargo'. In the interior many found work on the stations, 'for which they [received] fair wages, the men shearing, shepherding, boundary riding, horse-breaking etc etc – the women as domestic servants'.[98] There was a similar high level of employment in the south-west of

Western Australia, with the local blacks working for the settlers or living by kangaroo hunting.[99] In her study of New South Wales Aboriginal policy between 1880 and 1909, S. L. Johnson estimated that at the census of 1882 over 80 per cent of Aboriginal families were self-supporting, either through wage labour or a combination of casual employment with commercially oriented hunting and gathering.[100] A very similar conclusion was drawn by Anna Haebich in her thesis on the Aboriginal communities in Western Australia's south-west.[101] In 1900 most Aboriginal families were self-supporting, gaining their living from a similar combination of rural occupations. In New South Wales, South Australia and Western Australia an indeterminate number of families were farming land they had either purchased or leased. Johnson estimated that as many as 100 Aboriginal men were self-employed farmers or selectors in New South Wales in the 1880s.[102] While the range of skill and ability probably varied as much among black workers as among white, there is no doubt that Aborigines excelled at many rural occupations. By the end of the nineteenth century there had been long family association with work in the bush, while retained traditional skills and knowledge often gave black workers an edge on their white counterparts. J. E. Hammond, a pioneer of the south-west of Western Australia, paid tribute to Aboriginal workers he had known:

> As horsemen and stockmen natives are very useful. Several
> natives once worked with me continuously in this capacity for

two years, and I found that they could do in the bush on one horse what a white man could not do. This work on horseback was work that they liked. A lot of it was in the bush; and that was natural to them . . . In the days of hand reaping and threshing with flails, some of the old settlers engaged native men and women as harvest hands. They made really good reapers. I well remember two black women who beat all other reapers in their section of Pinjarra district . . . The natives also made good marksmen. I have never seen a white man do with the rifle in the bush what I have seen a native do. Seldom did a native miss. If he did not kill at the first shot, he would wound and track up his game and get it at the second shot. One great advantage that the native had over the white man was that he could creep much closer to the game than the white man could do. Having a keener eye and knowing more about the habits of the wild animals, the native could tell at once if the game were alarmed and, as soon as he saw that an animal was startled, not the slightest movement would he make until the animal seemed to think that all was safe again.[103]

Working and wandering

Despite the active participation of many Aborigines in the rural workforce, there were others who returned to the bush as often as they could, combining occasional work with hunting and gathering. In Victoria in the late 1880s about 300 blacks refused to live on the government or church reserves, preferring 'to roam about the country' and especially along the banks of the Murray. Their way of life was described by a local police magistrate:

> They would do a little work now and then, but not keep to it regularly. There were a good many employed as shepherds and stockriders, for which class of work they seem particularly qualified . . . some of them would do some fencing and do it very well, but only for a time. After doing a small amount of work they would invariably go home for a change. They liked to wander about in the woods, hunting and fishing and so on.[104]

Johnson estimated that during the 1880s about a quarter of New South Wales Aborigines were what she called 'workers and wanderers', that is, they combined labour with hunting and gathering in the manner of their grandparents in the 1840s.[105] But the wandering wasn't aimless and often seems to have been confined within traditional tribal boundaries or within their 'runs', as they were called in Western Australia.[106]

Numerous other traditions were preserved. Corroborees and initiations were still being performed in many districts at the end of the nineteenth century. Even the desire to own land had a partly traditional emphasis, both in where it was sought and its intended use. A government official in southern New South Wales wrote in 1883:

> I have known blacks in Braidwood and coast districts very intelligent, who have been and now are excellent farm labourers, and whose aspirations at all times were to be allowed some land they might call their own in reality; which they might cultivate unmolested for the use of themselves and their families; and

where aborigines of surrounding districts might meet periodically for the purpose of holding corroborees and other exhilarating games.[107]

At the end of the nineteenth century, Aborigines worked in the European economy and sought land in order to own it in the European way. However, they did so not in order to 'imitate white men' but to remain as distinctively Aboriginal as circumstances allowed. The situation was much as it had been fifty years before, when William Thomas observed that the 'nationality' of Port Phillip clans had been weakened but not 'broken up'. Many sought acceptance from white neighbours and more distant authorities, but it was acceptance for what they were and not what interfering Europeans would have them be. Life on the fringes of white society was fraught with difficulty and hardship, but given the circumstances it was where many Aboriginal people preferred to be.

six

AMALGAMATION OR SEGREGATION?

FROM THE EARLIEST years of settlement, Europeans argued the point about whether Aborigines should be incorporated with or excluded from the mainstream of settler society, that is, whether they should be assimilated or segregated. Both views had committed advocates and earnest followers; each had seasons of support and periods of official favour. Assimilationist views generally held sway during the first part of the nineteenth century. But the failure of early policy initiatives, recurrent frontier skirmishes and hardening racial attitudes strengthened the hand of those who believed the Aborigines should be confined to the fringes of society. Segregation became the dominant idea in the late nineteenth century, and for several generations Aborigines were forced to live on closed reserves or missions. The history of these people is still to be told. For the moment, attention will be focused on the attempts to assimilate the dispossessed clans and their reaction to that endeavour.

Imitating white men

A number of governors were apostles of assimilation. Even
before he arrived in Australia, Phillip determined that he would
'endeavour to persuade' the Aborigines to 'settle near us' in
order that they could be furnished 'with every thing that can
tend to civilize them'.[1] Macquarie thought it would only
require 'the fostering Hand of Time, gentle Means and Conciliating Manners' to bring the local blacks 'into an important
Degree of Civilisation'.[2] On the other side of the continent,
Western Australia's Governor Hutt argued that if the Aborigines and colonists were 'destined to occupy this land in
common as British subjects they ought to be encouraged to
mingle as one people'.[3] South Australia's Governor Hindmarsh
addressed the clans around Adelaide in the following manner:

> Black Men,
>
> We wish to make you happy. But you cannot be happy unless
> you imitate white men. Build huts, wear clothes, work and be
> useful.
>
> Above all things you cannot be happy unless you love God
> who made heaven and earth and men and all things.
>
> Love white men. Love other tribes of black men. Learn to
> speak English.[4]

Amalgamation, then, could only occur in one way: black
would imitate white. The arrogance was vast, the cultural
self-confidence quite invincible. But underpinning the expectation of the easy assimilation was a cluster of ideas more
attractive to today's taste, including the assumption that there

were no fundamental barriers to Aboriginal 'advancement', that underlying the great differences in custom and behaviour there was a bedrock of human equality. It was, wrote Captain Tench while reflecting on his time in the infant colony, 'by fortuitous advantage of birth alone' that the Europeans 'possess superiority, that untaught unaccommodated man, is the same in Pall Mall as in the wilderness of New South Wales'.[5] To Robert Dawson, manager of the Australian Agricultural Company, the problem lay not in the Aborigines but in their unpromising environment, for, he wrote in 1830, 'local situation and climate have more to do with the civilization of savage tribes than has generally been imagined'.[6] The surgeon Peter Cunningham pursued similar ideas, arguing that:

> We may, I think, in a great measure impute their present low state of civilization, and deficiency in the mechanical arts, to the nature of the country they inhabit, the kind of life they lead, and the mode of government they live under. Civilization depends more upon the circumstances under which man is placed than upon any innate impulse of his own.[7]

The Aborigines were not, then, innately different or inferior. They were humanity as nature had made them; 'unwrought upon by civilization – unpolished by the influence of the arts and sciences – unformed, unmoulded, into anything like shape of mind'.[8] The state of nature, as witnessed in Aboriginal Australia, was merely the 'state of a rational being placed in various physical circumstances which have contracted or expanded his faculties in various degrees'.[9] The maritime explorer James Grant concurred, observing that the mind of man 'in a state of nature' appeared to be the 'resa tabula [clean slate] of the philosophers; it has not been wrought upon by education; it is wax, of the purest and softest kind, fit to receive and preserve any impression'.[10] Given this situation, the task of 'improvement' and assimilation appeared to be straightforward. There was, Governor Macquarie explained to his superiors in Britain, every expectation of early success as the minds of the blacks in contact with the settlers 'gradually open to Reason and Reflection'.[11]

Idleness and independence

That was the theory. To the embarrassment of those who spoke of easy amalgamation and to the encouragement of their ideological opponents who argued all along that nothing could be done with 'savages', the practice was much more difficult. 'After the attempts of more than thirty years', the New South Wales chief justice Barron Field wrote, 'to civilize the natives of New South Wales and Van Diemens Land, they are exactly in the same state in which we found them.' The difficulties, in Field's view, were social and economic. The most 'persevering attempts' had been made to 'induce them to settle, to avail themselves of the arts of life', but they could not 'be fixed' nor was it possible by any 'kindness or cherishing to attach them'.[12] Other prominent colonists mulled over the problem. The Reverend Samuel Marsden wrote home to the secretary of the Church Missionary Society explaining that they 'seem to have all they wish for, Idleness and Independence. They have no wants, to stimulate their Exertions and until they have, I fear they will remain the same.'[13] His colleague Bishop Broughton attributed the situation of the blacks not to 'any unconquerable dullness of intellect, but merely to their love of erratic liberty'.[14] The commissioner of crown lands on the Darling Downs concluded that the 'roving life' of local clans still had charms for them 'too powerful for any inducement that the habits and custom of civilization can offer to overcome'.[15] The official protector of Aborigines at Perth told the colonial secretary that the bush had 'so many attractions' that local blacks preferred 'the precarious subsistence it affords to the food of the white man which must be earned by labour'.[16]

Voluntary labourers

Work appeared to be the panacea, providing discipline, training in punctuality and subordination, while at the same time augmenting the supply of labour. Macquarie expected the Aborigines to become 'progressively Useful to the Country' when employed either as 'Labourers in Agricultural Employ or among the lower Class of Mechanics'.[17] New South Wales's Governor Gipps wrote to the Colonial Office considering the 'means by which the Aborigines may be induced to become voluntary labourers for wages'. It was by such employment that 'the civilization of the Aborigines of the continent must be worked out'.[18] Governor Hutt reached a similar conclusion at much the same time, believing that the question of 'civilization or non-civilization' could only be satisfactorily addressed 'by discovering some method of overcoming [their] repugnance to regular work'.[19] The protector of Aborigines at Perth wrote a few years later that

> one of the best means of ameliorating the condition of the native population, and gradually raising them in the scale of civilization was to encourage them in a desire for steady employment.[20]

Missionaries agreed with secular officials about what needed to be done. The leading Methodist clergyman Joseph Orton called for 'assiduous, unremitting efforts to induce them to profitable industry',[21] while his Anglican counterpart, John Harper, argued that

> It will only be by keeping them employed, that their minds will be made susceptible of Religious impressions . . . They must also be brought to settle upon a spot were they will always be under inspection of their teachers.[22]

The frustrating thing was that Aborigines living in the 'settled' districts gave abundant evidence of their capacity to learn new skills and to master many of the tasks performed by white workers. George Augustus Robinson, chief protector of Aborigines at Port Phillip in the 1840s, had a broad overview of black communities all over Victoria. As far as they were employed, he told the superintendent of the settlement,

> they have been found faithful guides, able Bullock drivers, Efficient Shepherds, Stockkeepers, and Whalers, good Boatmen,

> Horsemen and Houseservants, Husbandmen, Policemen, Handi-
> crafts, and other useful employments [sic].[23]

The missionary Lancelot Threlkeld noted that in New South
Wales local blacks chose 'employments most congenial to
their habits and tastes'. In the towns they engaged in 'fishing,
shooting, boating, carrying wood and water, acting as messengers or guides'.[24] On the other side of the continent, a
local magistrate wrote an article for an English missionary
journal commenting that it was 'wonderful to see how readily
the bush natives can comprehend and adapt themselves' to
European society. They soon came 'to ride, to shoot, to reap,
even to plough and to take care of sheep, and keep them free
from scab'.[25] South Australia's protector of Aborigines,
Matthew Moorhouse, wrote with tempered enthusiasm,
explaining that the blacks around Adelaide '*could* be taught to
work at anything, but that neither he nor any other human
being could *teach them to like it*'.[26]

ʃ Taming the capricious hunter

While reporting on the condition of the local Aborigines in
1849, the commissioner of crown lands at Moreton Bay
observed:

> I myself have made repeated trials with Boys of every age and
> have invariably found the same result viz. an insuperable aversion
> to submit to the habits of civilized life neither food, clothing or
> even pecuniary recompense which they much value will induce
> them to settle down for more than a few days at a time; every

species of labour seems to be irksome to them unless perhaps
the tracking of cattle or the occasional acting of shepherds.[27]
That, then, was the challenge. How to turn 'the capricious
hunter . . . into the steady labourer',[28] how to induce him
to 'submit to the restraints which are imposed on ordinary
labourers'.[29]

It wasn't just the work itself which the Europeans wanted
to extract from an unwilling indigenous population. There was
an extensive hidden agenda as well. Work, it was assumed,
would induce discipline, punctuality, acceptance of authority
and a sedentary lifestyle, which would, in turn, facilitate religious instruction and eventual conversion to Christianity. The
problem was that the Aborigines were aware of the hidden
agenda and strenuously resisted the imposition of the restraints
which circumscribed the life of the steady labourer and which
flew in the face of many aspects of traditional culture. The
resulting struggle, though often hidden from view, small-scale
in nature and local in manifestation, can be traced throughout
the history of white–Aboriginal relations.

One of the first problems confounding the Europeans was
the fact that, as Samuel Marsden expressed it, the Aborigines
had 'no wants'. The thing to do, it was thought, was to create
a need for European commodities and then require the blacks
to work in order to supply that need and so 'feel the sweets
of property'.[30] Officials of the South Australian Colonization
Commission believed that 'every new want which they
acquire' would eventually prove 'a permanent stimulus to the

degree of industry requisite for its gratification'.[31] In New South Wales Mr Justice Barton suggested a number of steps needed 'to get these wanderers to settle down'. The first was to 'give them a taste' for the 'enjoyments and serenity of civilized life' and then to 'make it necessary that they should work in order to obtain these benefits'.[32] Governor Hutt went one step further, issuing an edict that no Aborigine could enter Perth unless he was wearing a woollen shirt, which had to be 'earned by labour'. It was to be a practical lesson 'of the value of acquiring property'.[33]

Aborigines could not be induced to become settled labourers quite as easily as that, however. The importance of sharing in Aboriginal society meant that everyone received some return whether they worked or not. One of Port Phillip's protectors of Aborigines, William Thomas, noted that 'their humane disposition one to each other shields the indolent (As they always divide among their fellows the fortune of the day)'.[34] For similar reasons the blacks had no difficulty with begging from the Europeans wherever and whenever they felt the need. They shared with each other and expected the whites to do the same, especially as the whites were overburdened with possessions. South Australia's protector of Aborigines told the governor that he found it a 'difficult task to make them believe that begging lessens them in the estimation of Europeans' and that their 'supplies would be much more certain and more creditable, if produced by cultivation from their own ground'.[35]

The Aborigines' ability to escape to the bush was even more crucial in allowing them to avoid the 'restraints' of wage labour than their 'humane disposition'. Whenever they wished, the blacks could walk away from the towns, farms and stations and live from the land, even when it could no longer sustain the traditional economy on a permanent basis. The more sympathetic Europeans appreciated the situation. Robert Dawson, for instance, thought it extremely unlikely that the Aborigines would willingly 'yield up a life of liberty in such a climate, and in the forest which supports them without labour and toil, quietly placing their necks in the yoke of servitude, at the bidding of men whose bodies differ from them only in colour'.[36] While discussing the problem of inducing Aborigines to work, a prominent New South Wales settler observed that two hours hunting and fishing

> will supply them with all they want for the day; why then should they vex themselves with the drudgery of labour? They are not fools. They are not labourers at all, and for the same reason that any other gentleman is not viz. that he can live without labour. So also can they, and as comfortably as they wish to live.[37]

∫ Unmeaning toil

Aborigines often found white work tedious and boring and without apparent purpose. 'They do not court a life of labour,' a settler explained, 'that of our shepherds and hutkeepers – our splitters and bullock drivers – appears to them one of unmeaning toil.'[38] A contemporary noted that the blacks quickly exhibited 'symptoms of impatience, and a sensation of irksomeness under the monotony of every day labour'.[39]

William Thomas spent several frustrating years trying to get local Aborigines to work on his reserve. There are many entries in his diaries and letters which reflect his difficulties. In November 1840 he tried to force all the men present to work by refusing flour to those who wouldn't perform. In response they told him they would return to the mountains to live 'like before white man came' when they took it in turns to hunt and 'people didn't have to work every day'. In April 1841 Thomas was still having trouble. He wrote despairingly in his journal:

> Blacks very independent say plainly them & women no work, I find this very often the case on Monday. Blacks declare that they will not render any assistance . . . the men one & all sit smoking & sleeping all day appeared to delight in being contrary & ridicule work.

Things were no better five months later. 'Their prevailing disposition & character as labourers', he wrote, 'is indolence . . . preferring sleep & saunter to work'.[40] The German missionary William Schmidt told a similar story when giving evidence to the 1845 Select Committee on Aborigines. The exchange began with the question,

What proportion of them are either regularly or occasionally employed by the settlers, and in what way?

If they are employed at all by the settlers, they are employed either as stockmen, or doing little jobs about the house . . .

Have any of them been employed latterly in that way?

There have been cases where the blacks have worked in that way, so long as they have continued at a certain station.

For how long at a time have you known any native continue at regular employment?

The longest time at our place, has been from five to seven weeks.

What habits have they bearing upon their aptitude for employment?

They are able to perform almost any species of manual labour with no difficulty.

Are they inclined to do so?

Sometimes they are, sometimes they are not.

They are not inclined to regular labour?

No, they work just according to their own inclination.[41]

Possibly the best account of a white man's problems with an Aboriginal workforce was provided by Jack Maclaren, who attempted to establish a coconut plantation on Cape York at the turn of the century. There were plenty of potential workers, but they had access to abundant bush food and he was not in a position to use force. He found it difficult to persuade his workers to appear on successive days. 'We worked yesterday and are tired and would rest, they would say, adding pointedly that in their habitual mode of life they worked not at all, and hunted only when need for food was on them.' Maclaren retorted by threatening to cut off the supply of tobacco, flour and other European commodities and insisting that the only way to acquire them was 'by working all day and every day'. The blacks took much longer over their meals than the impatient plantation manager thought appropriate. He was even critical of the time they took to chew their food. After lunch he tried to stop the camp from having a siesta:

> A lunch-time visit to the camp was one of my daily duties – and a most irksome one, there being few things I disliked more than the lengthy and provoking business of awakening sleeping natives. It was such a dreadfully thankless task.

Even during 'working' hours his labourers would curl up and go to sleep if it suited them to do so. Sexual intrigue disrupted the working day, as did hunting and foraging. Maclaren explained how

> their labours were often interrupted by the fact that it was their age-old habit never to pass by food. Should a man in the course of his cutting away the undergrowth come across the thin trailing vine of a wild yam, he would at once abandon his attack on the undergrowth in favour of digging the tuber, a matter which might occupy an hour or more. Should a tree when it was felled prove to have in it a wild bee's nest, the men who found it would do more felling till the nest was cut out. Should they disturb a wallaby or other animal, all hands would immediately set off in pursuit, abandoning axes for the spears they kept always by them, streaming off through the timber, calling directions one

to another regarding flanking the quarry and heading it off, and returning not for an hour, or several hours may be. To my remonstrances concerning these interruptions they paid little heed, save to remark that the wasting of food was not their fashion, and that because they worked for me was no reason why they should no longer dig yam, dig out bees or hunt wallabies.[42]

Since the settlers typically paid their black workers as little as possible, often in food and tobacco and invariably at a far lower rate than they would give to whites for doing comparable tasks, there was a deal of hypocrisy in their complaints. Even despite these conditions there were many cases of employers breaking promises, agreements and even heads when pressed to provide fair recompense. Whites found it all too easy to justify cheating and violence by convincing themselves that they were only dealing with savages. Missionary Threlkeld noted in 1838 that many who had 'attempted to employ the Blacks . . . expected the severest labor to be performed for a mere trifle'.[43] Writing of his experience in Western Australia, George Grey listed among the 'evils which the natives suffer' an 'uncertain and irregular demand for their labour' combined with a 'very insufficient reward for the services they render'. As an example of these circumstances he related the story of a man

who worked during the whole season, as hard and as well as any white man, at getting in the harvest for some settlers, and who only received bread, and sixpence a day, whilst the ordinary labourers would earn at least fifteen shillings. In many instances, they only receive a scanty allowance of food, so much so, that some settlers have told me that the natives left them because they had not enough to eat.

The evil consequence of this is, that a native finding he can gain as much by the combined methods of hunting and begging, as he can by working, naturally prefers the former and much more attractive mode of procuring subsistence, to the latter one.[44]

∫ That friendly subservience

The problems entailed in turning the capricious hunter into the steady labourer went deeper still. The Aborigines had to be taught 'to have some idea of the respective relations of Master and Servant'.[45] In the minds of upper-class colonial officials and employers that meant obedience and deference, 'that friendly subservience to the wants and wishes of the settlers'.[46] One way or another the blacks had to be 'brought into habits of order and subordination' and 'taught to bow the knee'.[47] But many things which were taken for granted by Europeans – and particularly by members of the elite – made little sense to Aborigines schooled in traditional society. The Aborigines had the temerity to think that when they worked it was the employer who principally benefited. This was a difficulty addressed by Edward S. Parker, protector of Aborigines at Port Phillip, when discussing plans for projected mission stations. He wrote that

in all cases where they are employed they should be made to feel that their occupation is for their own benefit, rather than for the benefit of the employer. They appear generally to feel that they owe us nothing and that they are under no obligation to work. If the suspicion therefore be aroused in their minds that they are working [more] for the benefits of whites than their own advantage they will speedily recede from their employment.[48]

What was more, the Aborigines were singularly reluctant to 'bow the knee'. Settlers who knew something about traditional society realised that within the constraints of kin relations the blacks were both egalitarian and independent. They were 'a people owning no chief – a literally pure democracy';[49] all members of the clan were 'held to be equal'.[50] They were, the explorer Thomas Mitchell argued, 'undegraded by any scale of graduated classes'.[51] A pioneer missionary lamented: 'were there the least subordination it would be better'.[52]

This 'aversion to acknowledge superiority' was perceived as a 'great evil when the Aborigines came in contact with the colonists'.[53] A Victorian missionary observed that because they had 'no-one in authority over themselves' the blacks 'did not understand exalted rank'. Indeed, it was 'difficult to get into a blackfellow's head that one man is higher than another'.[54] While reflecting on his missionary experience in New South Wales, James Gunther noted that the blacks that he was familiar with displayed a 'feeling of independence and even haughtiness with an appearance of dignity'. He related this to their 'peculiar form of government', admitting 'of no distinctions of rank' while allowing each man 'a share in their consultations and decisions as to any questions arising among them'.

Inevitably these customs influenced the way in which the blacks related to the whites. 'As they have no titles for distinction', Gunther explained,

> nor a proper name for a chief so they have neither a word in their language to signify a servant . . . no man has an idea of serving another. This idea of their own dignity and importance is carried so far that they hesitate long before they apply the term MR. to any European even though they know full well the distinction we make [between master and servant].[55]

∫ Fruits of friendship

Despite all the drawbacks, as we have seen above, Aborigines did work for Europeans in all parts of the continent. Dire necessity forced the issue sometimes, as did the need for tobacco or other desirable European commodities. On other occasions force, or fear of force, thrust them into the workforce or kept them there longer than they would have wished. When they could, however, they worked for people of their choice at congenial tasks for reasons of their own. A woman pioneer of New England observed that nothing could really repay the local clans 'for performing any labour' beyond what was necessary to provide for their immediate wants, despite the fact that local stations would have willingly employed them on a semi-permanent basis. Her husband engaged a number of black shepherds for some months, and others 'would come and work occasionally in the garden or vineyard, expecting merely food for their services'. However, the local people:

all looked on working for us as a personal favour, and gave us to understand as much, for it was only when my husband was unable to get European servants that he could induce them to shepherd for him; even then they always stipulated that in a certain number of days, weeks, or at the outside, 'moons', he would get 'white fellow' to relieve them of their uncongenial occupation. No doubt they like the white man's food well enough, yet they prefer trusting for their subsistence to the precarious gains of a hunter, rather than the weekly 'ration cart' of an employer.[56]

Aborigines worked out of a sense of obligation – as a favour – to particular individuals, not because they felt they should be 'industrious'. Work was not a matter of an unequal exchange between master and servant but merely one aspect of a reciprocal relationship. Long-term bosses were not seen as masters so much as de facto kin – as classifactory uncles or brothers rather than representatives of a higher and more powerful class. In such a relationship, Aborigines might adopt certain mannerisms expected of them by the boss and suggestive to the European of deference, but that was as far as it went. It did not mean that all 'gentlemen', let alone all white men, were similarly respected. 'Affection made them willingly perform acts of service', observed the historian G. W. Rusden, but they were performed 'as the fruits of friendship rather than as tasks of servants'.[57] The visiting Quaker missionary G. W. Walker observed that the Aborigines were:

more easily led than driven; for, though they are very tractable and accessible to kindness, it is easy to perceive that they consider themselves a free people. If they do service for others, they do it through courtesy. There is nothing that is servile or abject in their character when they are not under the influence of fear.[58]

European awareness of Aboriginal motivation varied widely. Some no doubt thought they had subdued the capricious hunter and inculcated habits of deference and obedience. Others saw deeper into the matter and were even able to make use of their status as de facto kin. While he was the manager of the Australian Agricultural Company, Robert Dawson developed good relations with the local blacks. He explained how

It was always with me a pleasing and an important duty to conciliate and to do them strict justice; and while I caused my authority to be respected when necessary, I took infinite pains to ingratiate myself with them upon all proper occasions. I danced and sang with them, and I entered into all their other sports and gambols as an applauding spectator; I accompanied them to their fights; gave names to their children; conferred upon them offices and badges of distinction; and supplied them with muskets and ammunition, with which to pursue their sports. I gave them food in return for their services, and a hearty welcome wherever and whenever I met them. In return for all this, I was treated as one belonging to and almost necessary to them. I was known and talked of by them far and near, and designated as bingeye (brother), from whom much had been received, and much was still expected. Every person who knows any thing of human nature, must be aware that man, in his wild state, is not to be conciliated, or tamed into respectfulness of demeanour and usefulness of conduct, by other than similar means to these.[59]

While many wanted to tame the blacks into respectful-ness of demeanour, few were willing to go to the lengths of Dawson. Force seemed a much easier and quicker way, and in frontier districts it became an increasingly acceptable and increasingly common means to recruit and sustain a work-force. By the last decades of the nineteenth century outback pastoralists felt quite comfortable in promoting their own chosen methods in the local press, one writing to the *North West Times*:

> Let a native once be told that you cannot punish him, and good-bye to all authority over him and his usefulness, pamper him and pet him as much as you like, and give him clothes every day of the week, he will only work when he likes, as he chooses, let him know on the other hand that corporal punishment will inevitably follow wilful disobedience of orders, and you have a valuable servant.[60]

∫ Blacks and boors

When members of the colonial elite talked of assimilation they assumed that the Aborigines would be absorbed into the working class. They were to be landless wage labourers. When Gipps argued that the civilisation of the Aborigines was most likely to be advanced through contact with Europeans and 'by being placed as nearly as possible on a par with them'[61] he did not mean on a par with everyone – only the lower orders. When the penal reformer Alexander Maconochie said that through service with the police select blacks would achieve equality and amalgamation, he only meant equality, with some Europeans. While they talked the language of racial equality, they were not for one moment advocating social equality – not by a long shot. The elite were more sharply aware of distinctions based on class and status than those based on race. Their hierarchical view of the world allowed them to advocate amalgamation without thinking that Aborigines would ever be their equals. For that matter, policies of racial assimilation were useful in other ways as well. By stressing that the colonial working class should intermingle with the indigenous tribes, the colonial elite were also emphasising their own elevation above the poor and powerless. Successful assimilation would maintain the social distance between ruler and ruled, master and servant, and help preserve cherished status distinctions under threat in the new world.

Thus, when the educated and well-to-do colonists favourably compared blacks and workers, they were emphasising both their racial tolerance and their sense of social distance from the poor and underprivileged. The influential arch-conservative G. W. Rusden argued that when comparing the Aborigines with 'only the lower and uneducated European', it was hazardous to affirm that 'the black is inferior to

the white' when in intelligence, good humour and loyalty the
Aborigine 'often put to shame the boors among the vaunting
Caucasian invader'.[62] It is hard to determine which was the
stronger – his contempt for the 'boors' or his admiration for
the indigenes. Similar views were commonly expressed
during the 1830s and 1840s. Aborigines were 'but little
inferior in intellect to the uneducated peasantry of Europe';[63]
they were 'fully equal to a large majority of peasantry of
civilized communities'.[64] Thomas Mitchell thought that in
'manners and general intelligence' the blacks appeared
'superior to any class of white rustic [he had] seen'.[65] The
magistrates at Bungonia believed that in every respect the
local tribespeople were 'as intelligent as the working people
around us'.[66] Many colonists, author John Dixon argued, had
'poor pretensions to rank above' the blacks.[67] The Aborigines' intelligence, missionary Threlkeld believed, was 'equal
to our own, when in an uncultivated state'.[68]

Despite such sentiments, the Aborigines were marked out
for low status while they retained identifiable racial
characteristics. Unlike the irreverent colonial working class,
they could not presume to social equality. It was therefore
possible to be familiar with a black servant in a way unthink-
able with a white one. It did not threaten the social distance
between master and servant. The Port Phillip pioneer Edward
Curr observed that Aboriginal servants were 'generally treated
by the educated squatter with a familiarity . . . in which the
labourer never shared'.[69] The colonial official J. H. Wedge

allowed his servant Mayday to live with him in his tent, some-thing that he would not have considered with a white servant.[70] The Queensland native police officer J. O'C. Bligh told the 1861 Select Committee that he was 'on much more familiar terms' with the troopers than he 'could be with white men'.[71] A squatter who observed native police commandant Frederick Walker at work said that 'he was more familiar' with the men 'than we consider it right to be with servants, for instance'.[72]

Some took the argument a step further, claiming that gentlemen and blacks shared an affinity not experienced by working-class whites. The Queensland magistrate H. B. Sheri-dan believed that the gentleman 'gets on much better with the blacks than an ordinary man', because there was a 'natural good breeding in the black which coincided with a similar quality in the other'.[73] Fellow colonist Ebenezer Thorne thought the blacks had a dignity of gesture and gracefulness 'that we look for in vain among our labouring classes and that we usually connect with the idea of a gentleman'.[74]

Immoral example

Despite the talk among officials, landowners and missionaries about inducing the Aborigines to become 'ordinary labourers for wages', they were wary about the 'bad' influence of irreverent, assertive colonial workers. They wanted black dependants who approximated an idealised upper-class version of how servants should behave. A prominent Western District settler outlined the problem. 'In their contact with the white man', he wrote, 'they have acquired all the vices of the labouring population . . .'[75] The missionary William Porter lamented that the convict–emancipist rural workers

> pull down and destroy whatever we attempt to build. Or in other words – whatever good impressions we may succeed in making on the minds of any of the natives; they soon erase them, by their filthy conversation, or immoral example.[76]

G. A. Robinson firmly believed that work and industry would assist in 'the great work of this amelioration'. But the implementation would have to wait until the 'depraved' white workers were replaced by a 'more honest and industrious peasantry'.[77]

One solution was to keep white and black servants apart. Thus J. H. Wedge did not allow his 'boy' Mayday 'to live with or associate with servants'.[78] Thomas Mitchell considered the problem when bringing guides back in from the bush and toyed with the idea of sending a young black couple to southern Europe, where they could learn to cultivate Mediterranean crops. After ten years away they could be repatriated when, speaking a foreign language, they 'would be less open to the influences that interpose between employers and employed' in the Australian colonies.[79] Similar ideas ran through the organisation of the native police forces. The troopers were to be kept away from the white working class to ensure they could not be 'tampered with'. Regulations drawn up at Port Phillip were quite clear about who troopers could associate with and relate to:

At the same time that the men of the corps are taught to consider themselves superior to the other blacks, they must be made to discriminate between the different classes of white people, showing respect to the upper and well conducted, and prevented from associating with those who may instruct them in vicious and disorderly habits.[80]

The establishment of institutions appeared to be the most effective way of keeping the blacks away from the white working class and at the same time inculcate habits of order, obedience and industry. The Reverend Robert Cartwright proposed such an institution to Governor Macquarie in 1819, the object of which was

to keep these black Natives entirely separate from our own people till the Institution is become sufficiently strong, and the work of civilization so far advanced as to be proof against the evil practices and examples of our countrymen. The only security for their gradual and real improvement . . . is to keep them as much and as long separate as possible from the bad example of those around them.[81]

Thirty years later, a prominent settler advocated the establishment of Aboriginal schools, which would 'alter in many instances the original bend of the mind'. While the bending was taking place, however, it 'would be absolutely necessary to remove them from the licentious intercourse with the labouring population till their principles were in a measure formed'.[82] Such plans found expression in many of the missions established during the second half of the nineteenth century. At Poonindie in South Australia, Matthew Hale brought Aborigines together in 'one little community apart from the vicious portion of white population'.[83] In Western Australia, the Spanish bishop Salvado moved his mission to its final site at New Norcia at the first appearance of white shepherds 'so as to keep the natives out of contact with corrupting influences'.[84]

∫ *That antipathy of races*

It is difficult to find out what the 'labouring population' thought of all this because they left few first-hand records of their attitudes. No doubt opinion about the blacks differed widely and changed over time, and we can't always be sure that gentlemen commentators or officials were fair in their assessment of their 'inferiors' or even if they knew what they were talking about. Ordinary workers probably mixed with the Aborigines more than did their 'betters', but that does not mean that they were necessarily more tolerant, sympathetic or understanding of the blacks' tragic circumstances. James Gunther suggested something of the complexity of the relationship. The convicts, he noted, 'either make too familiar with the Natives and teach them all their tricks and vices, or, they abuse and vex them'.[85]

As with the elite, working-class people's attitudes were enmeshed in their evolving views about their place in the class and status relationships of the society at large. In one sense, though, their attitudes and behaviour were the reverse of those of their 'betters'. While officials and landowners equated Aborigines and white labourers, the workers stressed the difference between them. When the elite sought thereby to extend the social distance between master and servant by amalgamation of the 'ordinary sort of people' with the physically distinct and culturally different native population, their social inferiors did exactly the opposite. They exaggerated the distance between themselves and the blacks in order to accentuate the social proximity between gentlemen and workers. Being at the bottom of the hierarchy of power and status, feeling themselves degraded 'by the scale of graduated classes', they felt compelled to emphasise their superiority over the blacks. The perceptive Edward Curr observed that the Aboriginal worker was 'a good deal bullied by the white labourer, who lost no opportunity of asserting his superiority over him'. The South Australian doctor and newspaper editor Richard Penny gave a good deal of thought to the way in which class relations in European society militated against the successful assimilation of the Aborigines. 'All the efforts for civilizing the native', he wrote,

> have been with the object of his becoming a portion of our labouring civilized population, and forming an integral part of it; and it has been this, that has caused all such attempts to end in failure. The two races can never amalgamate – the white labourer, and the native (be he ever so useful), can not be brought to work together on equal terms. We could never succeed in incorporating the native with the mass of the

labouring population, for there is always enough of that antipathy of races existing, to induce the settler to place the native, however deserving, in an inferior position to his white servants, and to give him the more menial offices to perform; but if the settler, being a friend of the aboriginal cause, and not disposed to make any distinction, but that of merit, the servants themselves would not perform those offices, whilst they could shift it on that of the blacks; therefore, if the native were to accept the terms of civilization that we offer him, everything would conduce to keep him in the lowest scale of society; he would be constantly subject to all sorts of oppression, and would make but a bad exchange for his native independence.[86]

Fear of economic competition fanned worker hostility to the Aborigines, which is hardly surprising given the standard policy of paying them very much less than white workers for comparable tasks, or not paying them at all. While reporting on the murder of Aboriginal servants by white stockmen in northern New South Wales in 1848, the local commissioner of crown lands attributed the attacks to a spirit of brutality, a desire for excitement and a 'feeling of animosity against the Natives and those who employ them arising from the idea that the rate of wages is lowered by their unpaid services'.[87] At much the same time Edward Parker concluded that there existed 'an aversion on the part of most European labourers to see the natives taught to work, avowedly for the reason that a successful result might interfere with the price of

labour'.[88] A generation later a north Queensland pioneer
wrote to the *Port Denison Times,* referring to

> the jealousy of many working men, who, to use their own
> expression, don't wish to see the bread taken out of a white
> man's mouth by a nigger, and endeavour in many cases to entice
> or frighten them from any work they may be employed in.[89]

At times, opposition to the use of Aboriginal labour
took on a more overtly political form. In 1865 a public
meeting was called in Maryborough to protest at the use of
Aboriginal labour both in the town itself and on the wharf.
Advertised with the slogan 'White Labour versus Black',
it attracted a large working-class audience. To great applause
a local orator declared that

> The storekeepers had committed a great wrong against the
> people in Maryborough in employing the blacks (loud cheers) —
> it might be necessary for settlers in the bush to employ them;
> it might have once been necessary in Maryborough, but it was
> disgraceful now for the sake of a few paltry pounds to employ
> this cheap and dirty labour (Great cheering).[90]

∫ Ever a servant

It has been suggested that Aborigines were often willing
enough to enter into a master–servant relationship with
particular Europeans when the option of economic independence no longer existed. They might 'bow the knee' to individuals they knew personally and who provided something
in return. That didn't mean they were willing to accept

a position of institutional inferiority as members of an under-class from which escape was impossible because their assigned role was determined by skin colour and other physical char-acteristics.

Members or the colonial elite apart, the majority of the settlers believed that every European was a master or a mistress when dealing with the blacks. That was the clear message of the ubiquitous and overwhelming determination of the whites to 'keep the blacks down', to 'keep them in their place'. The 'superiority of the white race has always been asserted', a Western Australian clergyman wrote in 1881, 'often arrogantly, not unfrequently with contempt or violence'.[91] The Quaker missionaries Backhouse and Walker concluded that the attempts at assimilation had failed because those Aborigines whom the Europeans had sought to 'civilise' had been 'placed in situations where they felt themselves looked down upon by the whites'.[92] Among Europeans the Aborigine became, in the words of George Grey, 'ever a servant – ever an inferior being',[93] or as Thomas Mitchell phrased it, 'a mere outcast, obliged to beg a little bread'.[94] Richard Penny remarked that among his own clan an Aborigine was 'an individual of some impor-tance', while 'amongst civilized men he [found] himself placed in the lowest scale of society'.[95] Despite the fine words about civilisation and Christianity, the reality was that all Europeans offered to the Aborigines was the life of the poor and powerless at the bottom of the 'scale of graduated classes', with virtually no chance of social mobility or of the 'improvement' that well-meaning whites talked so much about.

This was not always immediately apparent to blacks who 'came in' to the settler's world. Experience of traditional society encouraged them to think that Europeans would share their material abundance and deal with them in terms of equality. Service with exploring expeditions or with the native police often shielded young black men from a full appreciation of their situation. The return from the bush and the social limbo of the long expedition must have been a traumatic experience, and may help explain the fate of ex-police troopers who found that their relative status had not been raised by service as Maconochie had supposed. In 1856 William Thomas observed: 'of all the 40 fine blacks from time to time in the Native Police' there were 'but 3' still alive. 'I may safely say', he wrote, 'that 8 out of 10 have died thro [sic] drink or disease brought on by it.'[96]

George Grey discussed the case of the Western Australian Aborigine Miago, who sailed with the Europeans on the famous English surveying vessel the *Beagle* during a voyage to the north-west coast. While on the expedition Miago was 'apparently perfectly civilized', but on his return to Perth he rejoined his kin in the bush. In answering those who related this behaviour to an instinctive 'call of the wild', Grey referred to the 'immense boundary placed by circumstances' between white and black, 'which no exertions on their part can overpass'. He explained that when Miago arrived back from the north he

> had amongst the white people none who would be truly friends of his, – they would give him scraps from their table, but the very outcasts of the whites would not have treated him as an equal – they had no sympathy with him – he could not have married a white woman, – he had no certain means of subsistence open to him, – he never could have been either a husband or a father, if he had lived apart from his own people; – where, amongst the whites, was he to find one who would have filled for him the place of his black mother . . . ? what white man would have been his brother? – what white woman his sister? He had two courses left open to him, – he could either have renounced all natural ties, and have led a hopeless, joyless life amongst the whites . . . or he could renounce civilization and return to the friends of his childhood, and to the habits of his youth. He chose the latter course and I think I should have done the same.[97]

Seeking acceptance

Miago had the option of returning to his people and leaving the Europeans behind. For children raised by white families the situation was much more difficult. In most cases they had lost contact with their kin and had learnt little or nothing of their natural parents' language or customs. Yet no matter what they did they were not accepted by the Europeans. It was a desperate and often tragic situation. Even education failed to provide a way through the barriers of status, class and race. 'The learning brought no profit', wrote James Bonwick of young Tasmanians who had received some schooling, 'since an educated Black always felt he was treated as a *Nigger* by the unlettered whites.'[98]

The desire for acceptance was often so great that the young Aborigines came to feel hostility to other blacks and eventually to their own blackness. This was the case with James Bath, who was regarded as 'the first of the savage inhabitants . . . introduced to civil society'. His parents were both shot by settlers when they were attacking the infant settlement of Toongabbie. Adopted by the convict George Bath 'as a foundling', James had a series of guardians before working for William Miller, who owned a ship that plied the Hawkesbury. The young man became an expert sailor and in the 'art of fowling acquired a dexterity but rarely equalled'. In fact, the writer of his obituary observed, 'with his early alienation from his sooty kindred' he seemed to have 'undergone a total change of dispossession [sic] from that which forms their characteristic' as he was 'docile, grateful, and even affable; he took much pride in cleanliness of dress, spoke none but our language and . . . gave undoubted proofs of Christian piety'. At the same time, Bath viewed his origins

> with abhorrence, and never suffered to escape an occasion
> whereby he might testify a rooted and unconquerable aver-
> sion to all of his colour – also esteeming the term *Native* as
> the most illiberal and severe reproach that could possibly
> be uttered.[99]

Thomas Bungeleen had a similar experience of life half a century later in Victoria. Raised by Europeans after the severe disruption of Kurnai society in Gippsland, he became a 'civilised' native held up by humanitarians as an example of what might be achieved with the blacks if they were properly trained and educated. But Bungeleen, who died at eighteen, had a brief, troubled life and like James Bath 'could not bear to be reminded of his colour'. He was deeply offended when it was suggested that he marry a black girl, and broke a walking stick 'over a lad's back for calling him a blackfellow'. His adoptive father recalled that

> when a boy [he] would often run to me after washing his hands vigorously, and holding them up for my inspection say, 'I think they are getting a little whiter – are they not, father?[100]

John Bungaree was another tragic figure. He was well educated at Sydney College, spoke good Latin and behaved as 'a gentleman in elegant society'. Plans to send him to an English university fell through and he worked as a stockman before joining Frederick Walker's native police despite the strenuous opposition of a former employer. Bungaree negotiated a much higher wage than the ordinary troopers and entered the force as a sergeant.[101] But all was not well. While out on patrol he said to his lieutenant,

> I wish I had never been taken out of the bush, and educated as I have been, for I *cannot be a white man*, they will never look on me as one of themselves; and I *cannot be a blackfellow*, I am disgusted with their way of living.[102]

∫ *Sexual politics*

Sexual relations between black and white intensified inequalities felt sharply enough in other areas of life. The almost impenetrable barriers of prejudice preventing intimacy between Aboriginal men and European women made 'amalgamation' even less likely than it was in the first place. The situation was noted in the early years of settlement. In 1814 the Reverend William Shelley provided Governor Macquarie with a 'few ideas' on the 'civilization of the Natives'. It was a subject which 'frequently occupied' his thoughts. The problem, he argued, was that young Aboriginal men had not been provided with the means with which they 'could make themselves respectable in their new society'. They were, as a result, 'generally despised, especially by *European females*; thus all attachment to their new society was precluded'. Young men, Shelley believed,

> live in a prospect of Marriage, and have ambition and pride to be respectable in their own Society. No European Woman would marry a *Native*, unless some abandoned profligate. The same may be said of Native Women received for a long time among Europeans. A Solitary individual, either Woman or Man, educated from infancy, even well, among Europeans, would in general, when they grew up, be rejected by the other Sex of Europeans, and must go into the Bush for a Companion.[103]

In Western Australia Governor Hutt made a similar observation. Writing of a young 'civilised' Aborigine who had returned to the bush, he argued that the only alternative was to become 'a solitary outcaste'. His European acquaintances might 'tolerate him', but they would not 'acknowledge him as a member of their society'. What is more, Hutt explained, 'he cannot intermarry, and thus connect himself by any link of social affection with [the Europeans]'.[104]

We can only assume that young Aboriginal men were quickly made aware of their pariah status in European society. In 1814 a 'well known native' was asked why he rejoined his 'native acquaintances' when he returned from his regular voyages on European vessels during which he 'always acquitted himself well'. His reply 'went no further than to oppose one interrogatory to another':

> Will you, said he, keep me company; or will any white man or woman keep me company? white women will marry white men; but no white woman will have me; then why wish me to keep away from my own people, when no other will look upon me.[105]

Friendship between white and black children was common when they grew up together, even between Aboriginal boys and European girls. In her reminiscences about her childhood on a central Queensland station, the novelist Rosa Praed explained that she had learnt a great deal about the bush from a 'half-caste' boy called Ringo, who was 'the first object' of her 'youthful affections'.[106] But such attachments had to be broken well before the onset of puberty. John Green, an official involved in managing Aboriginal reserves, discussed this question when giving evidence to a Victorian Royal Commission in 1877. He had, he said, 'known several cases where aboriginal and half-caste children have been kept in European families and educated as same as one of the family'. All would go well, he explained,

> until they came to an age that they would like to make love. As soon as this was known by mamma or papa, there must be something done to stop it, so the white daughter or son is told they must not make so free with the darky; they must remember that, although he or she has been educated in the family, it would be degrading to make love with them. So the cold shoulder is soon turned on the darky; they very soon feel it, and a change seen in the darky; instead of one of the most cheerful they will mope about until they can find a chance to join their friends the aborigines.[107]

Aborigines played sexual politics too, and used the prospect of cohabitation or marriage to bring young men back from the Europeans. The young Tasmanian Kickerter-poller, or Tom Birch, was brought up by the settlers but was apparently enticed away by a girl while working on a property at Lovely Banks and in 1826–27 played a major part in attacks on Europeans. G. A. Robinson discerned that young black men returned readily to the bush at puberty for the 'purpose of cohabitation with the opposite sex'. Matthew Moorhouse believed that 'civilised' young men were 'invariably enticed into bush life, from being promised unlimited intercourse with the young women'. The inducement, he believed, 'was too powerful for them and I have not seen one of the young men who could resist it'.[108] The missionary

James Gunther recorded an incident in his journal that illustrated the considerations which weighed with young men who
returned to their tribe and accepted initiation. He discovered
that two of his potential converts, Bungary and Cochrane, had
'conformed to the practice of making incisions in the skin,'
despite their earlier and avowed opposition to the practice.
When reproached for their 'apostasy', the boys explained that
the women thought that those without marks on their skins
were 'ugly fellows'. 'Aha,' Gunther replied, 'you wish to please
the women.' Bungary was abashed at this charge, but Cochrane
'in his usual candour called out "Certainly we do".'[109]

The bushman–ethnographer F. J. Gillen recorded a similar
incident half a century later in Central Australia. It concerned
a young man who had been taken away from his people at
Charlotte Waters and worked on a station for ten or twelve
years. When he eventually returned he spoke perfect English
but had almost forgotten his own language. Gillen related that
one day that young man came to him and said,

> 'I think I will go and get cut' – that means the process of circum-
> cision and sub-incision which the blacks undergo – and I said,
> 'Look here, Jim, you are a fool to submit to that.' He said in
> reply, 'Well, I can't put up with the cheek of the women and
> children. They will not let me have a lubra, and the old men will
> not let me know anything about my countrymen.[110]

Future research may uncover evidence of relationships
or even marriages between Aboriginal men and European
women, but they seem to have been rare. The squatter Jacob

Lowe told Queensland's 1861 Select Committee on the Native Police that he had met an Aborigine in his district called Billy Bird who was married to a white woman.[111] The social pressures on such relationships must have been enormous, as the tragic career of the black bushranger Jimmy Governor shows.[112] Governor was the son of an itinerant bush worker and an Aboriginal or part-Aboriginal mother. Unlike many such liaisons, the Governors seem to have had a permanent relationship. Jimmy was comparatively well educated by the standards of rural New South Wales in the late nineteenth century. He read and wrote proficiently and was an avid reader of popular novels. A skilled bush worker, he turned his hand to fencing, well-sinking and horse breaking and worked for a period as a police tracker. In other words, he was like many other part-Aborigines growing up at the time in the long-settled districts of south-east and south-west Australia.

Governor sought respectability and acceptance as a white man. He remarked that he was 'never a loafer like some blackfellows', always 'worked and paid' for what he got, and was 'as good as any white man'. His wife explained that Jimmy was 'particularly touchy about his colour' and indeed did not 'like to be called a black-fellow'.[113] When public hysteria about the black bushrangers was at its height, a Sydney journalist conducted a long interview with Governor and reported that

the outlaw [had] no trace in his speech of the unusual dialect of the Aboriginal. His language is just the same as that of any white

Australian . . . his grammar is not, of course, of the most elegant description, but his only dialect is the dialect of the average bush labourer.[114]

Governor's life veered sharply away from the experience of part-Aboriginal people in rural Australia when in December 1898 he married a white girl, Ethel Page. The marriage outraged white opinion and the young couple suffered constant harassment. Ethel said that she 'had to put up with a great many taunts because of my marriage'. In despair she 'went down on her knees to ask God to take her away because of what people were saying'.[115] Taunts about the relationship were a major reason for Governor's murder of the family of his employer Mawbey and for his eventual trial and execution. He informed the police that Ethel had told him that Mrs Mawbey had said to her that 'a white who married a black was not fit to live'. Governor explained, 'that made me very wild so we went and killed them'.[116] In a statement to the court he went into more detail. He recalled that he said to his wife on the fateful night:

'I am going to see Mrs Mawbey about those words she has been saying, I'll take her to court if she doesn't mind herself.' I went up to the house. I said '. . . Did you tell my missus that any white woman who married a blackfellow ought to be shot? Did you ask my wife about our private business? Did you ask her what sort of nature did I have – black or white?' With that Mrs Mawbey and Miss Katz [the tutor] turned around and laughed at me with a sneering laugh, and before I got the words out of my mouth . . . I struck Mrs Mawbey on the mouth with this nullah-nullah. Miss Katz said 'Pooh, you black rubbish, you want shooting for marrying a white woman.' With that I hit her with my hand on the jaw, and I knocked her down. Then I got out of temper and got hammering them, and lost control of myself. I do not remember anything after that.[117]

European attitudes and behaviour produced quite a different outcome when it came to relations between white men and Aboriginal women. Here the rules were reversed. From the earliest years of settlement male settlers cohabited with black women, either as a result of force or of negotiation followed by payment in cash or kind. With the rapid expansion of the pastoral industry run by a 'nomad-tribe' of single men, the practice became even more widespread. The pioneer missionaries looked on with horror. John Watson noted in his journal in July 1834: 'there is scarcely a man within 40 miles of us Bond or Free who is not living in adultery with these unhappy females'.[118] His colleague John Gunther despaired because the women were engaged in 'frequent and almost constant intercourse with voloptuous [sic] Europeans'.[119] Conditions remained much the same in frontier areas until well into the twentieth century. Women were raped, chained up, held against their will and forced to live with and work for white men. While frontiersmen were often fiercely protective of 'their gins', they rarely developed long-term relationships with the women in question, much less married them or took responsibility for the children they fathered.

In 1845 over seventy prominent citizens from all parts
of the colony were asked to give their views about the place
of the Aborigines in New South Wales society. One question
put to them directly addressed the issues in hand: 'Is there
any disposition on the part of the white labouring population
to amalgamate with the Aborigines so as to form families?'[120]
The overwhelming impression of those who responded to
the inquiry was that although there was widespread evidence
of sexual relations between white men and black women,
there was almost no desire for amalgamation. Clerical
respondents were shocked by the trade in sex. The Reverend
Wilson of Portland Bay concluded 'unhesitatingly that promiscuous sexual commerce' between local women and the
shepherds and bullock drivers existed 'to an almost incred-
ible amount'. At the other end of the colony, Brisbane's
Reverend Gregor concluded that 'abominable intercourse
[was] common and open to a disgusting extent'. The
Reverend Meares at Wollongong was a little more dispas-
sionate about the matter, explaining that

> There is no desire on the part of the white labouring population
> to amalgamate, in a *legitimate* way, with the Aborigines; cases
> have occurred in which white men working among the moun-
> tains, as cedar cutters have co-habited with black women for
> months together; in one instance for two years, but the connec-
> tion has always ceased immediately on their return to a settled
> part of the district.[121]

The respondents came up with only nine instances of permanent relationships. Four of them were marriages between European men and 'half-caste' women. In four cases there were children and in two, large families. On the Hawkesbury John Lewis and his wife, Biddy, the daughter of an English seaman, had a family of seven children ranging in age from two to nineteen. The magistrates at Goulburn reported that in their district another couple had lived together for the previous fifteen years. They had several children and the family was 'in comfortable circumstances'.[122] There were a few examples of similar relationships in Tasmania. Fanny Cochran Smith and Dolly Dalrymple both enjoyed successful marriages with emancipated convicts and were apparently accepted in island society. On the Bass Strait islands, the sealers and their Aboriginal wives established dynasties despite the well-documented brutality of many of the Europeans. The extreme isolation of the islands and the need for mutual dependence in a hostile environment cemented relationships that on the inland frontier were shifting and transitory.

For the young women, sexual relations with the Europeans did not lead to amalgamation; they were sexually but not socially acceptable. A Victorian missionary observed that 'while white men would ridicule the idea of getting *married* to an Aboriginal half-caste, a good many unprincipled fellows would not be slow in accomplishing their ruin'.[123] All too often, liaisons led to degradation, disease and premature death.

Even when white men sought to marry their Aboriginal lovers intense social pressures intervened. Tribal husbands — or future husbands — and other relatives sought to break up long-term liaisons or else attempted to milk the relationship for all it was worth. Would-be white husbands were derided and ridiculed in European society. Clergymen sometimes refused to conduct interracial marriages. William Thomas recorded the fate of a shepherd who travelled all over the colony of Victoria in a vain attempt to find a clergyman who would marry him and his black lover. All refused. Eighteen months later the shepherd was dead and the woman had returned to her people.[124] In 1845 the Presbyterian clergyman the Reverend G. Stewart explained why he had refused to conduct an interracial marriage:

> I was applied to in one instance to marry a white man to an Aboriginal woman, but she had lived from her infancy with the whites; I declined, however, to marry them, as from the woman not having a christian education she could not understand the nature of the marriage convenant.[125]

If anything, the social pressure against interracial marriage increased during the nineteenth century, and by the early twentieth century state governments intervened to make it even less likely. The prominent missionary Mrs J. Matthews told the 1913 South Australian Royal Commission on the Aborigines that 'much unhappiness comes from them [the blacks] mixing with white people'. She told the story of a family:

who had a very nice half-caste girl in their service, and as soon as she grew up one of the sons wanted to marry her. The mother sent her off to Point Macleay [an Aboriginal mission] and the attachment was broken off. I saw the girl afterwards living with her native people in the camp. It would not be wise to encourage such a union, and it would have brought a great deal of trouble to that family. I know of a case where a white gardener took a native girl and lived with her but he could not mix with white society afterwards.[126]

∫ An unwise step

Clearly, personal relations with Europeans – even the most intimate relationships – did not provide a way to achieve equality or acceptance in the new society. Nor did white education, as careers as various as those of John Bungaree and Jimmy Governor indicate. Communities all over Australia resisted the entry of Aboriginal children into the expanding network of state primary schools. When the census was taken in New South Wales in 1882, only 9 per cent of Aboriginal children were being educated compared with 70 per cent or so of their European contemporaries.[127]

What made the situation worse was that many of those responsible for, or just interested in, Aboriginal education had come to accept the view that Aborigines should acquire no more than practical skills and rudimentary literacy. Bishop Salvado of New Norcia believed it might be possible to teach reading and writing in addition to work skills, but as the blacks could 'never hope to have the same status as a white man, it [was] useless to teach them those things which will not be useful to them'.[128] Queensland's northern protector of Aborigines, Walter Roth, believed that no useful results could possibly accrue by teaching the blacks composition, fractions, decimals or indeed 'any other subjects that [would] enable them to come into competition with Europeans'.[129] These views were probably reasonable reflections of public opinion in the late nineteenth century. Then, even more than in the early colonial period, the Europeans could find no place for educated or successful blacks. The bushman and ethnographer John Mann told a meeting of the Royal Australian Geographical Society in 1883 that Aborigines who were taken from their families as children were capable of receiving a good education

> and in this respect many compare favourably with the whites; but it is a question whether educating them beyond a certain standard is advisable, for when they grow up no white person likes to place them on an equal footing, notwithstanding their learning.[130]

Colonial authorities and missionaries responsible for training young Aborigines were similarly convinced that there was no place in the wider society for skilled black workers. In 1869 R. Brough-Smyth, an influential member of the Victorian Aborigines Protection Board and an 'expert' on the Aborigines, remarked that the 'more he considered the proposal that the blacks and half-castes should be taught useful trades' the more convinced he became 'that it would prove an unwise step'. No skilled tradesman, he argued, 'could exert himself in a society where he would be always regarded as an inferior – as a creature that by some extra-ordinary act of nature had come to be nearly like other men'. He could 'never join the recreations of his fellow workmen, and he would be subjected to slights which might not be intended to give pain, but would surely wound'.[131] In 1877 the Victorian missionary the Reverend F. W. Spieseke spoke out against amalgamation. The Aborigines, he explained, would 'ever have to take a dependent inferior position' and that made them dissatisfied.[132] The chief protector of Aborigines in Western Australia, H. C. Prinsep, argued in favour of compulsory education for half-castes that should include 'merely such an amount of reading, writing and numbers as would be of service to them in their position of humble labourers, the position which they cannot hope to rise from for at least three generations'.[133]

In 1913 similar sentiments were expressed by many of those responsible for Aboriginal 'welfare', in evidence given to the South Australian Royal Commission on the Aborigines. W. J. Bussell, vice-president of the Aborigines Friends Association, did not think it prudent to 'encourage too many half-castes to take up trades, because we do not want to provoke strife' and 'as long as there is colour present, there is an objection' from the wider community. The superinten-dent of the Point Pearce Mission said simply that 'people do not want Aborigines in trades'. 'White men', he observed, 'object to work at trades along with Aborigines. The Objection to colour comes in, and the Aborigines feel it.' He explained to the commissioners that

> Even at shearing sheds . . . the station owner would allot one side of the board to the natives and the other side to the white men. It is necessary to separate them for the peace of the workmen. That becomes a practical difficulty in the way of the natives learning trades, such as being carpenters.

Attempts to place young men in factories in Adelaide had also run up against the caste barrier. 'When the native gets among white people he is isolated,' the secretary of the Aborigines Friends Association explained, 'they do not like him, they will have nothing to do with him, and he gets lonely.' T. W. Fleming, the association's president, concurred, observing that even when employed, half-castes were always the first to be put off. The 'objection to colour' was so very strong that he 'did not think it will ever cease to be a difficulty'. Witnesses from the other states gave similar evidence. The superintendent of the Barambah reserve in Queensland said that, while the local blacks were 'fairly expert' at milking, there was no point in establishing a dairy. He explained why:

> There is not the slightest doubt, if we were to have a dairy farm and we sent cream to the creamery, that objection would be raised. People would urge that the cream from this settlement would not be so clean as the cream from dairies of the whites.

They would be prejudiced against the cream from here. I do not think it would be wise to start a dairy farm.

'Friends' of the Aborigines regretted this situation, but saw no way of changing it. Some just accepted things as they were. Mrs Garnett, wife of the superintendent at Point Pearce, opposed training of girls in dressmaking and cookery, because it would be both an expensive exercise and a needless one, 'because there is such a demand for them as raw material. They can all wash dishes and scrub floors.'[134]

∫ A home of our own

Aboriginal attempts to achieve independence on the land were similarly frustrated. From the very earliest stage of settlement some clans sought to gain access to land by way of the white authorities – or rather to have their own land rights given some recognition. The Methodist missionary at Buntingdale near Geelong, Francis Tuckfield, reported that the local blacks

> seem to be acquainted . . . with the relative possession of the Black and White populations – They are conscious of what is going on – they are driven from this favoured haunt and from their other favoured haunt and threatened if they do not leave immediately they will be lodged in gaol or shot. It is to the Missionaries they come with their tales of woe and their language is – 'Will you now select for us also a portion of land? My country all you gone. The white men have stolen it'.[135]

All over Australia, Aborigines who had grown up since
the arrival of the Europeans and become skilled in rural
occupations attempted to gain access to land either commu-
nally or individually. In the late 1850s the Kulen people of
central Victoria sought land 'to farm and sit down on like
white men, to manage we ourselves'. They assured protector
William Thomas that they would cultivate and 'set down on
the land like white men'.[136] The Kurnai in Gippsland similarly agitated for 'a spot which they can call their own'.[137]
Over the border in southern New South Wales, the black
communities living around Braidwood pressed for land they
could call their 'own in reality'.[138]

Individuals also attempted to select land, perhaps in
greater numbers than we presently suppose. In 1861 an
Aborigine called Bird unsuccessfully applied for land in
Queensland. He may well have been the Billy Bird who
married a European wife. In support of his application he
indicated that he had both horses and cattle. The Brisbane
papers reported that he was probably a rustler and 'while
being fluent and apparently intelligent [he couldn't] be placed
with whites'.[139] Fifteen years later, James Diper, William
Nilepi and Charles Ghipaia from the Bundaberg region tried
without success to select land. Others were prepared to
make similar applications, 'but not in such numbers as to
embarrass the Government'. In a letter which linked traditional ownership with a desire for European tenure, the
Catholic priest Francis McNab explained that the three men:

conceive and maintain that because they and their ancestors, from time immemorial, have occupied and possessed those lands . . . for their use and benefit, especially of residence, hunting, fishing [etc.] . . . they ought to be acknowledged, without expense, the rightful owners of specific homesteads.[140]

Small numbers of Aboriginal families established successful farms in many parts of the country in the second half of the nineteenth century either on land leased or purchased outright. But they received little encouragement. The flourishing farming communities at Coranderrk in Victoria and Poonindie in South Australia were broken up as a result of official policy. Alfred Cameron, a successful farmer on land he bought in the Coorong district of South Australia, gave vent to his frustrations before the 1913 Royal Commission. He explained that

For the last twelve years I have been applying to the Protector for land. I tried the land board, and I failed there. I could always produce £100, but the board granted land to young fellows who only had £25, and to some who only had 25s.[141]

A few years later, Walter Tripp attempted to establish himself on a small property but the protector determined that, while he was 'a decent hard-working man', it was doubtful if he 'or any other Aboriginal would prove a success on land of their own'.[142]

Apart from those tragic figures brought up and then rejected by Europeans, Aborigines did not wish to imitate white men. They might admire some aspects of the new society and appreciate the convenience of iron, tools, guns and horses and the pleasures of smoking and drinking, but generally speaking they liked their own ways best and sought to preserve as much as they could in the enforced compromise between old and new. Increasingly young people sought a place in the white people's world, if only because failure to do so led to poverty and powerlessness – to all the degradation produced by 'the scale of graduated classes'.

The pity of it was that whites couldn't deliver on the promise of amalgamation and 'improvement'. The social pressures within their society, combined with a strengthening current of racism, conspired to push the Aborigines to the bottom of European society. No matter what Aborigines tried – education, sexual intimacy, acquisition of new skills, acceptance of Christianity, even land ownership – all failed to break through the caste barrier, which kept them as securely in a depressed underclass as the fences and regulations of closed reserves kept the inmates away from the rest of society.

Even European ancestry didn't help. 'Half-castes' were said to inherit the worst characteristics of both races. 'If it is a male,' explained W. H. Willshire, South Australia's best-known frontier policeman, 'it is born for the gallows or to be shot; if a female, she becomes a wanton devoid of shame . . . I hold out no gleam of hope for such a repulsive breed.'[143] Even a greater infusion of 'European blood' didn't help. W. E. Dalton, the secretary of South Australia's

Aborigines Friends Association, believed that 'the quadroon is a person with the colour taint in him for all time'.[144] The widely respected 'expert' Daisy Bates wrote in 1921 that 'as to half-castes' it didn't matter how early they were 'taken away and trained' because 'with very few exceptions the only good half-caste is a dead one'.[145]

Such ideas were commonplace in the late nineteenth century and early twentieth century. Buttressed by Social Darwinism, racism came to dominate white Australia's response to the Aborigines and continued to do so until after the Second World War. The widespread conviction that 'full bloods' were destined to die out hampered any serious consideration of long-term policy. The 'half-caste problem' could best be solved, it was commonly believed, by biological rather than sociopolitical means – they could be 'bred out' of existence.

As it burgeoned in the late nineteenth century, Australian nationalism took a strong racial emphasis, drawing strength from pride of race and the 'blood tie' with Britain. There was no place in nationalist rhetoric for the indigenous Australians. The White Australia Policy always had two faces. One looked outward, prohibiting the entry of non-Europeans. The other turned inward, controlling the movement and the marriages of Aborigines and Islanders.

Even the democratisation of the colonies worked to the blacks' disadvantage. In the first half of the nineteenth century it was possible for the elite of landowners and colonial officials to assume that the Aborigines would assimilate with the 'ordinary sort of people'. By the end of the century such sentiments were far less acceptable. As the differences in status between master and servant, rich and poor diminished (although they clearly didn't disappear), there was no longer a place for racial minorities, either immigrant or indigenous. The gap between white and black grew wider as the nineteenth century progressed and by the new century appeared unbridgeable. But while these changes were taking place Aborigines were being rapidly absorbed within the European economy, either as fringe dwellers in the farming districts and on the outskirts of country towns, or as part of the permanent workforce which pioneered the vast areas of north Australia.

CONCLUSION

IN THE SOUTH-EAST and south-west of the continent
Aborigines assisted the pioneers. In the north and the centre
they were the pioneers, a fact which clearly emerges from
this and other recent studies of the Aboriginal contribution
to northern development. In her thesis on Aboriginal labour
in the north Queensland cattle industry between 1897 and
1968, Dawn May observed that there was little doubt that
'the bulk of the stockmen and domestics in the remote areas
before World War I were black – probably in the vicinity of
five to every one European'.[1] The same would have been
true for the Northern Territory and Western Australia in the
late nineteenth and early twentieth centuries.

The importance of black labour clearly challenges the
still-popular view that pioneering was the exclusive achievement of Europeans and that the Aborigines contributed
nothing to the successful colonisation of the continent. The
reluctance to embrace the black pioneers is not surprising

given the pervasive influence of white racism and the enduring power of a national legend that suggests that the outback moulded uniquely Australian values, attitudes and personality types. The development of these traits was supposedly most apparent between 1870 and 1914, the very time when Aboriginal labour was so important.

Acceptance of the black worker also carries other lessons incompatible with self-congratulatory nationalist legends. The brutality and exploitation they endured provides powerful evidence to suggest that the violence that accompanied the dispossession persisted long after Aboriginal resistance had been crushed, that the settlers were, by and large, cruel and inclement conquerors. The tough, adaptable frontiersman of popular memory was, as often as not, a racist bully who bashed and kicked his 'boys' and 'busted' gins whenever the whim took him. Even the famed egalitarianism of the frontier seems with the new perspective to have been, in part, the rough camaraderie of a small racial aristocracy lording it over a powerless, subject population.

The black pioneers have not always been appreciated in Aboriginal communities either. Indeed, activists who have praised the tribesmen and women who resisted the Europeans have ignored, or disowned, the ones who worked with and assisted them. Black troopers, stockworkers and servants have been condemned either as collaborators and traitors to the Aboriginal cause or as people with wills so weak that they lacked minds of their own and became, as a result, willing tools of the whites. The evidence clearly suggests, however, that for all its importance, vigour and longevity, Aboriginal resistance was never the only theme in forming the black response to the European invasion. From the earliest years of settlement blacks were on both sides of the frontier, the same skills, the same bushcraft being used to enhance and to resist alike the progress of the pioneer. And while we have come to accept the brutality of the white frontiersman, we cannot avoid making the same judgement about the Aboriginal stockmen, troopers and trackers who were so often by their side. They too were engaged in the destruction of tribes that impeded the pioneer's path. They too had blood on their hands. In northern New South Wales and Queensland the troopers of the native police played a major part in the process of dispossession – in an area covering one-quarter of the continent and home to as many as one-third of the total indigenous population. Precision is impossible in such matters, but it seems likely that as many as one in four of all Aborigines killed in frontier skirmishing fell victim to guns shouldered by other Aborigines. The Kooris of New South Wales played a major role in crushing tribal resistance in south and central Queensland. The Murris from those regions did much the same a decade or two later in north Queensland while wearing the uniform of the native police. Following that, individual Murris rode with the white frontiersmen right across the north of the continent, inflicting their share of destruction on the way. Within living memory

the violent reputation of the 'Queensland boys' was spoken
of with great fear by old blacks in the Territory.

But the majority of the Aborigines who were 'with the
white people' were not directly involved in frontier conflict.
They sought security in a difficult and threatening world and
in doing so made many adaptations to, and compromises
with, European society. Many remained locked in poverty.
By the end of the nineteenth century there were also numerous men and women who had developed skills in a wide
range of occupations, spoke good English and had adopted
many of the ways of the colonists. There are numerous
photographs of such people – individuals, families and
other groups – in collections all over Australia. They appear
self-confident and well nourished. As often as not they are
dressed in fashionable, well-fitting clothes and hats, with
stylish haircuts, the men with modish moustaches and often
sporting waistcoats and watch-chains. They are often better
dressed than struggling selectors and other poor whites in
photos taken at much the same time.

These were the people who wanted to be accepted as
equals by the Europeans but who were perpetually beaten
back by the racism of colonial society and the impenetrable
caste barrier erected in its name. For the most part they
didn't want to deny their kin and their Aboriginal heritage
or to forget where they had come from. They wanted to
be accepted as they were and in doing so they looked forward to, and indeed were the frustrated pioneers of, what

in recent times has become known as the multicultural society.

The two themes of resistance and assistance, of confrontation and collaboration, are threaded through the history of the Aboriginal response to the Europeans over the last two hundred years. But then the same themes run through the history of practically all those people who have been faced with the problem of dealing with European imperialism over the past four centuries. Both responses were important in Australia; neither predominated. Individuals, clans and communities adopted both at various times depending on events and circumstances. Neither was more 'Aboriginal' than the other if we use as our measure the way Aboriginal people have behaved over the last two hundred years. From the beginning, Aborigines have followed the diverging paths worked out by Bennelong and Pemulwy in the early days of the settlement at Sydney Cove.

While reminiscing about his life on the frontier, the South Australian pioneer Simpson Newland recalled two Aboriginal men known to him as Barpoo and Old Solomon, who never compromised with the Europeans. Solomon, he explained, 'never took kindly to the whites'. He 'clung to the customs of his forefathers' and steadfastly refused to work 'whatever the inducement offered'. Barpoo 'never unbent' to the white man. 'Indeed from first to last he refused to hold any intercourse with the hated [European], much less work for him, wear his clothes, or even eat his food.'

Other Aborigines followed a very different way. Writing of New South Wales in the 1820s, Robert Dawson recalled meeting a young Aboriginal man on the road from Sydney to Botany Bay,

> and not far from the latter place, saw coming towards me a black man, with an exceedingly clean dress, consisting of a short white smock-frock, with a blue linen collar turned down, a coloured neckerchief tied round his neck, a pair of white trousers, and a good hat; he had also a stick across his shoulder, with several wild ducks upon it. Seeing him so neat and orderly, I took him in the first instance for a foreign black, but on observing him more closely, saw he was a native and about twenty years of age. I felt too much interested in such an unexpected sight not to stop him and ask him many questions. He spoke our language as plainly and as intelligibly as an Englishman, and informed me he was a labourer, and usually worked at Botany Bay for Mr. Gordon Brown . . . He said that Mr. Brown having nothing for him to do at that time, he had been employing himself in shooting ducks, to carry to the Sydney market; that he never was idle, and did not mind what he did so that he could turn an honest penny. I remarked how clean his dress was, and asked who washed it for him. He always did it himself, he said, and endeavoured to be as clean as he could when he went to town.[3]

The two great themes of confrontation and collaboration are deeply rooted in the past and both also lead into the future. One points to further integration, accelerated intermarriage and greater achievement in mainstream society, with Australians of Aboriginal descent gaining the equality and acceptance sought so often by their forebears. Such a future has its supporters and its detractors. Hazel Mackellar, a leading spokesperson for the Aborigines of south-west Queensland, wrote recently that:

> In looking to the future, I don't believe the way forward is in blacks being separate from whites. What we simply desire is to be treated equally and without prejudice by Australians. The future lies in cooperation and not conflict.[4]

The other theme of resistance points in the opposite direction, towards separatism, sovereignty and black nationalism and leading ultimately to an independent Aboriginal state. Such an outcome was recently espoused by the leading activist Michael Mansell, who argued:

> Aboriginal people ought not to sell ourselves short by perceiving ourselves in terms of a unit of Australian society – an ethnic or minority [sic] – who are just getting a hard time. We are in fact a nation of people and we ought to stand up and acknowledge it.[5]

Whether one of these two great themes will ultimately prevail is impossible to predict. What is more certain is that they will persist well into the future. If they are to be reconciled it will be by future generations, in circumstances at present unforeseen.

Notes

RGSSA	*Journal of the Royal Geographical Society of Australia, South Australian Branch*
SAPP	*South Australian Parliamentary Papers*
SMH	*Sydney Morning Herald*
TSA	Tasmanian State Archives
VLAV&P	*Victorian Legislative Assembly Votes and Proceedings*
VPP	*Victorian Parliamentary Papers*
WAHS	*Journal of the Western Australian Historical Society*
WAPP	*Western Australian Parliamentary Papers*
WAVP	*Western Australia Votes and Proceedings*

INTRODUCTION TO
FIRST EDITION

1 H. Reynolds, *The Other Side of the Frontier*, Townsville, 1981; Ringwood, 1982.
2 Ibid., p. 2.
3 H. Reynolds, *Frontier*, Sydney, 1987.

CHAPTER ONE

1 T. L. Mitchell, *Three Expeditions into the Interior of Eastern Australia*, 2, London, 1839, pp. 338–9.
2 W. Murdoch, *The Making of Australia*, Melbourne, n.d., p. 129.
3 E. Favenc (ed.), *The Story of Our Continent*, Sydney, n.d., p. 1.
4 J. Finney, *History of the Australian Colonies*, Sydney, 1901, p. 191.
5 Favenc, *The Story of Our Continent*, p. 1.
6 C. H. Eden, *Australia's Heroes*, London, 1875, p. 2.
7 A. E. Calvert, *The Exploration of Australia*, 2, London, 1895, p. 386.
8 E. Favenc, *The Explorers of Australia*, Christchurch, 1908, p. ix.
9 M. Clarke, *History of the Continent of Australia*, Melbourne, 1877, p. 6.
10 Favenc, *Explorers*, p. vii.
11 E. Berry, *Australian Explorers*, Brisbane, 1893, p. 39.
12 Mitchell, *Three Expeditions*, vol. 2, p. 333.
13 Berry, *Australian Explorers*, p. 1.
14 J. L. Stokes, *Discoveries in Australia*, 1, London, 1846, p. 400.
15 L. Leichhardt, *Journal of an Overland Expedition*, London, 1847, p. 354.
16 C. D. Haynes, Fire in the Mind – Aboriginal Cognizance of Fire-Use in North Central Arnhem Land, unpub. paper, 48th ANZAAS Congress, Melbourne, August 1977.
17 N. B. Tindale, 'Ecology of Primitive Aboriginal Man in Australia', in A. Keast, *et al.* (eds), *Biography and Ecology in Australia*, Hague, 1959, p. 42.
18 J. Oxley, *Journals of Two Expeditions into the Interior of New South Wales*, London, 1820, pp. 5, 174.
19 Ibid., pp. 168,174.
20 W. H. Hovell, 'Journal of a Journey from Lake George to Port Phillip, 1824–25', VII, 1921, p. 330.
21 Stokes, *Discoveries*, 1, pp. 1, 339.
22 T. L. Mitchell, *Journal of an Expedition into the Interior of Tropical Australia*, London, 1848, p. 202.
23 Leichhardt, *Journal*, p. 77.
24 *SAPP*, 2, 1858, 151, p. 2.
25 E. J. Eyre, *Journals of Expeditions of Discovery*, 2, London, 1845, p. 168.
26 G. Grey, *Journals of Two Expeditions of Discovery*, 1, London, 1841, p 110.
27 C. Sturt, *Two Expeditions into the*

Interior of Southern Australia, 2, London, 1833, p. 61.

28 A. C. Gregory, *Journals of Australian Exploration*, Brisbane, 1884, p. 207.

29 N. J. B. Plomley (ed.), *Friendly Mission*, Hobart, 1966, pp. 515, 905.

30 Expedition in Search of Gold . . . , *QVP*, 111, 1876, p. 400.

31 J. B. Jukes, *Narrative of a Surveying Voyage of HMS Fly*, London, 1857, pp. 24, 56, 66.

32 Eyre, *Journals*, l, p. 332, 2, p. 17.

33 J. M. Stuart, *The Journals of John McDouall Stuart*, London, 1864, p. 175.

34 R. Austin, *Journal of Assistant Surveyor R. Austin*, Perth, 1855, p. 8.

35 *The Burke and Wills Exploring Expedition*, Melbourne, 1861, p. 21.

36 Stokes, *Discoveries*, l, p. 400.

37 J. F. Campbell, 'John Howe's Exploratory Journey', *JRAHS* 14, 1928, p. 235.

38 M. J. Currie Journal, 8 June 1823, quoted by D. Bell, 'From Moth Hunters to Black Trackers', BA Hons, Monash University, 1975, p. 42.

39 J. S. Roe, 'Journal of an Expedition from Swan River Overland to King George Sound', *Perth Gazette*, 3 July 1836.

40 *Inquirer*, 14 October 1868.

41 Mitchell, *Three expeditions*, 1, p. 12.

42 Ibid., p. 201.

43 *SAPP*, 1858, 1, p. 4, 2 (151), p. 10.

44 Western Australia, CSO/1848/ 173/36, Battye Library, Perth.

45 Report of an Expedition under Surveyor-General J. S. Roe, *JRGS*, 22, 1852, p. 1.

46 Mitchell, *Journal of an Expedition*, p. 32.

47 Eyre, *Journals*, 2, p. 211.

48 Ibid., p. 247.

49 *Inquirer*, 21 September 1864.

50 See for instance D. Lindsay, 'An Expedition Across Australia from South to North', *Proceedings Royal Geographical Society*, 11, 1889, p. 660.

51 L. H. Wells, *Journal of Explorations in Western Australia*, Adelaide, 1899, p. 163.

52 Ibid., p. 162.

53 D. W. Carnegie, *Spinifex and Sand*, London, 1898, p. 432.

54 Ibid., p. 267.

55 Ibid., p. 232.

56 Austin, *Journal of R. Austin*, p. 8.

57 'Dr. John Harris-Browne's Journal of the Sturt Expedition, 1844–45', *South Australiana*, 5 (1), March 1966, p. 30.

58 Sturt, *Two Expeditions*, 2, pp. 49, 121, 126.

59 Mitchell, *Three Expeditions*, 1, p. 201.

60 C. Sturt, *Expeditions into Central Australia*, vol. 1, London, 1849, p. 44.

61 Ibid., p. 45.

62 Ibid., pp. 109–10.

63 S. Hallam, *Fire and Hearth*, AIAS, Canberra, 1975, pp. 65, 76.

64 Mitchell, *Three Expeditions*, 2, p. 162.

65 Sturt, *Two Expeditions*, 2, p. 217.

66 W. Tench, *Sydney's First Four Years*, Sydney, 1961, pp. 225, 227.

67 *HRNSW*, 5, 1897, pp. 749, 759.

68 J. Grant, *The Narrative of a Voyage of Discovery*, London, 1803, p. 127.

69 Tench, *Sydney's First Years*, p. 227.

70 Grant, *Narrative of a Voyage*, p. 127.

71 P. Cunningham, *Two Years in New South Wales*, Sydney, 1966, p. 189.

72 M. Flinders, *Voyage to Terra Australis*, 1, London, 1814, p. 235.

73 *HRNSW*, 5, p. 753.

74 Tench, *Sydney's First Years*, pp. 225–6.

75 Mitchell, *Journal of an Expedition*, p. 64.

76 E. Giles, *Australia Twice Traversed*, 2, London, 1889, pp. 109–10.

77 Leichhardt, *Journal*, p. 5; Grey, *Journals of Two Expeditions of Discovery*, vol. 1, London, pp. 315.

78 Mitchell, *Tropical Australia*, p. 275.

79 Leichhardt, *Journal*, p. 118.

80 H. S. Russell, *The Genesis of Queensland*, Sydney, 1888, p. 334.

81 Leichhardt, *Journal*, pp. 115–16.

82 *Port Phillip Herald*, 9 June 1840.

83 J. Black, *North Queensland Pioneers*, Townsville, n.d., p. 55.

84 *Argus*, 31 August 1850.

85 *QVP*, 3, 1876, p. 379.

86 Mitchell, *Journal of an Expedition*, pp. 145–50.

87 Ibid., p. 414.

88 Ibid., p. 135.

89 Mitchell, *Three Expeditions*, 2, p. 35.

90 Ibid., p. 94.

91 Ibid., p. 68.

92 Mitchell, *Journal of an Expedition*, p. 63.

93 Ibid., p. 113.

94 Mitchell, *Three Expeditions*, 2, p. 36.

95 Roe, 'Journal of an Expedition', p. 37.

96 W. H. Tietkins, *Journal of the Central Australian Exploring Expedition*, Adelaide, 1891, p. 25.

97 Ibid., p. 41.

98 P. E. Warburton, *Journey Across the Western Interior of Australia*, London, 1875, p. 177.

99 J. Forrest, *Explorations in Australia*, London, 1875, p. 237.

100 E. Giles, *Australia Twice Traversed*, 2, London, 1889, p. 199.

101 Report of the Commissioners Appointed into . . . the Burke and Wills Expedition, *VPP*, 1861–2, 3, no. 17, p. v.

102 G. W. Rusden, *History of Australia*, 3, London, 1883, p. 197.

103 *Burke and Wills Expedition*, p. 35.

104 Ibid., p. 33.

105 Ibid., p. 15.

106 Report of Burke & Wills Commission, pp. 11, 13.

107 *Burke and Wills Expedition*, pp. 27, 28, 30.

108 *HRNSW*, 5, p. 514.

109 Cunningham, *Two Years*, p. 193.

110 The Diary of James Coutts Crawford, *South Australiana*, 4 (1), March 1965, p. 3.

111 *Perth Gazette*, 3 August 1839.

112 Select Committee on the Condition of the Aborigines, *NSWLCV&P* 1845, p. 45.

113 R. Henning, *The Letters of Rachel Henning*, D. Adam (ed.), Ringwood, 1977, p. 161.

114 Select Committee on Queensland Native Police, *QVP*, 1861, p. 26.

115 N. Gunson (ed.), *Australian Reminiscences and Papers of L. E. Threlkeld*, AIAS, Canberra, 1974, p. 354.

116 Return to an Address by Dr. Thomson . . . on Aborigines, *NSWLCV&P*, 1843, p. 510.

117 G. A. Robinson papers, 61, A/7082, Mitchell Library, p. 93.

118 J. Atkinson, *An Account of the State of Agriculture and Grazing in New South Wales*, London, 1826, p. 136.

119 N. B. Tindale, 'Ecology of Primitive Aboriginal Man in Australia', in A. Keast *et al.* (eds), *Biography and Ecology in Australia*, Hague, 1959, p. 40.

120 G. A. Robinson papers, 61, p. 93.

121 J. E. Hammond, *Winjan's People*, Perth, 1938, pp. 76–7.

122 G. C. McCrae, 'The Early Settlement of the Eastern Shore of Port Phillip Bay', *Victorian Historical Magazine*, 1, 1911, p. 25.

123 J. F. Mann, 'A Few Notes on Australian Aborigines', 1904, Newspaper Cuttings, Aborigines, 2, Mitchell Library, Sydney p. 50.

124 Mitchell, *Three Expeditions*, 1, p. 31.

125 Cunningham, *Two Years*, p. 194.

126 M. Doyle (ed.), *Extracts from the Letters and Journals of George Fletcher Moore*, London, 1834, p. 95.

127 G. F. Moore, 'A New River Discovered on a Recent Excursion to the Northward', *Perth Gazette*, 14 May 1836.

128 Ibid.

129 A. T. Magarey, 'The Australian Aborigines Water Quest', *Proceedings Royal Geographical Society, South Australia*, 2, 1895, p. 68.

130 A. T. Magarey, 'Tracking by the Australian Aborigines', *Proceedings Royal Geographical Society, South Australia*, 3, 1897, p. 126.

131 E. B. Kennedy, *Four Years in Queensland*, London 1870, p. 68.

132 *Rockhampton Morning Bulletin*, 12 Feb. 1894.

CHAPTER TWO

1 R. C. Praed, *Australian Life: Black and White*, London, 1885, p. 35.

2 M. Durack, *Kings in Grass Castles*, London, 1959, pp. 145, 291, 306; *Sons in the Saddle*, Melbourne, 1985, pp. 63, 155; J. Sullivan, *Banggaiyerri: The Story of Jack Sullivan*, AIAS, Canberra, 1983, p. 37.

3 H. Holthouse, *S'pose I Die: The Story of Evelyn Maunsell*, Sydney, 1973, pp. 65, 143.

4 Report of G. H. Stockland for 1852, Col. Off. Papers, CO201/467, no.163.

5 D. May, *From Bush to Station*, Townsville, 1983, pp. 159–61.

6 Report of a Commission into ... [the] Native Prisoners of the Crown, *WAVP*, 1884, no. 32, p. 18.

7 *QVP*, 1902, 1, pp. 1131, 1171; D. May, 'Aboriginal Labour in the North Queensland Cattle Industries, 1897–1968', PhD thesis, James Cook University, 1986, p. 407.

8 *WAPP*, 1901, 2 (26), 1903–4, 2 (32), p. 160.

9 A. McGrath, 'We Grew Up the Stations', PhD thesis, La Trobe University, 1983, p. 12.

10 *Queenslander*, 15 June 1895.

11 Quoted in S. Hunt, *Spinifex and Hessian*, Perth, 1986, pp. 97–8.

12 May, *From Bush to Station*, pp. 57–8.

13 Queensland Home Office, A/44679, COL/144, QSA.

14 *QPP*, 3, 1913, p. 1085.

15 Reports of the Resident Magistrate . . . on Special Duty to the Murchison and Gascoyne Districts, WAVP, 1882, no. 33.

16 Report on Stations Visited by the Travelling Inspector of Aborigines, *WAPP*, 2, 1901, no. 26, pp. 16–48.

17 Report of Constable Pollet, Police Dept, PD 268/87, Battye Library.

18 A. W. Bucknell, 'Some Aboriginal Beliefs and Customs', *Australian Museum Magazine*, 5 (1), Jan.–March 1933, p. 36.

19 Quoted in May, *From Bush to Station*, p. 59.

20 A. S. Haydon, 'Slavery in Queensland', *Queenslander*, 12 April 1884.

21 *QPP*, 2, 1906, p. 913.

22 Ibid., 1, 1904, p. 847.

23 May, *From Bush to Station*, p. 83.

24 McGrath, 'We Grew Up the Stations', p. 128.

25 3 November 1883, quoted in May, *From Bush to Station*, p. 81.

26 Qld Colonial Secretary, In Letters, COL/A713, 12790 of 1892.

27 Ibid., enclosing letter John Swan to Charles Lilly, 21 December 1891.

28 Ibid.

29 *Queenslander*, 18 April 1891.

30 May, *From Bush to Station*, p. 81.

31 Durack, *Kings in Grass Castles*, p. 145.

32 J. Bardsley, *Across the Years*, Sydney, 1987, p. 127.

33 S. Hunt, *Spinifex and Hessian*, Perth, 1986, pp. 106–7.

34 *SAPP*, 2, 1899, no. 77, p. 90.

35 Quoted by Hunt in *Spinifex and Hessian*, p. 106.

36 Report on Aborigines West of the Warrego, COL/144, QSA, p. 7.

37 Constable Reside, Boulia to Inspector Brannerly,

10 December 1898, COL/140, QSA.

38 *Queenslander*, 19 November 1898.

39 A. Meston, Aboriginals West of the Warrego, COL/140, QSA, p. 7.

40 Quoted in May, *From Bush to Station*, p. 83.

41 Bardsley, *Across the Years*, p. 129.

42 D. Daly, *Digging, Squatting and Pioneering Life in the Northern Territory of South Australia*, London, 1887, p. 68.

43 Quoted in May, *From Bush to Station*, p. 84.

44 Holthouse, *S'pose I Die*, p. 88.

45 K. L. Parker, *My Bush Book*, ed. M. Muir, Adelaide, 1982, p. 87.

46 Holthouse, *S'pose I Die*, p. 56.

47 Ibid., p. 85.

48 A. J. Allingham, 'Victorian Frontierswomen: The Australian Journals and Diaries of Lucy and Eva Gray, 1868–72, 1881–92', MA thesis, James Cook University, 1987, pp. 344–54.

49 Bardsley, *Across the Years*, p. 108.

50 Holthouse, *S'pose I Die*, pp. 56–7.

51 Bardsley, *Across the Years*, p. 108.

52 Hassell, *My Dusky Friends*, Fremantle, 1975, p. 9.

53 Parker, *My Bush Book*, p. 146.

54 Ibid. Parker's first book, *Australian Legendary Tales*, was first published in London in 1896. A second book, *More Australian Legendary Tales*, was published two years later. Ethel Hassell's

manuscript was written at much the same time but was not published until 1975.

55 Hassell, *My Dusky Friends*, p. 9.

56 Bardsley, *Across the Years*, p. 113.

57 Holthouse, *S'pose I Die*, pp. 92–3.

58 Bardsley, *Across the Years*, p. 109.

59 Holthouse, *S'pose I Die*, p. 57.

60 Bardsley, *Across the Years*, p. 48.

61 *Queenslander*, 21 January 1897.

62 See speeches by A. H. Palmer, *Queensland Parliamentary Debates*, 33, 1880, pp. 1137–8; S. Burt, *Western Australia Parliamentary Debates*, 2, new series, 1892, p. 398.

63 Harold Meston to Protector of Aborigines, 20 December 1902, COL/144, QSA.

64 A. Meston, Aboriginals West of the Warrego, COL/140, QSA, p. 6.

65 May, *From Bush to Station*, p. 81.

66 H. Meston to Protector of Aborigines, 20 December 1902, Home Office, COL/144, QSA.

67 23 May 1885.

68 Corporal Payne, Roebourne, quoted by Hunt in *Spinifex and Hessian*, p. 98.

69 The case was the Gribble libel case, see S. Hunt, 'The Gribble Affair: A Study in Colonial Politics', *Studies in Western Australian History*, 8, December 1984, pp. 42–51.

70 W.A. Col. Sec., ACC 388, 'The Gribble Case', Battye Library.

71 Hunt, *Spinifex and Hessian*, p. 148.

72 Quoted in M. A. Bain, *Full Fathom Five*, Perth, 1982, p. 17.

73 E. W. Streeter, *Pearls and Pearling Life*, London, 1886, p. 156.

74 A. V. Bligh, *The Golden Quest*, Sydney, 1938, p. 35.

75 Ibid.

76 Ibid.

77 Bain, *Full Fathom Five*, p. 28.

78 The Gribble Case, Col. Sec., ACC 388, Battye Library, p. 11.

79 Corporal Payne, 15 September 1883, Col Sec., CSO/1582.43, Battye Library.

80 Ibid.

81 Statement of Jacky in R. M. Angelo's report from Roebourne, Colonial Office Dispatches, ACC 391. no. 67, Battye Library.

82 Gould to Col. Sec., 30 November 1878, quoted by B. W. Shepherd, 'A History of the Pearling Industry of the North-West Coast of Australia', MA thesis, University of Western Australia, 1975, p. 85.

83 *WAPP*, 2 (26), 1901, p. 49; 2 (32), 1903–4, p. 19.

84 Ibid.

85 *QPP*, 2, 1903, p. 456.

86 *QVP*, 2, 1894, p. 920.

87 Qld Col. Sec., COL/A333, 1385 of 1882.

88 C. Anderson, 'Aborigines and Tin Mining', *Mankind*, 13 (6), April 1983, pp. 473–98.

89 *QVP*, 4, 1891, p. 269.

90 Royal Commission on Mining, *QVP*, 4, 1897, p. xliv.

91 *WAPP*, 2 (26), 1901, p. 24.

92 W. A. Roth to Commissioner of Police, 24 June 1898, Col. Sec., COL/139, QSA.

93 McGrath, 'We Grew Up the Stations'; May, 'Aboriginal Labour . . .'.

CHAPTER THREE

1 P. Cunningham, *Two Years in New South Wales*, Sydney, 1966, p. 189.

2 J. T. Bigge, *Report . . . into the State of the Colony in New South Wales*, London, 1822, p. 117.

3 Charles Symmons to Col. Sec., 18 January 1853, CSO In Letters: Aborigines 1853/36/255, Battye Library, Perth.

4 Cunningham, *Two Years*, p. 195.

5 *HRNSW*, 6, p. 3.

6 W. Tench, *Sydney's First Four Years*, Sydney, 1961, p. 210.

7 Ibid., p. 215.

8 N. J. B. Plomley (ed.), *Friendly Mission*, Hobart, 1966, p. 262.

9 Select Committee on Native Police, *QVP*, 1861, p. 111.

10 Select Committee on the Condition of the Aborigines, *NSWLCV&P*, 1845, p. 18.

11 E. J. Eyre, *Journals of Expeditions of Discovery*, 2, London, 1845, p. 247.

12 'Reminiscences of the Early Sixties by an Ex-Officer', *Queenslander*, 10 June 1899.

13 *Sydney Gazette*, 14 May 1814.

14 *Sydney Gazette*, 30 March 1816.

15 *The Colonist*, 16 February 1839.

16 Col. Sec. In Letters, CSO/1/323, TSA.

17 *Hobart Town Courier*, 5 April 1828.

18 E. Dumaresq to Col. Sec., 6 November 1829, CSO/1/316, TSA.

19 *Colonial Times*, 26 February 1830.

20 A. Reid to Col. Sec., 2 January 1829, CSO/1/323, TSA.

21 Thomas Hooper to T. Anstey, 19 August 1830, CSO/1/316, TSA.

22 T. A. Lascelles to Col. Sec., 10 June 1829, CSO/1/316, TSA.

23 Van Diemens Land. Return to an Address . . . on the subject of Military Operations, 1831, 19 (259), p. 72.

24 Cunningham, *Two Years*, p. 195.

25 Lt. de la Condamine to Captain Foley, 8 September 1826, *HRA*, 1, 12, p. 616.

26 Arthur Papers, V19, mss A/2179, Mitchell Library.

27 Tasmanian Aborigines, mss A/612, Mitchell Library, p. 249.

28 Plomley, *Friendly Mission*, p. 473.

29 A. H. Campbell, *John Batman and the Aborigines*, Malmsbury, n.d., pp. 31–6.

30 Maconochie's plan was published in the Hobart paper *Murray's Review*, 16 January 1838 and was reprinted in N. J. B. Plomley (ed.), *Weep in Silence*, Hobart, 1987, pp. 1003–8.

31 Ibid., p. 1008.

32 The history of the Port Phillip force has been examined by M. Fels in her book *Good Men and True: The Aboriginal Police of the Port Phillip District, 1837–1853*, Melbourne, 1988. There is no corresponding study of the Queensland force. The New South Wales era is covered by L. E. Skinner, *Police of the Pastoral Frontier*, St Lucia, 1975. The only comprehensive study is the unpublished BA Hons thesis by N. Taylor, 'The Native Mounted Police of Queensland, 1850–1900', James Cook University, 1970.

33 Fels, *Good Men and True*, p. 85.

34 A. J. Vogan, *The Black Police*, London, 1890, pp. 170–1.

35 Walker to Col. Sec., 16 October 1849, Letters re Moreton Bay, mss A2/19, 49/10488, Mitchell Library; Walker to Col. Sec., 1 July 1854, Letters re Moreton Bay/Native Police, mss A2/48, Mitchell Library.

36 Plunkett to Col. Sec., 18 November 1850, Government Resident, Moreton Bay: Letters from Col. Sec., QSA 48/101, RES/2, Brisbane.

37 Skinner, *Police*, p. 54.

38 Walker to Col. Sec., 1 March 1852, *NSWLCV&P* no. 1, 1852, p. 789.

39 Select Committee on Native Police Force, *QVP*, 1861, p. 151.

40 *Queensland Guardian*, 27 July 1861.

41 *Courier* (Brisbane), 25 July 1861.

42 Select Committee on Native Police, p. 29.

43 *Queensland Guardian*, 4 May 1861.

44 Select Committee on the Native Police, 1861, p. 156.

45 J. G. Gill, Governor Bowen and the Aborigines, *Queensland Heritage*, 2 (7), 1972, p. 22.

46 *QVP*, 1864, p. 453.

47 Gill, Governor Bowen, p. 21.

48 The various estimates of costs will be found in: Select Committee on the Native Police Force, *NSWLAVC&P*, 1856–57,1, p. 7; Select Committee on Murders . . . on the Dawson River, *NSWLAV&P*, 1858, 2, pp. 861–3, 905. Select Committee on the Native Mounted Police, op. cit., pp. 50, 51,121. Report on the North Queensland Aborigines by W. Parry-Okeden, *QVP*, 1897, 2, p. 15.

49 See the proposal by Captain M. C. O'Connell, Select Committee on Murders, pp. 861–2.

50 E. B. Kennedy, *Four Years in Queensland*, London, 1902, p. 127.

51 Report on the North Queensland Aborigines, p. 17.

52 Select Committee on the Native Police, 1861, pp. 131,154.

53 Kennedy, *Four Years*, p. 102.

54 Select Committee on the Native Police, 1861, p. 31.

55 Ibid., p. 158.

56 Ibid., p. 131.

57 Walker to Col. Sec., 31 December 1849, *NSWLCV&P*, 1850, p. 586.

58 Select Committee on the Native Police Force, 1856–57, p. 11.

59 Dana to La Trobe, 22 November 1842, Select Committee on Aborigines, Australian Colonies, *BPP*, 1844, p. 288.

60 Select Committee on the Native Police, 1861, p. 81.

61 Report on the North Queensland Aborigines, p. 17.

62 Select Committee on the Native Police, 1861, p. 55.

63 Ibid., p. 74. See also the evidence of C. R. Haley, p. 81 and J. L. Zillman, p. 78.

64 R. Evans, K. Saunders, K. Cronin, *Exclusion, Exploitation and Extermination*, Sydney, 1975, p. 61.

65 Ibid.

66 Walker to Col. Sec., 12 July 1849, Letters re Moreton Bay, mss A2/19, Mitchell Library.

67 *Queensland Guardian*, 27 July 1861.

68 T. L. Mitchell, *Journal of an Expedition into the Interior of Tropical Australia*, London, 1848, p. 25.

69 *Moreton Bay Free Press*, 24 August 1852.

70 F. Walker to Col. Sec., 1 March 1852, *NSWLAV&P*, p. 790.

71 Select Committee on Murders . . . on the Dawson River, *NSWLAV&P*, p. 880.

72 Select Committee on the Native Police Force, 1856–57, p. 25.

73 C. Eden, *My Wife and I in Queensland*, London, 1872, p. 114.

74 R. Gray, *Reminiscences of India and North Queensland*, London, 1913, p. 79.

75 Select Committee on the Native Police Force, 1856–57, p. 36.

76 *Rockhampton Bulletin*, 5 August 1865.

77 Select Committee on the Police, *QVP*, p. 11.

78 Report on the North Queensland Aborigines, p. 16.

79 Ibid., p. 15.

80 Ibid.

81 Instructions of Commandant to Officers . . . of Native Police, January 1858, Select Committee on the Native Police Force, p. 151.

82 N. J. B. Plomley, *Weep in Silence*, Hobart, 1987, p. 1005.

83 Select Committee on the Aborigines and Protectorate, *NSWLCV&P*, 1849, p. 2.

84 Gill, Governor Bowen and the Aborigines, p. 10.

85 G. S. Lang, *The Aborigines of Australia*, Melbourne, l865.

86 *QVP*, 3, 1876, p. 106.

87 For an assessment of the Canadian treaties see J. Friesen, 'Magnificent Gifts: The Treaties of Canada with the Indians of the North West', Royal Society of Canada, *Transactions*, 5 (1),1986, pp. 41–51.

88 See R. McGregor, 'Answering the Native Question: The Dispossession of the Aborigines of the Fitzroy District, West Kimberley, 1880–1905', BA Hons thesis, James Cook University, 1985. B. Shaw, 'Heroism against white rule: The "Rebel" Major', in E. Fry, *Rebels and Radicals*, Sydney, 1983, pp. 8–26.

89 Fels, *Good Men and True*, pp. 71–106.

90 Select Committee on the Murders . . . on the Dawson River, p. 27.

91 Select Committee on the Police, *QVP*, 1860, 1, p. 34.

92 Skinner, *Police*, p. 53.

93 Dana to La Trobe, 19 January 1843, Aborigines: Australian Colonies, BPP, 1844, p. 290.

94 Ibid., p. 293.

95 Ibid.

96 Gill, Governor Bowen, p. 9.

97 Skinner, *Police*, p. 54.

98 E. S. Parker, *The Aborigines of Australia*, Melbourne, 1854, p. 71.

99 *See* R. Evans, *et. al.*, *Exclusion, Exploitation and Extermination*, Sydney, 1975, p. 379.

100 G. Grey, *Journals of Two Expeditions of Discovery*, 1, London, 1841, p. 364.

101 Ibid., p. 293.

102 Select Committee on the Murders . . . on the Dawson River, p. 865.

103 A. J. Boyd, *Old Colonials*, London, 1882, p. 195.

Chapter Four

1   W. Tench, *Sydney's First Four Years*, Sydney, 1961, p. 148.

2   Ibid.

3   J. B. Marsden, *Memoirs of the Life and Labours of the Rev. Samuel Marsden*, London, n.d., p. 84.

4   N. J. B. Plomley (ed.), *Friendly Mission*, Hobart, 1966, pp. 833, 910, 911, 913.

5   E. J. Eyre, *Autobiographical Narrative of Residence and Exploration in Australia 1832–1839*, London, 1984, p. 105.

6   Ibid., pp. 114–15.

7   Ibid., p. 124.

8   Ibid., p. 174.

9   Ibid. ch. 1.

10 R. Dawson, *The Present State of Australia*, London, 1830, pp. 107, 205.

11 *Sydney Gazette*, 25 April 1828.

12 R. Henning, *The Letters of Rachel Henning*, Ringwood, 1977, pp. 161, 194–5.

13 N. Wade-Broun, *Memoirs of a Queensland Pioneer*, Sandgate, 1944, p. 18.

14 M. Durack, *Kings in Grass Castles*, London, 1959, p. 275.

15 A. J. Allingham, 'Victorian Frontierswomen: The Australian Journals and Diaries of Lucy and Eva Gray, 1868–1872, 1881–1892', MA thesis, James Cook University, 1987, p. 163.

16 *Port Denison Times*, 3 April 1869.

17 Journal of Joseph Hann, (typescript), James Cook University, p. 110.

18 Allingham, 'Victorian Frontierswomen . . .', p. 199.

19 Ibid.

20 *QVP*, 2, 1903, p. 461.

21 J. Bardsley, *Across the Years*, Sydney, 1987, p. 83.

22 *QVP*, 1, 1904, p. 871.

23 Durack, *Kings in Grass Castles*, p. 291.

24 Qld Col. Sec. Correspondence, QSA, COL/A1483 of 1869, COL/A316, 2895 of 1881.

25 *QVP*, 1, 1904, p. 87.

26 J. Bonwick, *The Last of the Tasmanians,* London, 1870, p. 383.

27 A. Meston, Southern Protector of Aborigines to Under-Secretary, Home Office, 13 January 1903, *QSA*.

28 *Annual Report of the Chief Protector of Aborigines*, *QPP*, 2, 1906, p. 15.

29 *QVP*, 2, 1903, p. 452.

30 J. H. Binnie, *My Life on a Tropic Goldfield*, Melbourne, 1944, pp. 8, 11.

31 COL/A713 no.12790 of 1892, QSA.

32 *QVP*, 4, 1901, p. 1335.

33 Ibid., 2, 1903, p. 461.

34 Bardsley, *Across the Years*, pp. 71, 179, 180, 181.

35 *QVP*, 4, 1901, p. 1336.

36 Qld Colonial Secretary In Letters, COL/145, QSA.

37 *QPP*, 2, 1906, p. 924.

38 Meston to Under-Secretary.

39 Western Australia Col Sec. Correspondence, miscellaneous file ACC388.

40 *QPP*, 2, 1906, p. 920.
41 H. Finch-Hatton, *Advance Australia*, London, 1885, p. 145.
42 Bonwick, *The Last of the Tasmanians*, pp. 354–6.
43 Plomley, *Friendly Mission*, pp. 475–6.
44 *Sydney Gazette*, 7 July 1805.
45 Marsden, *Memoirs of the Life and Labours . . .*, p. 84.
46 Plomley, *Friendly Mission*, p. 446.
47 Ibid., p. 911.
48 *QVP*, 2, 1903, p. 461.
49 Ibid., 4, 1901, p. 1337.
50 *QPP*, 2, 1906, p. 914.
51 *QVP*, 2, 1903, p. 461.
52 Ibid.
53 Meston to Under-Secretary.
54 Durack, *Kings in Grass Castles*, p. 257.
55 Meston to Under-Secretary.
56 F. Bonney, 'On Some Customs of the Aborigines of the River Darling', *Journal of the Anthropological Institute*, 14, 1885, pp. 124–25.

CHAPTER FIVE

1 William Thomas to Col. Sec., 15 January 1853, 17 January 1854; Half-Yearly Reports, Thomas Papers, Mitchell Library.
2 E. B. Addis, Geelong, 28 December 1841, Aborigines: Australian Colonies, *BPP*, 1844, p. 182.
3 E. J. Eyre, *Journals of Expeditions of Discovery*, 2, London, 1845, p. 373.
4 'Live and Let Live'. The Case of the Aborigines, *Queenslander*, no. 20, July 1895.
5 Norton to Col. Sec., 10 April 1896, Colonial Secretary's In Letters, COL/143, QSA.
6 *Rockhampton Bulletin*, 21 January 1871.
7 Ibid., 17 January 1871.
8 Diary of Abijon Good, James Cook University Archives.
9 Ibid., 28 September, 4 October.
10 A. Meston, Report on the Western Aboriginals, COL/144, QSA.
11 J. Wegner, 'The Aborigines of the Etheridge Shire, 1860–1940', in H. Reynolds (ed.), *Race Relations in North Queensland*, Townsville, 1978, p. 156.
12 C. H. Haggar to Col. Sec., 10 September 1889, COL/A/89/9668, QSA.
13 *Queenslander*, 18 January 1890.
14 J. S. Norton to Col. Sec., 10 April 1896, COL/143, QSA.
15 R. F. Woodcraft to Col. Sec., 26 June 1902, COL/143, QSA.
16 A. Meston, Report on the Aboriginals of Queensland, *QVP*, no. 4, 1896, p. 732.
17 Travelling Inspector's special inspection tour to Broome, March 1903, *WAPP*, 2 (32), 1902–3, p. 18.
18 Annual Report of the Chief Protector of Aborigines, *QPP*, 1, 1905, p. 750.
19 *Church News*, 28, 1896, p. 41.
20 R. B. Mitchell, Reminiscences, 1856–66, mss. B757, Mitchell Library, p. 104.

21 *Moreton Bay Courier*, Gladstone correspondent, 27 April 1861.

22 Report of the Northern Protector of Aborigines, *QVP*, 2,1903, p. 466.

23 J. Bardsley, *Across the Years*, Sydney, 1987, p. 23.

24 Annual Report of the Chief Protector of Aborigines, *QPP*, 1, 1905, p. 750.

25 *Queenslander*, 8 April 1893.

26 N. A. Loos, 'Aboriginal–European Relations in North Queensland, 1861–1897', PhD thesis, James Cook University, 1976, p. 437.

27 *Cleveland Bay Express*, 25 June 1870.

28 Candidus, 'The Aboriginal Abomination', *Port Denison Times*, 7 August 1869.

29 *Queensland Guardian*, 13 July 1861.

30 Bardsley, *Across the Years*, p. 24.

31 Reprinted in the *Queenslander*, 11 June 1870.

32 J. H. W. 'The Nigger Nuisance', *Northern Territory Times*, 13 February 1874.

33 *Rockhampton Morning Bulletin*, 24 January 1871.

34 *Ravenswood Miner*, 24 February 1872.

35 *Queenslander*, 10 December 1887.

36 Aborigines, Australian Colonies, 1844, *BPP*, p. 420.

37 Reports of Protector of Aborigines, *SAA*, 6R6/24/6, pp. 132, 712.

38 *Brisbane Courier*, 25 October 1924

39 *Courier Mail*, 18 February 1939.

40 J. S. Hassall, *In Old Australia*, Brisbane, 1902, pp. 187–8.

41 *Cooktown Courier*, 20 July 1888.

42 P. Cunningham, *Two Years in New South Wales*, Sydney, 1966, p. 187.

43 *Cleveland Bay Express*, 5 June 1869, quoted in the *Queenslander*, 19 June 1869.

44 See report of Government Resident, Port Lincoln, SAA, 6R6/24/6, pp. 382, 454; *Hunter River Gazette*, 11, 18 December 1841, 8 January 1842; *Portland Mercury*, 2 August 1843; *Portland Gazette*, 21 April 1847.

45 Letterbooks of Commissioner, Crown Lands, Wide Bay, 1 January 1855–13 December 1857, 30/11, QSA.

46 *Maryborough Chronicle*, quoted in the *Queenslander*, 6 March 1869.

47 Spero Meliora, 'Queensland and her Blacks', *Queenslander*, 12 January 1884.

48 *Maryborough Chronicle*, 9 January 1863.

49 *Cleveland Bay Express*, 13 August 1870.

50 *Northern Argus* reported in *Queenslander*, 24 August 1867.

51 *Queenslander*, 5, 13 February 1892.

52 W.A. Col. Sec.'s files C80/1853/36, p. 255.

53 Bourke & District Historical Society, *The History of Bourke*, 3, 1971, p. 172.

54 Report on Stations Visited by the Travelling Inspector of Aborigines, *WAPP*, 3, 1901, p. 26.

55 *Queenslander*, 20 May 1871.

56 J. W. Craig, *Diary of a Naturalist*, Paisley, 1908, p. 150.

57 *The History of Bourke*, p. 172.

58 The Diary of Lucy Gray, *Queensland Heritage*, 1 November 1964, p. 14.

59 Here and There in Queensland, *Illustrated Sydney News*, 24 October 1885.

60 Report on flogging by Constable King of an Aboriginal, Qld Col. Sec., COL/A 2894 of 1876, QSA.

61 D. T. Seymour, General Order no. 596, 28 October 1876, POL/4, QSA.

62 Quoted in Loos, 'Aboriginal European Relations . . .', p. 433.

63 *Endeavour Times*, 22 August 1891.

64 *Port Denison Times*, 27 October 1877.

65 Ibid., 10 April 1869.

66 J. Phillips to Col. Sec., 3 December 1852, Western Australia CSO In Letters, Jan.–June 1852, 231, p. 36, Battye Library.

67 Qld Col. Sec., In Letters, COL/A187, 2122 of 1873, QSA.

68 Annual Report of the Chief Protector of Aborigines, *QPP*, 3, 1908.

69 In the 1940s anthropologists investigated the Aboriginal communities in the small town in northern New South Wales, discovering conditions that were very similar to those noted in the nineteenth century. See for instance: M. Reay, 'A Half-Caste Aboriginal Community in North-Western New South Wales', *Oceania*, 15 (4), June 1945; M. Reay & G. Sitlington, 'Class and Status in a Mixed-Blood Community', *Oceania*, 18 (3), March 1948; G. Sitlington, 'Mixed Blood Aborigines at Moree, New South Wales', *The Aborigines Protector*, 2 (4), June 1948; M. Reay, 'Colour Prejudice at Collarenebri', *The Aborigines Protector*, 2 (3), 1947; C. Kelly, 'The Reaction of White Groups to Aborigines', *Social Horizons*, July 1943.

70 Cunningham, *Two Years*, p. 188.

71 Eyre, *Journals of Expeditions*, 2, p. 446.

72 A. Pope, 'Aboriginal Adaption to the Early Colonial Labour Markets', *Labour History*, 54, May 1988, p. 9.

73 Cunningham, *Two Years*, p. 188.

74 The replies were published in Report of the Select Committee on the Aborigines, *NSWLCV&P*, 1845, and Replies to Circular Letters Addressed to the Clergy, *NSWLCV&P*, 1846.

75 Select Committee on the Aborigines, *NSWLCV&P*, p. 46.

76 Replies to Letters Addressed to the Clergy, *NSWLCV&P*, p. 565.

77 Select Committee on the Aborigines, *NSWLCV&P*, p. 38.

78 Replies to Letters Addressed to the Clergy, *NSWLCV&P*, p. 562.

79 Select Committee on the Aborigines, *NSWLCV&P*, p. 36.

80 Replies to Letters Addressed to the Clergy, *NSWLCV&P*, p. 558.

81 Ibid., p. 571.

82 Select Committee on the Aborigines, *NSWLCV&P*, p. 35.

83 Ibid., p. 46.

84 Ibid., p. 29.

85 Ibid., p. 41.

86 Ibid., p. 23.

87 Ibid., p. 26.

88 Ibid., p. 36.

89 Replies to Letters Addressed to the Clergy, *NSWLCV&P*, p. 560.

90 Ibid., p. 576.

91 Select Committee on the Aborigines, *NSWLCV&P*, p. 35.

92 Replies to Letters Addressed to the Clergy, *NSWLCV&P*, p. 558.

93 Select Committee on the Aborigines, *NSWLCV&P*, p. 28.

94 Replies to Letters Addressed to the Clergy, *NSWLCV&P*, p. 565.

95 Ibid., p. 574.

96 Ibid., p. 559.

97 There were reports every year by the Protection Boards in the three colonies. There was a Royal Commission on the Aborigines in Victoria in 1877. See *VPP*, 1877–8, 3, no. 76.

98 Quoted by S. L. Johnson, 'The New South Wales Government Policy towards the Aborigines, 1880–1909', MA thesis, University of Sydney, 1970.

99 Report of the Aborigines Protection Board, *WALCV&P*, 1888, 8.

100 Johnson, 'NSW Government Policy', p. 66.

101 A. Haebich, 'A Bunch of Cast-Offs, PhD thesis, Murdoch University, 1988, p. ix.

102 Johnson, 'NSW Government Policy', p. 66.

103 J. E. Hammond, *Winjan's People*, Perth, 1933, pp. 74–5.

104 See the evidence of C. E. Strutt, P. M., Royal Commission on the Aborigines in Victoria, 1877.

105 Johnson, 'NSW Government Policy', p. 78.

106 Haebich, 'A Bunch of Cast-Offs', p. 246.

107 Quoted by Johnson, 'NSW Government Policy', p. 70.

CHAPTER SIX

1 *HRNSW*, 1, p. 39.

2 *HRA*, 1 (8), p. 368.

3 Quoted in W. McNair & H. Rumley, *Pioneer Aboriginal Mission*, Perth, 1981, p. 24.

4 Quoted in P. B. Walsh, 'The Problems of Native Policy in South Australia in the Nineteenth Century', BA Hons thesis, University of Adelaide, 1966, p. 19.

5 W. Tench, *Sydney's First Four Years*, Sydney, 1961, p. 294.

6 R. Dawson, *The Present State of Australia*, London, 1830, p. 194.

7 P. Cunningham, *Two Years in New South Wales*, Sydney, 1966, p. 202.

8 H. Melville, *History of Van Diemens Land* . . ., (1836), Sydney, 1965, p. 61.

9 Translator's preface to M. Labillardiere, *Voyages in Search*

of La Perouse, 1791–1794,
London, 1800, p. v.

10 J. Grant, *Narrative of a Voyage of Discovery* . . ., London, 1803, p. 170.

11 *HRA*, 1 (8), p. 368.

12 B. Field (ed.), *Geographical Memoirs of New South Wales*, London, 1826, pp. 203–4.

13 Marsden to D. Coates, 21 November 1825, Bonwick transcripts, series 1, box 53, Mitchell Library.

14 Report from the Select Committee on Aborigines, 1836, p. 17.

15 C. Rolleston, Report on the State of the Aborigines for 1850, Col. Off. papers, C01/201/442.

16 R. H. Bland to Col. Sec., 4 January 1843, Select Committee on Aborigines: Australian Colonies *BPP*, 1844, p. 417.

17 *HRA*, 1 (8) p. 368.

18 Gipps to Russell, 7 April 1841, Aborigines: Australian Colonies, p. 368.

19 Hutt to Stanley, 8 April 1842, Aborigines: Australian Colonies, *BPP*, 1844, p. 412.

20 Symmonds to Col. Sec., 18 September 1848, WA Col. Sec., CSO 1848/173/36.

21 J. Orton journal, 3 December 1844, A1715, Mitchell Library.

22 Harper to Newstead, 23 April 1827, Bonwick transcripts, series 1, box 53, Mitchell Library.

23 Robinson to La Trobe, 14 December 1839, NSW Col.

Sec., files, CSO/4/1135.1.

24 L. E. Threlkeld papers, A382, Mitchell Library.

25 W. Cowan, The Natives of Western Australia, *Colonial Intelligencer and Aborigines Friend*, 1867–71, p. 53.

26 *Examiner*, 1 February 1843.

27 Col. Off. papers, C01/201/430.

28 Dr Collie, in Select Committee on Native Inhabitants, *BPP*, 1837, p. 129.

29 Governor Gipps, in Aborigines: Australian Colonies, *BPP*, 1844, p. 119.

30 C. J. Griffiths to Select Committee on the Protectorate, *NSWLCV&P*, 1849, p. 17.

31 South Australian Colonization, fourth annual report.

32 NSW & Vic. Misc. P., 1817–73, A1493, Mitchell Library.

33 Quarterly Report of Protector of Aborigines, 31 March 1842, W.A. Col. Sec. In Letters, 1842/198.

34 W. Thomas Journal, 18 September 1841, W. Thomas papers, uncatalogued mss 214/2, Mitchell Library.

35 Report of Aborigines Protector, 10 February 1842, SA Col. Sec., Letters Received, GRG/24/6.

36 Dawson, *Present State*, p. 194.

37 G. Wyndham, Answers to Questionnaire of Immigration Committee, A/611, Aborigines Mitchell Library.

38 Select Committee on the Aborigines, *NSWLCV&P*, 1845, p. 17.

39 W. Westgarth, *A Report on the Condition, Capabilities and Prospects of the Australian Aborigines*, Melbourne, 1846, p. 23.

40 William Thomas Papers – small diary, 18 November 1840, journal, 12 April 1841, 18 September 1841, uncat. mss 214, Mitchell Library.

41 Select Committee on Aborigines, *NSWLCV&P* p. 17.

42 J. Maclaren, *My Crowded Solitude*, Sun Books edn, Melbourne, 1966, pp. 37–40.

43 L. Threlkeld, annual report for 1838, Threlkeld papers, A382, Mitchell Library.

44 G. Grey, *Journals of Two Expeditions of Discovery*, 2, London, pp. 367–8.

45 E. S. Parker, in Papers of the Port Phillip Protectorate, box 12, Vic. PRO.

46 Charles Symmons Annual Report, CSO/36/1856, W.A. Col. Sec. files, p. 348.

47 W. Thomas, Report of the Yarra Aboriginal Mission for 1846; Journal, 18 September 1841, mss 214, Mitchell Library.

48 E. S. Parker, 'Statement' in Port Phillip Protectorate papers, box 12, Vic. PRO.

49 C. Symmons, Quarterly Report on the Aborigines, 30 June 1841, W.A. Col. Sec. In Letters, 1841/95.

50 G. Taplin, *The Folklore, Manners, Customs and Languages of the South Australian Aborigines*, Adelaide, 1879, p. 12.

51 T. L. Mitchell, *Journal of an Expedition into the Interior of Tropical Australia*, London, 1848, p. 65.

52 W. Walker to R. Watson, 5 December 1821, Bonwick transcripts, box 52, Mitchell Library.

53 Taplin, *The Folklore* . . . , p. 12.

54 J. Bulmer, 'Some Account of the Aborigines of the Lower Murray, Wimmera and Maneroo', *Proceedings Royal Geographical Society of Victoria*, 1 (V), March 1888, p. 30.

55 J. Gunther, Lecture on the Aborigines, B. 505, Mitchell Library.

56 A Lady, *My Experiences in Australia*, London, 1860. Extract in I. McBride (ed.), *Records of Time Past*, AIAS, Canberra, 1978, pp. 248–9.

57 G. W. Rusden, *History of Australia*, vol. 2, London, p. 237.

58 J. B. Walker, *Early Tasmania*, Hobart, 1902, p. 249.

59 Dawson, *Present State*, pp. 272–3.

60 *North West Times*, 27 March 1894.

61 Gipps to Russell, 7 April 1841; Aborigines: Australian Colonies, *BPP*, 1844, p. 106.

62 Rusden, *History*, 1, pp. 85–6.

63 Return to an address . . . comprising Government Expenditure on the Aborigines, *NSWLCV&P*, 1843, p. 506.

64 Ibid., pp. 19, 20.

65 T. L. Mitchell, *Three Expeditions*

into Eastern Australia, vol. II, London, 1834, p. 340.

66 Select Committee on the Aborigines, *NSWLCV&P*, 1845, p. 35.

67 J. Dixon, *The Condition and Capabilities of Van Diemens Land*, London, 1839, p. 23.

68 Threlkeld, annual report, op. cit.

69 E. Curr, *Recollections of Squatting in Victoria*, Melbourne, 1883, p. 299.

70 J. Bonwick, *The Last of the Tasmanians*, London, 1870, p. 356.

71 Select Committee on Native Police, 1861, QVPLA, p. 156.

72 Select Committee on Murders by the Aborigines on the Dawson River, *NSWLAV&P*, 1858, p. 864.

73 Select Committee on Native Police, 1861, p. 26.

74 E. Thorn, *The Queen of the Colonies*, London, 1876, p. 308.

75 Select Committee on . . . the Protectorate, *NSWLCV&P*, 1849, p. 22.

76 William Porter Journal, 22 February 1841, Church Missionary Society papers, C.N./ 070.

77 Robinson to La Trobe, 30 August 1841, Aborigines: Australian Colonies, BPP, 1844, p. 132.

78 Bonwick, *Last of*, p. 356.

79 Mitchell, *Journal of an Expedition*, p. 416.

80 Aborigines and Native Police 1835–44, CSO 4/1135.1, NSW Archives.

81 Cartwright to Macquarie, 6 December 1819, Return to an Address . . . [re] the Moral and Religious Instruction of the Aboriginal Inhabitants . . . , 1831.

82 Select Committee on . . . the Protectorate, *NSWLCVP*, 1849, p. 37.

83 James Gunther Journal, 23 April 1838, Church Missionary Society papers, C.N./047; M. Hale, *The Aborigines of Australia*, London, 1889, p. 10.

84 E. J. Stormon (ed.), *The Salvado Memoirs*, Perth, 1977, p. 71.

85 James Gunther Journal, 23 April 1838.

86 *Examiner*, 3 December 1842.

87 Bligh to Col. Sec., 16 September 1848, Letters Relating to Moreton Bay, NSW Col. Sec., 48/10740, QSA.

88 E. S. Parker, Annual report for 1848, Port Phillip Aboriginal Protectorate Papers, box 11, PRO.

89 *Port Denison Times*, 5 August 1876.

90 *Maryborough Chronicle*, 7 January 1865.

91 C. G. Nicolay, *The Handbook of Western Australia*, 2nd edn, London, 1896, pp. 221–2.

92 Letter to Directors, London Missionary Society, Reports of J. Backhouse and G. W. Walker, B706, Mitchell Library.

93 Grey, *Journals*, 2, p. 371.

94 Mitchell, *Three Expeditions*, p. 416.

95   *Examiner*, 3 December 1842.

96   Thomas to Col. Sec., 19 January 1856, Half-Yearly Reports, Thomas Papers.

97   Grey, *Journals*, 2, pp. 370–1.

98   J. Bonwick, *The Lost Tasmanian Race*, London, 1884, p. 207.

99   *Sydney Gazette*, 2 December 1804.

100 J. T. Hinkins, *Life Among the Native Race*, Melbourne, 1884, p. 73. See also P. D. Gardner, 'A Melancholy Tale', *Victorian Historical Journal*, 52, (2), May 1981, pp. 101–12.

101 L. E. Skinner, *Police of the Pastoral Frontier*, St Lucia, 1975, pp. 85–8, 129–30, 407.

102 W. Ridley in evidence to Select Committee on Native Police, 1861, p. 116.

103 Shelley to Macquarie, 8 April 1814, *HRA*, 1 (8), pp. 370–1.

104 Hutt to Russell, 1 March 1842, Aborigines: Australian Colonies, *BPP*, 1844, p. 403.

105 *Sydney Gazette*, 1 January 1814.

106 R. C. Praed, *Australian Life: Black and White*, London, 1885, p. 34.

107 Royal Commission on the Aborigines, *VPP*, 3 (76), 1877–8, p. 532.

108 H. J. B. Plomley (ed.), *Weep in Silence*, Hobart, 1987, p. 11 and *Friendly Mission*, Hobart, 1966, pp. 104, 109; C. Mattingley, *Survival in Our Own Land*, Adelaide, 1989, p. 149.

109 J. Gunther Journal, 1 April– 31 December 1839.

110 Select Committee on the Aborigines Bill, *SAPP*, 1899, no. 77, p. 101.

111 Select Committee on Native Police, 1861, p. 414.

112 See B. Davies, *The Life of Jimmy Governor*, Sydney, 1979.

113 *Sydney Morning Herald*, 23 November 1900.

114 Article from *Evening News*, in NSW Police File, 4/8581.

115 *Sydney Morning Herald*, 23 November 1900.

116 Ibid.

117 Ibid., 24 November 1900.

118 J. Watson Journal, 17 July 1834, Church Missionary Papers, C.N./093.

119 J. Gunther to D. Coates, 12 December 1839, ibid., C.N./047.

120 The answers to a 'circular letter' can be found in Report of Select Committee on the Aborigines, *NSWLCV&P*, 1845, and Replies to Circular Letters Addressed to the Clergy, *NSWLCV&P*, 1846.

121 Replies to Circular Letters, pp. 554, 562, 567.

122 Ibid., pp. 562, 563, Select Committee, 1845, pp. 26, 31, 36, 37.

123 J. Stahe, Report on Lake Condah Mission, *VLAV&P*, 1889, 4, 129.

124 Language and Customs of the Australian Aborigines, p. 94, W. Thomas Papers.

125 Replies to Circular Letters, p. 580.

126 *SAPP*, 3 (26), 1915, p. 58.

127 S. L. Johnson, 'The New South Wales Government Policy

Towards Aborigines,
1880–1909', MA thesis,
University of Sydney, 1970,
p. 103.

128 Report of Aborigines
Department, *WAPP*, 1899,
2 (40), p. 5.

129 Report of Northern Protector of
Aborigines, *QPP*, 1,1904, p. 867.

130 J. F Mann, Notes on the
Aborigines of Australia, *Journal
of the Geographical Society of
Australia*, 1, 1885, p. 41.

131 Annual Report of the Aborigines
Protection Board, *VPP*, 4, 1869,
p. 19.

132 Royal Commission on the
Aborigines, *VPP*, 1877–78,
3 (76), p. 99.

133 Quoted in A. Haebich, 'A Bunch
of Cast-Offs', PhD thesis,
Murdoch University, 1985,
p. 85.

134 Royal Commission on the
Aborigines, *SAPP*, 2 (26), 1913,
pp. 18, 21, 52, 55, 70, 81.

135 Francis Tuckfield Journal,
La Trobe Library, 655, p. 176.

136 D. Barwick, 'Coranderrk and
Cumeroogunga', in T. Epstein
(ed.), *Opportunity and Response*,
London, 1972, pp. 17, 21.

137 B. M. Atwood, 'Blacks and
Lohans', PhD thesis, La Trobe
University, 1984, pp. 98, 118.

138 M. Brennan, *Australian
Reminiscences*, Sydney, 1907,
p. 213.

139 *Moreton Bay Courier*,
16 December 1861.

140 *QVP*, 3, 1876, pp. 162–3.

141 Royal Commission on the
Aborigines, p. 38. Such refusals
were common; see Mattingley
(ed.), *Survival in Our Own Land*,
pp. 77, 123.

142 Ibid., p. 126; see also
A. Haebich, 'European Farmers
and Aboriginal Farmers in South
Western Australia', *Studies in
Western Australian History*,
8 December 1984, pp. 59–67.

143 W. H. Willshire, *Land of the
Dreaming*, Adelaide, 1896,
p. 35.

144 Royal Commission on the
Aborigines, *VPP*, p. 18.

145 *Sunday Times*, 2 October 1921,
quoted in Haebich, 'A Bunch of
Cast-Offs', p. 7.

CONCLUSION

1 May, 'Aboriginal Labour . . .',
p. 410.

2 H. Simpson-Newland, 'Some
Aborigines I Have Known',
*Papers and Proceedings of Royal
Geographical Society*, South
Australia, 1894–95, pp. 40–54.

3 Dawson, *The Present State of
Australia*, p. 332–3.

4 H. McKellar, *Matya-Mundu:
A History of the Aboriginal People
of South-West Queensland*,
Cunnamulla, 1984, p. 92.

5 M. Mansell, 'Aboriginal
Sovereignty', *Aboriginal Law
Bulletin*, 2 (37), April 1989, p. 5.

BIBLIOGRAPHY

OFFICIAL PRINTED SOURCES

Britain

House of Commons, Sessional Papers

1831, 19 (259): Van Diemen's Land. Return to an Address . . . for Copies of all Correspondence between Lieutenant-Governor Arthur and His Majesty's Secretary of State for the Colonies, on the Subject of the Military Operations lately carried on against the Aboriginal Inhabitants of Van Diemens land.

1831, 19 (261): New South Wales. Return to an Address . . . dated 19 July 1831 for Copies of Instructions given by His Majesty's Secretary of State for the Colonies, for Promoting the Moral and Religious Instruction of the Aboriginal Inhabitants of New Holland or Van Diemens Land.

1834, 44 (617): Aboriginal Tribes (North America, New South Wales, Van Diemen's Land and British Guinea).

1836, 7 (538): Report from the Select Committee on Aborigines (British Settlements).

1837, 7 (425): Report from the Select Committee on Aborigines (British Settlements).

1839, 34 (526): Australian Aborigines . . . Copies or Extracts of Despatches Relative to the Massacre of Aborigines of Australia . . .

1843, 32 (505): Papers Relative to the Affairs of South Australia (especially pp. 267–340).

1843, 33 (141): Port Essington: Copies or Extracts of Any Correspondence Relative to the

Establishment of a Settlement . . .
1844, 34 (627): Aborigines
(Australian Colonies) . . . Return
to an address . . . for Copies or
Extracts from the Despatches of
the Governors of the Australian
Colonies, with the Reports of
the Protectors of Aborigines . . .
to illustrate the Condition of the
Aboriginal Population of said
Colonies . . .
1897, 61 (8350): Western Australia:
Correspondence Relating to the
Abolition of the Aborigines
Protection Board.

New South Wales
Legislative Council: Votes and
Proceedings
1838: Report from the Committee on
the Aborigines Question.
1839, 2: Report from the Committee
on Police and Gaols.
1841: Report from the Committee on
Immigration with . . . Replies to
a Circular Letter on the
Aborigines.
1843: New South Wales (Aborigines).
Return to an address by Dr
Thomson . . . comprising details
of Government Expenditure
on Aborigines, 1837–43, and
a large collection of
correspondence relating to the
protectorate and the missions.
1844, 1: New South Wales
(Aborigines). Return to an
address by Sir Thomas Mitchell
. . . for numbers of whites and
Aborigines killed in conflicts
since the settlement of the Port

Phillip District.
1845: Report from the Select
Committee on the Condition of
the Aborigines.
1850, 1: The Native Police, Report of
the Commandant to the Colonial
Secretary.
1852, 1: Letter from Mr F. Walker,
Commandant, Native Police.
1853, 1: Return of Murders by
Aborigines in the Northern
Districts.
1855, 1: Report of Board of Enquiry
Held at Moreton Bay regarding
Commandant F. Walker.

Legislative Assembly: Votes and
Proceedings
1856–57, 1: Report from the Select
Committee on the Native Police
Force
1858, 2: Report from the Select
Committee on Murders by the
Aborigines on the Dawson River.

South Australia
Parliamentary Papers
1857–58, 2 (156): Explorations of
Mr S. Hack.
1857–58, 2 (193): Northern
Exploration.
1858, 1 (25): Northern Exploration:
Reports etc of Explorations . . .
by Babbage, Warburty, Geharty
and Parry.
1878, 4 (209): Journal of Mr Barlay's
Exploration.
1884, 3: Quarterly Report on the
Northern Territory.
1885, 4 (170): Report on the Pursuit
of the Daly River Murderers.

1888, 3 (53): Government Resident's
Report on the Northern
Territory for 1887.

1890, 2 (28): Government Resident's
Report on the Northern
Territory for 1889.

1892, 3 (129): Report on the
Mai-Nini Murder Trial.

1892, 3 (181): Government
Resident's Report on the
Northern Territory for 1891.

1899, 2 (77a): Report from the
Select Committee on the
Aborigines Bill.

1899, 2 (77): Minutes of Evidence on
the Aborigines Bill.

1900, 3 (60): Justice in the Northern
Territory; Letter from
Mr Justice Dashwood.

1901, 2 (45): Government Resident's
Report on the Northern
Territory for 1900.

1913, 2 (26): Report from the Royal
Commission on the Aborigines.

Tasmania
Legislative Council Journals and Papers
1863, no. 48: Half-Caste Islanders in
Bass's Straits, Report by the
Venerable Archdeacon Reibey.

1881, no. 75: First Discovery of Port
Davey and Macquarie Harbour
by Captain James Kelly in . . .
1815–16 and 1824.

Victoria
Legislative Council: Votes and
Proceedings
1858–59, D8: Report on the Select
Committee of the Legislative
Council on the Aborigines.

Parliamentary Papers
1877–78, 3 (76): Report of the
Royal Commission on the
Aborigines.

1882–83, 2 (5): Report of the Board
Appointed to Inquire into and
Report Upon . . . the
Coranderrk Aboriginal Station.

1873–84: Ninth to Twentieth Reports
of Board for the Protection of
Aborigines in the Colony of
Victoria, presented to both
Houses of Parliament.

Queensland
Votes and Proceedings of the
Legislative Assembly
1860: Report of Select Committee on
the Police.

1861: Report of Select Committee on
Native Police Force.

1863: Papers Regarding the Dismissal
of J. Donald Harris of the Native
Police.

1867, 1: Copies of Correspondence
. . . concerning the inquiry
into the case of C. J. Blakeney,
late Lieutenant of Native
Police.

1867, 1: Charges Against the Native
Police under the command of
Mr Sub-Lieutenant Hill.

1867, 2: Alleged Massacre of Blacks
at Morinish Diggings.

1872: Report of Acting Commandant
of Police for 1871.

1874, 2: Enquiry into the Claims
of Patrick Corbett.

1875, 1: Report of Commandant
of Police for 1874.

1876, 3: Report of the

North-Western Exploring Expedition.

1876, 3: Report of Expedition in Search of Gold . . . in the Palmer District by Mulligan and Party.

1878, 2: Report of the Aborigines Commissioners.

1881, 1: Report of Explorations in Cape York Peninsula by R. L. Jack.

1881, 2: Further Reports on the Progress of the Gold Prospecting Expedition in Cape York Peninsula.

1883–84: Report of Police Magistrate, Thursday Island on Pearl Shell and Bêche de Mer Fisheries in Torres Strait.

1885, 2: Reports of Mr Douglas's Cruise Among the Islands of Torres Strait.

1886, 2: Visit of Inspection of Various Islands in the G.S.S. *Albatross*.

1888, 3: Annual Reports of the Gold Fields Commissioners.

1889, 3: Annual Reports of the Gold Fields Commissioners.

1890, 3: Report on the Pearl and Pearl Shell Fisheries of North Queensland by W. Saville-Kent.

1890, 3: Annual Report of the Government Resident at Thursday Island.

1894, 2: Annual Report of the Government Resident at Thursday Island.

1896, 4: Report on the Aborigines of North Queensland by Mr A. Meston.

1897, 2: Report on the North Queensland Aborigines and the Native Police by W. Parry Okeden.

1900–1904: Annual Reports of Northern Protectorate of Aborigines.

1902, 1: Report of the Southern Protector of Aboriginals.

1903, 2: W. E. Roth: North Queensland Ethnography Bulletin no. 5.

Western Australia

Votes and Proceedings of the Legislative Council

1871, 2: Information Respecting the Habits and Customs of the Aboriginal Inhabitants of Western Australia.

1872, 5: Despatches between the Governor and the Secretary of State for the Colonies.

1875–76, 12: Correspondence Relative to the State of Affairs on the North-West Coast.

1880, A16: Report of the Government Resident, Roebourne on the Pearl Shell Industries of the North-West Coast.

1882, 33: Reports from the Resident Magistrate . . . in the Murchison and Gascoyne Districts.

1884, 32: Report of a Commission to Inquire into the treatment of Aboriginal Native Prisoners of the Crown.

1885, A15: Report of the Select Committee. . . Appointed to Consider and Report Upon . . . the Treatment and Condition of

the Aboriginal Natives of the
Colony.
1888, 27: Papers Respecting the
Necessity of Increased Police
Protection for the Settlers in the
Kimberley District.

Parliamentary Papers of Western
Australia
1901, 2 (26): Report on Stations
Visited by the Travelling
Inspector of Aborigines.
1902–3, 2 (32): Report of the
Aborigines Department.
1903–4, 2 (32): Report of the
Aborigines Department.
1905, 5: Report of the Royal
Commission on the Condition
of the Natives.

DOCUMENTARY COLLECTIONS

Historical Records of Australia, series 1,
1–25 and series 3, 1–6.
Historical Records of New South Wales,
1–7.

OFFICIAL MANUSCRIPT SOURCES

Archives Office of
New South Wales
Colonial Secretary's Correspondence:
In Letters (special bundles).
Aborigines, 4/7153.
Aborigines, 1833–35, 4/2219.1.
Aborigines, 1836, 4/2302.1.
Aborigines, 1837–39, 4/24433.1.
Aborigines, 1849, 4/1141.
Aborigines, 1849, 4/2831.1.
Aborigines, 1852, 4/713.2.
Aborigines and the Native Police

1835–44, 4/1135.1.
Aboriginal Outrages, 2/8020.4.
Port Phillip Papers, 1839, 4/2471.
Port Phillip Papers, 1840, P 1,
4/2510.
Port Phillip Papers, 1840, P 2,
4/2511.
Port Phillip Papers, 1841, P 1,
4/2547.
Port Phillip Papers, 1842, P 1,
4/2588 B.
Port Phillip Papers, 1842, P 2,
4/2589 B.
Port Phillip Papers, 1846, 4/2745–2.
Letters Received from and about
Wide Bay, 1850–57, 4/7173.
Raffles Bay, 4/2060.2.
Reports on the Border Police,
1843–46, 4/7203.
Letter from Moreton Bay, 1843,
4/2618.1.
Bathurst 1815–23, 4/1798.
Bathurst 1824, 4/1800.
Bathurst 1826, 4/1801.
Bathurst 1824–26, 4/1799.
Supreme Court Records.
Papers Relating to the Aborigines,
1796–1839, 1161.

Mitchell Library
Aborigines MSS A/611.
Letters from Government Officials,
MSS A/664.
Queensland Native Police: Answers to
Questionnaire, 1856, MSS
A/467.
Letterbook, Commissioner of Crown
Land, Darling Downs 1843–48,
MSS A/1764–2.
Somerset Letterbook no. 1, MSS
B/1414.

Tasmanian State Archives
Papers Relating to the Aborigines, 7578.
Reports on the Murders and Other Outrages Committed by the Aborigines, CSO/1/316.
Records Relating to the Aboriginals, CSO/1/317.
Reports of Mr G. A. Robinson Whilst in Pursuit of the Natives, CSO/1/318.
Papers of the Aborigines Committee, CSO/1/319.
Reports of the Roving Parties, CSO/1/320.
Suggestions Relative to the Capture of the Natives, CSO/1/323.
Papers Relating to the Black Line, CSO/1/324.

Battye Library, Perth
Swan River Papers, 9, 10.

Colonial Secretary: In Letters, Volumes concerned with the Aborigines
53, April, May 1837.
54, June, July 1837.
56, October 1837.
89, 1840.
95, 1841.
108, 1842.
173, 1848.

State Library of South Australia
Governors Despatches GRG/2/6/1.
Letterbook of the Government Resident, Port Lincoln 3/3/379.
Report of Attack on Barrow Creek Telegraph Station GRG/24/6/1874 Nos. 332, 347.

Colonial Secretary: In Letters, 1837–41, GRG/24/1; 1842–45, GRG/24/6.
Colonial Secretary's Letterbooks, GRG/24/4/3; GRG/24/4.
Protector of Aborigines Letterbook 1840–57, GRG/52/7.

Victorian Public Records Office
Records of the Port Phillip Aboriginal Protectorate, especially the boxes – Westernport, North-Western District, Mainly In-Letters, Mt Rouse.

Queensland State Archives
New South Wales Colonial Secretary, Letters Received Relating to Moreton Bay and Queensland, 1822–1860.
Microfilm copies of material from State Archives of NSW, Reels A2/1–A2/48 including the special bundles and A2/48 which contains Commissioner of Crown Lands re Aborigines in the District, 1854 Government Resident, Moreton Bay re complaints about the Native Police 1857.
Correspondence concerning the police firing on the Aborigines.
Native Police: Moreton Bay 1857, Reels A2/47.
Native Police Papers QSA/NMP 48/100, 48/111, 48/120.
Government Resident, Moreton Bay, QSA/RES/2 and 3 48/101, 48/102.
Letterbook of Commissioner for Crown Lands, Wide Bay and

Burnett, 24/9/53–30/12/54,
QSA/CCL/35/889 and
1/1/55–13/12/57,
QSA/CCL/30/11.
Letterbook of W. H. Wiseman,
5/2/55–30/5/60,
QSA/CCL/7/61.
Colonial Secretary: In Letters,
1860–1890, the QSA/Col/A
files and the Special Bundles
Relating to the Aborigines,
QSA/Col/139–QSA/Col/144.

**James Cook University Library,
Townsville**
Microfilm collection of the Joint
Copying Project of Colonial
Office Files re New South Wales,
Tasmania and South Australia.
Especially useful were the files:
New South Wales, Original
Correspondence, 1838–1849
and Queensland, Original
Correspondence, 1861–1900.

OTHER MANUSCRIPT SOURCES

Mitchell Library
Papers of Sir George Arthur,
especially 19, Letters received
1827–28, MSS A/21/2179, 20,
1829–30, MSS A2180 and 28
Aborigines, 1825–37, MSS
A2188, Tasmanian Aborigines,
MSS A612.
Papers of G. A. Robinson, especially
14.
Port Phillip Protectorate, 1839–40,
MSS A7035.
Port Phillip Protectorate.
Correspondence 54–57a and

other papers, 1839–49, MSS
A7075–7078–2.
Port Phillip Protectorate, Official
Reports, 59–61, 1841–49, MSS
A7078–MSS A7082.
J. D. Lang, Papers, 20, MSS 2240.
W. Gardner, Productions and
Resources of the Northern
Districts of NSW, 2 vols,
1842–54, MSS A176/1,
A176/2.
William Thomas Papers, especially his
journal for 1844–47, uncat. MSS
214/2 and 3.
E. J. Eyre, Autobiographical of
Residence and Exploration in
Australia, 1832–39, MSS
A1806.
Diary of John Gilbert,
18/9/44–22/6/45, MSS A2587.
Jesse Gregson Memoirs, MSS 1382.
A. Le Souef, Personal Recollections of
Early Victoria, MSS A2762.
Reminiscences of Mr James Nesbit,
MSS A1533.
A. C. Grant, Early Station Life in
Queensland, MSS A858.
Telfer, Reminiscences, MSS A2376.
J. Backhouse, G. Walker, Report of
a Visit to the Penal Settlement,
Moreton Bay, MSS B706.
H. W. Best Diary, 20/9/62–15/4/63,
MSS B515/1.
Arthur Bloxham Diary, May–July
1863, MSS B515/1.
Andrew Murray, Journal of an
Expedition 1859–1860, MSS
736.
R. B. Mitchell, Reminiscences
1855–66, MSS B575.
J. Raven, Reminiscences of a Western

Queensland Pioneer, MSS A2692.

J. F. Stevens, Histories of Pioneers, MSS 1120.

Bonwick Transcripts, series 1, boxes 49–53.

J. Backhouse, G. Walker, Reports, MSS B707.

Rev. W. Bedford, Papers 1823–43, MSS A76.

J. E. Calder, Papers, MSS A597.

J. Gunther, Journal 1836–65, MSS B504.

J. Gunther, Correspondence and Notes on New South Wales Aborigines, MSS A1450.

J. Gunther, Lecture on the Aborigines, MSS B505.

Hassall Correspondence, MSS A1677.

D. Matthews, Papers, MSS A3384.

J. Orton, Letterbook, MSS A1719.

R. Sadlier, Papers, MSS A1631.

T. H. Scott, Letterbooks, MSS A850.

L. E. Threlkeld, Papers, MSS A382.

R. Windeyer, On the Rights of the Aborigines of Australia, MSS 1400.

Tasmanian State Archives

Van Diemens Land Company Papers, Letters and Despatches, 1828–46, VDC 5/1–7.

Battye Library, Perth

Constance Norris, Memories of Champion Bay or Old Geraldton, Q994.12/GER.

L. F. Clarke, West Australian Natives: My Experiences With Them, PR 2766.

Mr William Coffin, Oral History Tape, PR 9893.

Reminiscences of Mr F. H. Townsend, PR 3497.

Report of the Rev. John Smithers re the Swan River Aborigines, 1840, PR 1785a.

Extracts from the Diary of Lieut. G. F. Dashwood in Perth, September 1832, PR 956/FC.

Diary of Dr S. W. Viveash, QB/VIV.

F. F. B. Wittenoom, Some Notes on his Life QB/WIT.

Journals of Trevarthon C. Scholl, 1865–66 QB/SHO.

L. C. Burgess: Pioneers of Nor'-West Australia, PR 40.

N. K. Sligo, Reminiscences of Early Westralian Goldfields, Q 994.1/SLI.

State Library of South Australia

Letters Written by John Mudge . . . whilst a trooper at Pt Lincoln and Mt Wedge, 1857–60, SAA 1518.

J. B. Bull Reminiscences 1835–94, SAA 950.

Extracts from the Diary of Mary Thomas, SAA 1058M.

Simpson Newland, The Ramingaries (Encounter Bay) Tribe of Aborigines, A571/A4.

Resolution of the Bush Club, 9/5/1839, A546/B8.

Papers of George Taplin, SAA 186/1/1–6. Journal, Letters Received, Lecture on Narrinyeri Tribe, History of Port Mackay.

La Trobe Library, Melbourne

W. Thomas, Brief Remarks on the

Aborigines of Victoria, 1839,
7838Lt.
Journal of Patrick Coady Buckley,
1844–1853, 6109, Box 214/7.
Diary of Neil Black, typescript,
September 1839–May 1840,
Box 99/1.
Foster Fyans Reminiscences,
1810–1842, 6940.
W. H. Hovell, Remarks on a Voyage
to Western Port, 7/11/26–
25/3/27 CY, 8, 1/32c.
The Journal of Francis Tuckfield,
655.
The Papers of James Dredge –
Notebook, 421959; Letterbook,
421/961.
H. Meyrick, Letters to his family in
England, 1840–47, 7959.

Oxley Library, Brisbane
Archer Family Papers, including
Durundur Diary, 1843–44,
Some Letters Mainly from
Australia, 1835–55.
Diary of Captain G. Griffin at
Whiteside, 1/1/47–16/5/49,
OM72–42.
Letter of T. W. Wells to H. C. A.
Harrison, 24/10/61,
OM66/2/f2.
Reminiscences of Mrs Adelaide
Morrison, OM69/8/f1.
Robert Hamilton, Diary at Mt Auburn
Station, 18/11/61–3/9/62,
OM68/28/Q2.
Harry Anning, Thirty Years Ago,
OM172/123.
Archibald Meston Papers, OM64/17.

National Library of Australia
Hagenauer Letterbooks, MSS 3343.
Microfilm of Australian Joint Copying
Project.
Church Missionary Society Records,
FM4 1453–1523.
James Gunther, Letters 1837–42,
Journals, 1837–40.
John Handt, Letters 1830–43,
Journals 1832–41, Report
1835. William Porter, Letters
1838–41, Journal 1838.
William Watson, Letters
1832–42, Journal 1832–37,
Reports 1832–40.
Methodist Missionary Society Records
FM4 1398–1421.
Correspondence – In: Australia,
1812–26, 1827–36, 1837–42.
London Missionary Society, FM
338–445.
Australian Letters 1798–1855.
Australian Journals 1800–1842
including W. Shelley, R. Hassall,
L. E. Threlkeld.
Matthew Hale Papers, FM4/1063.

Rhodes House, Oxford
Papers of the Anti-Slavery Society,
MSS British Empire S22.
Letterbook of J. P. Phillips,
1850–54, MSS Australia S1.

Newspapers

New South Wales
Atlas, 1844–45.
Australian, 1824, 1840–41, 1848.
Colonist, 1837–39.

Empire, 1851–52, 1855–58.
Hunter River Gazette, 1841–42.
Maitland Mercury, 1843–50.
Morning Chronicle, 1844.
Sydney Gazette, 1803–30.
Sydney Morning Herald, 1834–50
    (*Sydney Herald* before July 1842).

Tasmania

Colonial Times, 1825–31.
Hobart Town Courier, 1827–31.
Hobart Town Gazette, 1819–25.
Launceston Advertiser, 1829–31.
The Tasmanian, 1827–28.

Western Australia

Geraldton Express, 1886–90.
Inquirer, 1840–51, 1864–67.
Northern Public Opinion, 1893–98.
Pilbara Goldfields News, 1897–98.
Perth Gazette, 1833–40.

South Australia

Adelaide Examiner, 1842–43.
Adelaide Observer, 1844–49.
Port Augusta Dispatch, 1877–80.
South Australian Register, 1839–44.
Southern Australian, 1838–40.

Victoria

Geelong Advertiser, 1840–44.
Portland Gazette, 1845–47.
Portland Guardian, 1842–43.
Portland Mercury, 1842–44.
Port Phillip Gazette, 1838–46.
Port Phillip Herald, 1840.
Port Phillip Patriot, 1841–42.

Queensland

Burnett Argus, 1863.
Cairns Post, 1885–88.

Colonist (Maryborough), 1884–88.
Cooktown Courier, 1874–79, 1888.
Cooktown Herald, 1874–77.
Cooktown Independent, 1888–91.
Croydon Golden Age, 1896, 1898.
Darling Downs Gazette, 1858–59.
Herberton Advertiser, 1884–85.
Hodgkinson Mining News, 1877–88.
Mackay Mercury, 1868–80.
Maryborough Chronicle, 1860–80.
Moreton Bay Courier, 1846–62.
Moreton Bay Free Press, 1852–59.
North Australian (Brisbane), 1856–65.
North Queensland Telegraph, 1888.
Peak Downs Telegram (Clermont), 1876.
Port Denison Times (Bowen), 1867–83.
Queenslander, 1866–1900.
Queensland Figaro, 1885.
Queensland Guardian, 1861–63.
Queensland Times (Ipswich), 1864–66.
Ravenswood Miner, 1871–72.
Rockhampton Bulletin, 1865–76.
Torres Strait Pilot, 1897–1907.
Wide Bay and Burnett News, 1881–84.
Wide Bay and Burnett Times, 1859–60.
Wild River Times (Herberton),
    1886–89.

Northern Territory

Northern Territory Times, 1873–83,
    1887–89, 1890–95.

MISSIONARY JOURNALS

*The Colonial Intelligencer or Aborigines
    Friend*, 1847–48, 1867–71.
The Aborigines Friend, 1852–58,
    1863–65, 1878–82.
The Colonial Intelligencer, 1874–78.
Missionary Notes of the Australian
Board of Missions, 1895–1905.

Kirchliche Mitteilungen (Church News), 1886–1900.

Newspaper Cutting Books on the Aborigines and related topics in Oxley Library, Mitchell Library, State Library of South Australia. A number of the papers listed above were used for periods other than for those specified. But they were in such cases only consulted for a few issues at any one time. Numerous other papers were used for an issue or two but they have not been listed. Reference has been made to a few of these in the endnotes.

RESEARCH THESES

Attwood, B. M., 'Blacks and Lohans: A Study of Aboriginal–European Relations in Gippsland in the Nineteenth Century', PhD, La Trobe University, 1985.

Allingham, A. J., 'Taming the Wilderness: The First Decade of Pastoral Settlement in the Kennedy District', BA Hons, James Cook University, 1976.

Allingham, A. J., 'Victorian Frontierswomen: The Australian Journals and Diaries of Lucy and Eva Gray, 1868–72, 1881–82', MA, James Cook University, 1987.

Beckett, J., 'A Study of a Mixed Blood Aboriginal Minority in the Pastoral West of New South Wales', MA, ANU, 1958.

Bell, D., 'From Moth Hunters to Black Trackers: An Interpretive Analysis of the Black and White Experience', BA Hons, Monash University, 1975.

Bickford, R. A., 'Traditional Economy of the Aborigines of the Murray Valley', BA Hons, University of Sydney, 1966.

Biskup, P. 'Native Administration and Welfare in Western Australia 1897–1954', MA, UWA, 1960.

Brayshaw, H., 'Aboriginal Material Culture in the Herbert–Burdekin District', PhD, James Cook University, 1977.

Bridges, B., 'Aboriginal and White Relations in New South Wales 1788–1855', MA, University of Sydney, 1966.

Blundell, V. J., 'Aboriginal Adaption in North West Australia', PhD, University of Wisconsin, 1975.

Brown, R. B., 'A History of the Gilbert River Goldfield, 1869–1874', BA Hons, James Cook University, 1974.

Bury, W. R., 'The Foundations of the Pt McLeay Aboriginal Mission', BA Hons, University of Adelaide, 1964.

Critchett, J. F, 'A History of the Framlingham and Lake Condah Aboriginal Stations, 1860–1918', MA, University of Melbourne, 1980.

Christie, M. F., 'Race Relations between Aborigines and Colonists in Early Victoria, 1835–86', PhD, Monash University, 1978.

Crawford, I. M., 'William Thomas and the Port Phillip Protectorate',

MA, University of Melbourne, 1967.

Curthoys, A., 'Race and Ethnicity: A Study of the Response of British Colonists to Aborigines, Chinese and non-British Europeans in N.S.W. 1856–1881', PhD, Macquarie University, 1973.

Denholm, D., 'Some Aspects of Squatting in New South Wales and Queensland, 1847–1864', PhD, ANU, 1972.

Desailly, B., 'The Mechanics of Genocide', MA, University of Tasmania, 1978.

Eckermann, A. K., 'Half-Caste, Out Caste', PhD, University of Queensland, 1977.

Evans, G., 'Thursday Island, 1878–1914', BA Hons, University of Queensland, 1972.

Evans, K., 'Missionary Effort Towards the Cape York Aborigines, 1886–1910', BA Hons, University of Queensland, 1969.

Evans, R., 'European–Aboriginal Relations in Queensland, 1880–1910', BA Hons, University of Queensland, 1965.

Gale, F., 'A Study in Assimilation: Part Aborigines in South Australia', PhD, University of Adelaide, 1956.

Graves, A. A., 'An Anatomy of Race Relations', BA Hons, University of Adelaide, 1973.

Haebich, A., 'A Bunch of Cast-Offs: Aborigines of the South-West of Western Australia, 1900–1936', PhD, Murdoch University, 1985.

Hardley, R. G., 'Some of the Factors that influenced the Coastal Riverine and Insular Habits of the Aborigines of South-East Queensland and Northern New South Wales', BA Hons, University of Queensland, 1975.

Harrison, B. W., 'The Myall Creek Massacre', BA Hons, University of New England, 1966.

Hartwig, M. C., 'The Coniston Killings', BA Hons, University of Adelaide, 1960.

Hartwig, M. C., 'The Progress of White Settlement in the Alice Springs District and its Effect on the Aboriginal Inhabitants, 1860–1914', PhD, University of Adelaide, 1965.

Hocking, B., 'Native Land Rights', LLM, Monash University, 1970.

Hoskin, G., 'Aboriginal Reserves in Queensland', BA Hons, University of Queensland, 1968.

Hunt, S. J., 'The Gribble Affair: A Study of Australian Labour Relations in North-West Australia during the 1880s', BA Hons, Murdoch University, 1978.

Jenkin, G., 'The Aborigines Friends' Association and the Ngarrindjeri People', MA, University of Adelaide, 1976.

Johnston, S. L., 'The New South Wales Government Policy Towards the Aborigines, 1880–1909', MA, University of Sydney, 1970.

Kirkman, N., 'The Palmer River Goldfield, 1874–1884', BA

Hons, James Cook University, 1984.

Krastins, V., 'The Tiwi: A Culture Contact History of the Australian Aborigines on Bathurst and Melville Islands, 1705–1942', BA Hons, ANU, 1972.

Loos, N. A., 'Aboriginal–European Relations in North Queensland, 1861–1897', PhD, James Cook University, 1976.

Loos, N. A., 'Frontier Conflict in the Bowen District, 1861–1874', MA Qualifying, James Cook University, 1970.

McGrath, A., 'We Grew Up the Stations', PhD, La Trobe University, 1983.

McGregor, R., 'Settling the Black Question: Aborigines in the East Kimberley', BA Hons, James Cook University, 1985.

Milich, C., 'Official Attitudes to the South Australian Aborigines in the 1930s', BA Hons, University of Adelaide, 1967.

Murray-Prior, J., 'Women Settlers and Aborigines', BA Hons, University of New England, 1973.

O'Kelly, G. J., 'The Jesuit Mission Stations in the Northern Territory, 1882–1899', BA Hons, Monash University, 1967.

Pearson, M., 'The MacIntyre Valley: Field Archaeology and Ethnohistory', BA Hons, University of New England, 1973.

Pedersen, H., 'Pigeon: An Aboriginal Rebel', BA Hons, Murdoch University, 1980.

Prentis, M.D., 'Aborigines and Europeans in the Northern Rivers of New South Wales, 1823–1881', MA, Macquarie University, 1972.

Riddett, L. A., 'Kine, Kin and Country: The Victoria River District of the Northern Territory 1911–1966', PhD, James Cook University, 1988.

Rosewarne, S., 'Aborigines in Colonial Queensland', MA, University of Melbourne, 1976.

Rule, M., 'Relations between the Aborigines and Settlers in Selected Areas of the Hunter Valley', BA Hons, University of Newcastle, 1977.

Russo, G. H., 'Bishop Salvado's Plan to Civilize and Christianize the Aborigines, 1846–1900', MA, UWA, 1972.

Ryan, L., 'The Aborigines in Tasmania, 1800–1974', PhD, Macquarie University, 1976.

Sabine, N., 'An Ethnohistory of the Clarence Valley', BA Hons, University of New England, 1970.

Shelmerdine, S., 'The Port Phillip Native Police Corps as an Experiment in Aboriginal Policy and Practice, 1837–1853', BA Hons, University of Melbourne, 1972.

Shepherd, B. W., 'A History of the Pearling Industry of the North-West Coast of Australia', MA, UWA, 1975.

Smith, P., 'Yarrabah, 1892–1910', BA Hons, James Cook University, 1981.

Taylor, J. C., 'Race Relations in South East Queensland', BA Hons, University of Queensland, 1967.

Taylor, N., 'The Native Mounted Police of Queensland, 1850–1900', BA Hons, James Cook University, 1970.

Thorpe, W., 'Archibald Meston and the Aborigines: Ideology and Practice, 1870–1970', BA Hons, University of Queensland, 1978.

Walker, J. A., 'Aboriginal–European Relations in the Maryborough District, 1842–1903', BA Hons, University of Queensland, 1975.

Walker, K. G. T., 'The Letters of the Leslie Brothers in Australia 1834–54', BA Hons, University of Queensland, 1956.

Willmott, J., 'The Pearling Industry in Western Australia, 1850–1916', BA Hons, UWA, 1975.

CONTEMPORARY BOOKS, ARTICLES AND PAMPHLETS

Archer, T., *Recollections of a Rambling Life*, Yokohama, 1897.

Arden, G., *Latest Information with Regard to Australia Felix* etc., Melbourne, 1840.

Atkinson, J., *An Account of the State of Agriculture and Grazing in New South Wales*, London, 1826.

Austin, R., *Journal of Assistant Surveyor R. Austin*, Perth, 1855.

Backhouse, J., *A Narrative of a Visit to the Australian Colonies*, London, 1843.

Bagehot, W., *Physics and Politics*, London, 1872.

Balfour, H., 'On the Method Employed by the Natives of N.W. Australia in the Manufacture of Glass Spear Heads', *Man*, 1903.

Barnard, J., 'Aborigines of Tasmania' *AAAS*, 2, 1890.

Bartlett, T., *New Holland*, London, 1843.

Barton, R. D., *Reminiscences of an Australian Pioneer*, Sydney, 1917.

Bennett, M. M., *Christison of Lammermoor*, London, 1927.

Bennett, S., *The History of Australasian Discovery and Colonization*, Sydney, 1867.

Beveridge, P., *The Aborigines of Victoria and Riverina*, Melbourne, 1889.

Beveridge, P., 'On the Aborigines Inhabiting the . . . Lower Murray, Lower Murrumbidgee, Lower Lachlan and Lower Darling', *Journal of Royal Society of New South Wales*, 17, 1883.

Boldrewood, R., *Old Melbourne Memories*, Melbourne, 1884.

Bond, G., *A Brief Account of the Colony of Port Jackson*, Oxford, 1806.

Bonwick, J., *The Last of the Tasmanians*, London, 1870.

Bonwick, J., *Port Phillip Settlement*, London, 1883.

Bonwick, J., 'The Australian Natives' *JAI*, 16, 1887.

Boyd, A. J., *Old Colonials*, London, 1882.

Bradley, W., *A Voyage to New South Wales*,

1786–92, Sydney, 1969.

Braim, T. H., *A History of New South Wales*, 2 vols, London, 1846.

Breton, W. H., *Excursions in New South Wales, Western Australia and Van Diemens Land*, London, 1833.

Bridge, T. F., *Letters from Victorian Pioneers*, Melbourne, 1898.

Brock, D. G., *To the Desert With Sturt*, Adelaide, 1975.

Brown, P. L., (ed.), *The Narrative of George Russell*, London, 1935.

Bull, J. W., *Early Experiences of Life in South Australia*, Adelaide, 1884.

Bulmer, J., 'Some Account of the Aborigines of the Lower Murray, Wimmera and Maneroo', *Proceedings Royal Geographical Society of Victoria*, 1 (5), March 1888.

Bunbury, H. W., *Early Days in Western Australia*, London, 1930.

The Burke and Wills Exploring Expedition, Melbourne, 1861.

Burkitt, A. N., 'Observations on the Facial Characteristics of the Australian Aborigines', *AAAS*, 18, 1926.

Byerley, F. J., *Narrative of an Overland Expedition*, Brisbane, 1867.

Byrne, J. C., *Twelve Years Wanderings in the British Colonies*, 2 vols, London, 1848.

Calder, J. E., *The Native Tribes of Tasmania*, Hobart, 1875.

Calvert, A. F., *The Aborigines of West Australia*, London, 1894.

Campbell, J., *The Early Settlement of Queensland*, Brisbane, 1936.

Carnegie, D., *Spinifex and Sand*, London 1898.

Carrington, G., *Colonial Adventures and Experiences*, London, 1877.

Carron, W., *Narrative of an Expedition of the late Assistant Surveyor Mr E. B. Kennedy*, Sydney, 1849.

Chester, E., 'Early Days in Albany: Reminiscences of Mr E. Chester', *WAHS*, 1, 1931.

Chewings, E., *Back in the Stone Age*, Sydney, 1936.

Collins, D., *Account of the English Colony of New South Wales, 1798–1804*, 2 vols, London, 1802.

Crawford, J. C., 'The Diary of James Coutts Crawford', *South Australiana*, 1 (2), 1964, 1965.

Curr, E., *An Account of the Colony of Van Diemens Land*, London, 1824.

Curr, E., *The Australian Race; its origin, languages, customs*, 4 vols, Melbourne, 1886–1887.

Curr, E., *Recollections of Squatting in Victoria*, Melbourne, 1883.

Daly, D., *Digging, Squatting and Pioneering Life in the Northern Territory of South Australia*, London, 1887.

Darwin, C., *Journal of Researches* etc., London, 1839.

Davenport, S., 'Letters of Samuel Davenport 1842–1849', *South Australiana*, 6 (10), 1967, 1971.

Dawson, J., *Australian Aborigines; the languages and customs of several tribes of Aborigines in the Western District of Victoria*, Melbourne, 1881.

Dawson, R., *The Present State of Australia*, London, 1830.

De Brebant Cooper, F., *Wild Adventures*

in Australia and New South Wales, London, 1857.

De Satge, E. and O., *Pages from the Journal of a Queensland Squatter*, London, 1901.

Devanny, J., *Travels in North Queensland*, London, 1951.

Doyle, M. (ed.), *Extracts from the Letters and Journals of George Fletcher Moore*, London, 1934.

Dredge, J., *Brief Notices on the Aborigines of New South Wales*, Geelong, 1845.

Dumont d'Urville, J. J., *Voyage de la Corvette L'Astrolabe*, Paris, 1830.

Dunnett, J. S., 'Evaluation in Australia', *Empire Review*, 14, 1907–8.

Durack, P. M., 'Pioneering in the East Kimberleys', *WAHS*, 2 (14), 1933.

Easty, J., *Memorandum of the Transactions of a Voyage from England to Botany Bay*, Sydney, 1865.

Eden, C., *My Wife and I in Queensland*, London, 1872.

Eipper, C., *Statement of the Origin, Condition and Prospects of the German Mission to Aborigines at Moreton Bay*, Sydney, 1841.

Eyre, E. J., *Autobiography and Narrative of Residence and Exploration in Australia, 1832–1839*, ed. and introd. Jill Waterhouse, London, 1984.

Eyre, E. J., *Journals of Expeditions of Discovery*, 2 vols, London, 1845.

Fenwick, J., 'Diary of John Fenwick', *Queensland Heritage*, 2 (3), November 1970.

Field, B., *Geographical Memoirs of New*

South Wales, London, 1825.

Finlayson, Pastor, 'Reminiscences', *RGSSA*, 4, 1902–19.

Fison, L. & A. W. Howitt, *Kamilaroi and Kurnai*, facsimile edition, Oosterhout, 1967.

Flinders, M., *A Voyage to Terra Australis*, 2 vols, London, 1814.

Fraser, J., *The Aborigines of New South Wales*, Sydney, 1892.

Fremantle, C. H., *Diaries and Letters of Admiral Sir C. H. Fremantle*, London, 1928.

Froggatt, W. W., 'Notes on the Natives of West Kimberley, North West Australia', *Proceedings of Linnean Society of New South Wales*, 3, May 1888.

Giles, E., *Australia Twice Traversed*, 2 vols, London, 1889.

Gillen, F. J., 'The Natives of Central Australia', *RGSSA*, 4, 1898–1901.

Grant, J., *The Narrative of a Voyage of Discovery*, London, 1803.

Gray, R., *Reminiscences of India and North Queensland*, London, 1913.

Grey, G., *Journals of Two Expeditions of Discovery*, 2 vols, London, 1841.

Gribble, J. B., *Black but Comely: Aboriginal Life in Australia*, London, 1884.

Gribble, J. B., *Dark Deeds in a Sunny Land*, Perth, 1905.

Griffith, C., *The Present State and Prospects of the Port Phillip District*, Dublin, 1845.

Hale, M. B., *The Aborigines of Australia*, London, *c*.1889.

Hall, T., *A Short History of the Downs*

Blacks, Warwick, n.d.

Harris, A., *Settlers and Convicts*, 2nd edn, Melbourne, 1954.

Hawker, J. C., *Early Experiences in South Australia*, Adelaide, 1899.

Haydon, G. H., *Five Years Experience in Australia Felix*, London, 1846.

Haygarth, H. W., *Recollections of Bush Life in Australia*, London, 1848.

Henderson, C. C., 'The Mutation Theory of Evolution in History', *AAAS*, 13, 1912.

Henderson, J., *Excursions and Adventures in New South Wales*, 2 vols, London, 1851.

Henderson, J., *Observations on the Colonies of New South Wales and Van Diemens Land*, Calcutta, 1832.

Hives, F., *The Journal of a Jackeroo*, London, 1930.

Hodgen, M. T., *Early Anthropology in the Sixteenth and Seventeenth Century*, Philadelphia, n.d.

Hodgkinson, C., *Australia: From Port Macquarie to Moreton Bay*, London, 1845.

Hogson, C. P., *Reminiscences of Australia*, London, 1846.

Horne, G. & G. Aiston, *Savage Life in Central Australia*, London, 1924.

Hovell, W., 'Journal of a Journey from Lake George to Port Phillip, 1824–25', *JRAHS*, 7, 1921.

Howitt, A. W., *The Native Tribes of South-East Australia*, London, 1904.

Howitt, R., *Impressions of Australia Felix*, London, 1845.

Hull, H. M., *Experience of Forty Years in Tasmania*, London, 1859.

Hunter, J., *An Historical Journal of Events at Sydney and at Sea, 1787–1792*, Sydney, 1968.

Huxley, T. H., *Evidence as to Man's Place in Nature*, London, 1863.

Irwin, F. C., *The State and Position of West Australia*, London, 1835.

Jack, R. L., *Northmost Australia*, 2 vols, London, 1921.

Jorgensen, J., 'A Shred of Autobiography', *Hobart Town Almanack and Van Diemens Land Annual*, 1838.

Journal of Several Expeditions Made in Western Australia, London, 1833.

Jukes, J. B., *Narrative of the Surveying Voyage of HMS Fly*, London, 1847.

Kennedy, E. B., *The Black Police of Queensland*, London, 1902.

Kennedy, E. B., 'Extracts from the Journal of an Exploring Expedition into Central Australia', *JRGS*, 22, 1852.

Kennedy, E. B., *Four Years in Queensland*, London, 1870.

King, P. P., *Narrative of a Survey of the Inter-tropical and Western Coast of Australia*, 2 vols, London, 1827.

Kirby, J., *Old Times in the Bush in Australia*, Melbourne, 1894.

Kittle, S., *A Concise History of the Colony and Natives of New South Wales*, Edinburgh, 1816.

Knight, J. J., *In the Early Days*, Brisbane, 1895.

Labillardiere, M., *Voyage in Search of La Perouse, 1791–1794*, London, 1800.

Landor, E. W., *The Bushman or Life in*

a New Country, London, 1847.

Lang, G. S., The Aborigines of Australia, Melbourne, 1865.

Lang, J. D., Queensland, London, 1861.

Lawrence, W., Lectures on Comparative Anatomy, London, 1819.

Leichhardt, L., Journal of an Overland Expedition, London, 1847.

Leichhardt, F. W. L., The Letters of F.W. Ludwig Leichhardt, collected, translated and edited by M. Auroussean, 2 vols, Cambridge, 1968.

Lindsay, D., Journal of the Elder Scientific Exploring Expedition, 1891–2, Adelaide, 1892.

Lloyd, G. T., Thirty-three Years in Tasmania and Victoria, London, 1862.

Loyau, G. E., The History of Maryborough, Brisbane, 1897.

Lubbock, J., Pre-Historic Times, London, 1865.

Lumholtz C., Among Cannibals, London, 1889.

Lumholtz, C., 'Among the Natives of Australia', Journal of American Geographical Society, 21, 1889.

MacAllister, D., 'The Australian Aborigines', Melbourne Review, 3, 1878.

McCombie, T., Essays on Colonization, London, 1850.

McCombie, T., The History of the Colony of Victoria, Melbourne, 1858.

McCrae, G. C., 'The Early Settlement of the Eastern Shores of Port Phillip Bay', Victorian Historical Magazine, 1, 1911.

MacGillivray, J., Narrative of the Voyage of HMS Rattlesnake, London, 1852.

Mackaness, G. (ed.), Fourteen Journeys Over the Blue Mountains of NSW, 1813–41, Sydney, 1965.

Mackay, R., Recollections of Early Gippsland Goldfields, Traralgon, 1916.

McKillop, D., 'Anthropological Notes on the Aboriginal Tribes of the Daly River, North Australia', RGSSA, 5, 1893.

McKinlay, W., McKinlays Journal of Exploration, Melbourne, 1862.

McLaren, J., My Crowded Solitude, Sun Books edition, Melbourne, 1966.

McLean, J., 'Police Experiences with the Natives', RGSSA, 6, 1902–1903.

MacPherson, A., Mount Abundance, London, 1897.

Major, T., Leaves from a Squatters Notebook, London, 1900.

Mann. J. F., Eight Months with Dr Leichhardt, Sydney, 1888.

Mathew, J., Eaglehawk and Crow, London, 1899.

Mathew, J., Two Representative Tribes of Queensland, London, 1910.

Melville, H., The History of the Island of Van Diemens Land, London, 1835.

Merivale, H., Lectures on Colonization and Colonies, 2nd edn, London, 1928.

Meston, A., Geographical History of Queensland, Brisbane, 1895.

Meyrick, F J., Life in the Bush, 1840–47, London, 1939.

Mitchell, T. L., Journal of an Expedition into the Interior of Tropical

Australia, London, 1848.

Mitchell, T. L., *Three Expeditions into Eastern Australia*, 2 vols, London, 1834.

Moore, G. F., *Diary of Ten Years Eventfull Life of an Early Settler in West Australia*, London, 1884.

Moore, G. F., *A Descriptive Vocabulary of the Language in Common Usage Amongst the Aborigines of West Australia*, London, 1842.

Morgan, J., *The Life and Adventures of William Buckley*, ed. C. E. Sayers, London, 1967.

Morrell, J., *Sketch of a Residence Among the Aborigines of North Queensland*, Brisbane, 1863.

Morris, E. E., *A Dictionary of Austral English*, London, 1898.

Mudie, R., *The Picture of Australasia*, London, 1829.

Newland, S., *Memoirs of Simpson Newland*, Adelaide, 1928.

Newland, S., 'The Parkinjees or the Aboriginal Tribes on the Darling River', *RGSSA*, 2, 1887–1888.

Newland, S., 'Some Aborigines I Have Known', *RGSSA*, 1894–1895.

Nicolay, C. G., *The Handbook of Western Australia*, London, 1896.

Nott, J. C., & G. R. Gliddon, *Types of Mankind*, London, 1864.

Ogle, N., *The Colony of Western Australia*, London, 1839.

Oxley, J., *Journals of Two Expeditions into the Interior of New South Wales*, London, 1820.

Paine, D., *The Journal of Daniel Paine 1794–1797*, ed. R. J. Knight & A. Frost, Sydney, 1983.

Palmerston, C., 'Diary of Christie Palmerston', *Queensland Heritage*, 1 (8), May 1968.

Parker, E. S., *The Aborigines of Australia*, Melbourne, 1854.

Parker, K. L., *The Euahlayi Tribe*, London, 1905.

Peron, M. F., *A Voyage of Discovery to the Southern Hemisphere*, London, 1809.

Petrie, T., *Reminiscences of Early Queensland*, Brisbane, 1932.

Pitt-Rivers, A. C. F., *The Evolution of Culture*, Oxford, 1906.

Pitts, H., *The Australian Aborigines and the Christian Church*, London, 1914.

Plomley, N. J. B. (ed.), *Friendly Mission: The Tasmanian Journals and Papers of George Augustus Robinson, 1829–1834*, Hobart, 1966.

Porteus, S. D., 'Mentality of Australian Aborigines', *Oceania*, 4, 1933.

Praed, R. C., *Australian Life, Black and White*, London, 1885.

Pridden, W., *Australia, Its History and Present Condition*, London, 1843.

Pulleine, P. & H. Woolard, 'Physiological and Mental Observations on the Australian Aborigines', *Proceedings Royal Society of South Australia*, 54, 1930.

Ramsay-Smith, W., 'The Place of the Australian Aboriginal in Recent Anthropological Research', *AAAS*, 22, 1908.

Reilly, J. T., *Reminiscences of Fifty Years Residence in West Australia*, Perth, 1903.

Richardson, A. R., *Early Memoirs of the Great Nor-West*, Perth, 1914.

Richmond, F., *Queensland in the 'Seventies': Reminiscences of the Early Days of a Young Clergyman*, Singapore, 1927.

Ridley, W., *Kamilaroi and Other Australian Languages*, 2nd edn, Sydney, 1875.

Roberts, N., 'The Victorian Aborigine As He Is', *AAAS*, 14, 1913.

Robertson, W., *Cooee Talks*, Sydney, 1928.

Rolleston, H. D., 'Description of the Cerebral Hemispheres of an Adult Australian Male', *JAI*, 17, 1887.

Ross, J., 'The Settler in Van Diemens Land Fourteen Years Ago', *Hobart Town Almanack*, 1836.

Roth, H. L., *The Aborigines of Tasmania*, 2nd edn, Halifax, 1899.

Roth, W. G., *Ethnographical Studies Among the North-West-Central Queensland Aborigines*, Brisbane, 1897.

Rusden, G. W., *History of Australia*, 3 vols, London, 1883.

Russell, H. S., *The Genesis of Queensland*, Sydney, 1888.

Sadlier, R., *The Aborigines of Australia*, Sydney, 1883.

Schurmann, C. W., *Vocabulary of the Parnkalla Language*, Adelaide, 1844.

Searcey, A., *In Australian Tropics*, London, 1907.

Searcey, A., *In Northern Seas*, Adelaide, 1905.

Semon, R., *In the Australian Bush*, London, 1899.

Shann, E. O. G., *Cattle Chosen*, London, 1926.

Shenton, E., 'Reminiscences of Perth 1830–1840', *WAHS*, 1(1), 1927.

Siebert, O., 'Sagen und Sitten der Dieri und Nachbarstämme in Zentral-Australien', *Globus*, 47, 1916.

Sinnett, F., *The Rush to Port Curtis*, Geelong, 1859.

Smith, C., *The Booandick Tribe of South Australian Aborigines*, Adelaide, 1880.

Smyth, A. B., *The Journal of Arthur Bowes Smyth, 1787–1789*, ed. P. Fidcon, Sydney, 1979.

Smyth, R. B., *The Aborigines of Victoria*, 2 vols, Melbourne, 1876.

Spencer, H., 'Comparative Psychology of Man', *JAI*, 5, 1876.

Spencer, H., *The Principles of Sociology*, London, 1876.

Spiller, G., 'The Mentality of the Australian Aborigines', *The Sociological Review*, 6, 1913.

Stevenson, J. B., *Seven Years in the Australian Bush*, Liverpool, 1880.

Stokes, J. L., *Discoveries in Australia*, 2 vols, London, 1846.

Streeter, E. W., *Pearls and Pearling Life*, London, 1886.

Stuart, J. M., *Explorations Across the Continent of Australia 1861–1862*, Melbourne, 1863.

Sturt, C., *Narrative of an Expedition into Central Australia*, 2 vols, London, 1849.

Sturt, C., *Two Expeditions into the Interior of Southern Australia*, 2 vols, London, 1833.

Sutherland, A. G., *Victoria and Its Metropolis*, Melbourne, 1888.

Sutherland, G., *Pioneering Days: Across the Wilds of Queensland*, Brisbane, 1913.

Taplin, G., *The Narrinyeri, their Manners and Customs*, Adelaide, 1878.

Taplin, G. (ed.), *The Folklore, Manners, Customs and Languages of the South Australian Aborigines*, Adelaide, 1879.

Taunton, H., *Australind*, London, 1903.

Teichelmann, C. G., *Outlines of a Grammar, Vocabulary and Phraseology of the Aboriginal Language of South Australia*, Adelaide, 1840.

Tench, W., *Sydney's First Four Years*, introd. by L. F. Fitzhardinge, Sydney, 1961.

Threlkeld, L. E., *An Australian Language*, Sydney, 1892.

Threlkeld, L. E., *Australian Reminiscences and Papers*, ed. N. Gunson, Canberra, 1974.

Tietkins, W. H., *Journal of the Central Australian Exploring Expedition*, Adelaide, 1891.

Tuckey, J. H., *An Account of a Voyage to Establish a Colony at Port Phillip*, London, 1805.

Turnbull, J., *A Voyage Round the World* etc., 2nd edn, London, 1813.

Vogan, A. J., *The Black Police*, London, 1890.

Vogt, C., *Lectures of Man*, London, 1864.

Wake, C. S., 'The Mental Characteristics of Primitive Man, as Exemplified by the Australian Aborigines', *JAI*, 1, 1872.

Walker, J. B., *Early Tasmania*, Hobart, 1902.

Wallace, A. R., 'Mr Wallace on Natural Selection Applied to Anthropology', *Anthropological Review*, 16, 1867.

Wallace, A. R., 'The Action of Natural Selection on Man', *Half Hours with Modern Scientists*, New Haven, 1873.

Warburton, P., *Journey Across the Western Interior of Australia*, London, 1875.

Ward, A., *The Miracle of Mapoon*, London, 1908.

Welsby, T., *Collected Works*, 2 vols, Brisbane, 1907.

West, J., *History of Tasmania*, 2 vols, Launceston, 1852.

Westgarth, W., *Australia Felix*, Edinburgh, 1848.

Westgarth, W., *Australia*, Edinburgh, 1861.

Westgarth, W., *A Report on the Condition, Capabilities and Prospects of the Australian Aborigines*, Melbourne, 1846.

Westgarth, W., *Tracks of McKinlay and Party Across Australia*, London, 1863.

White, C., *An Account of the Regular Gradation in Man*, London, 1799.

Widowson, H., *The Present State of Van Diemens Land*, London, 1829.

Willshire, W. H., *The Aborigines of Central Australia*, Adelaide, 1891.

Wilson, T. B., *Narrative of a Voyage Round the World*, London, 1835

Windsor-Earl, G., 'On the Aboriginal

Tribes of the North Coast of Australia', *JRGS*, 16, 1846.

Windsor-Earl, G., *Enterprise in Tropical Australia*, London, 1846.

Withnell, J. G., *The Customs and Traditions of the Aboriginal Natives of North-Western Australia*, Roebourne, 1901.

Wild, J. J., Outlines of Anthropology, *AAAS*, 1, 1889.

Wood, K. M., 'A Pioneer Pearler – Reminiscences of John Wood', *WAHS*, 2 (12).

Woods, J. D. (ed.), *The Native Tribes of South Australia*, Adelaide, 1879.

Worgan, G. B., *Journal of a First Fleet Surgeon*, Sydney, 1978.

Young, S. B., 'Reminiscences of Mrs Susan Bundarre Young', *JRAHS*, 8, 1923.

Zillman, J. H. L., *Past and Present Australian Life*, London, 1889.

Modern Books, Articles

Allen, J., 'The Archaeology of Nineteenth Century British Imperialism', *World Archaeology*, 5 (1), June 1973.

Anderson, C., 'Aboriginal Economy and Contact Relations at Bloomfield River, North Queensland', *Australian Institute of Aboriginal Studies Newsletter*, 12, September 1979.

Anderson, R. H., 'The Effect of Settlement upon the New South Wales Flora', *Proceedings, Linnean Society of New South Wales*, 66, 1941.

Bach, J., 'The Political Economy of Pearl Shelling', *Economic History Review*, 14 (1), 1961.

Bain, M. A., *Full Fathoms Five*, Perth, 1982.

Baker, S. J., *The Australian Language*, Melbourne, 1966.

Bardsley, J., *Across the Years: Jane Bardsley's Outback Letterbook, 1896–1936*, ed. J. A. Young, Sydney, 1987.

Barwick, D., 'Coranderrk and Cumeroogunga' in T. Epstein (ed.), *Opportunity and Response*, London, 1972.

Basedow, H., *The Australian Aboriginal*, Adelaide, 1925.

Bates, D., *The Passing of the Aborigines*, London, 1938.

Bennett, M. M., *The Australian Aborigine as a Human Being*, London, 1930.

Bern, J., 'Ideology and Domination', *Oceania*, 50 (2), December 1979.

Berndt, R. M., 'A Preliminary Report of Fieldwork in the Ooldea Region', *Oceania*, 13, 1942–43.

Berndt, R. M., 'Surviving Influence of Mission Contact on the Daly River', *Neue Zeitschrift für Missionswissenschaft*, 8 (2–3), 1952.

Berndt, R. M. & C. H., *Arnhem Land: Its History and Its People*, Melbourne, 1954.

Berndt, R. M. & C. H., *From Black to White in South Australia*, Melbourne, 1951.

Biskup, P., *Not Slaves, Not Citizens: The Aboriginal Problem in Western*

Australia 1898–1954, St Lucia, 1973.

Blainey, G., *Triumph of the Nomads*, Melbourne, 1975.

Black, J., *North Queensland Pioneers*, Townsville, n.d.

Bridges, B., 'The Colonization of Australia: A Communication', *Teaching History*, November 1977.

Bridges, B., 'The Aborigines and the Land Question in New South Wales', *JRAHS*, 56 (2), June 1970.

Bridges, B., 'Pemulwy: A Noble Savage', *Newsletter of the Royal Australian Historical Society*, 88, 1970.

Bridges, B., 'The Native Police Corps, Port Phillip District and Victoria 1837–53', *JRAHS*, 57 (2), June 1971.

Broome, R., *Aboriginal Australians*, Sydney, 1982.

Campbell, A. H., *John Batman and the Aborigines*, Malmsbury, 1988.

Chase, A. K. & J. R. Von Sturmer, 'Mental Man and Social Evolutionary Theory', in G. E. Kearney et al., *The Psychology of Aboriginal Australians*, Sydney, 1973.

Christie, M. F., *Aborigines in Colonial Victoria*, Sydney, 1979.

Corris, P., *Aborigines and Europeans in Western Victoria*, Canberra, 1963.

Coutts, P. J. et al., 'Impact of European Settlement on Aboriginal Society in Western Victoria', *Records of the Victoria Archaeological Survey*, 4, August 1977.

Cribbin, J., *The Killing Times:*

The Coniston Massacre 1928, Sydney, 1984.

Davies, M., 'Settlers and Aborigines at Port Lincoln 1840–45', *South Australiana*, 18, 1979.

Docker, E. C., *Simply Human Beings*, Brisbane, 1964.

Donaldson, I. & T., *Seeing the First Australians*, Sydney, 1985.

Durack, M., *Kings in Grass Castles*, London, 1979.

Durack, M., *Sons in the Saddle*, London, 1983.

Evans, R. et al., *Exclusions, Exploitation and Extermination*, Sydney, 1975.

Farwell, G., *Land of Mirage*, London, 1950.

Fels, M., *Good Men and True: The Aboriginal Police of the Port Phillip District 1837–1853*, Melbourne, 1988.

Frost, A., 'New South Wales *terra nullius*: the British denial of Aboriginal land rights', *HS*, 19, 1981.

Gale, F., *A Study of Assimilation: Part Aborigines in South Australia*, Adelaide, 1964.

Gardner, P., 'The Journals of De Villiers and Warman', *Victorian Historical Journal*, 50, 1979.

Gardner, P., 'The Warrigal Creek Massacre', *JRAHS*, 66, 1980.

Gill, A., 'Aborigines, Settlers and Police in the Kimberleys 1887–1905', *Studies in Western Australian History*, 1, 1977.

Green, N., 'Aboriginal and Settler Conflict in Western Australia, 1826–1852', *The Push from the Bush*, 3, May 1979.

Green, N., *Broken Spears: Aborigines and Europeans in the Southwest of Australia*, Perth, 1984.

Gunson, N. (ed.), *Australian Reminiscences and Papers of L. E. Threlkeld*, Canberra, 1974.

Haddon, A. C., *Head Hunters: Black, White and Brown*, London, 1932.

Hallam, S., *Fire and Hearth*, Canberra, 1975.

Hamilton, A., 'Blacks and Whites: The Relationships of Change', *Arena*, 30, 1972.

Hamman, J., 'The Coorong Massacre', *Flinders Journal of Politics and History*, 3, 1973.

Hancock, W. K., *Australia*, Jacaranda edn, Brisbane, 1960.

Hasluck, A., 'Yagan the Patriot', *WAHS*, 7, 1961.

Hasluck, P., *Black Australians*, Melbourne, 1942.

Hassell, E., *My Dusky Friends*, Fremantle, 1975.

Haynes, B. T., *West Australian Aborigines, 1622–1972*, Perth, 1973.

Hercus, L., 'Tales of Nadu-Dagali (Rib-Bone Billy)', *Aboriginal History*, 1 (1), 1977.

Holthouse, H., *S'pose I Die: The Story of Evelyn Maunsell*, Sydney, 1973.

Hughes, I., 'A State of Open Warfare', *Lectures on North Queensland History*, 2nd series, Townsville, 1975.

Hunt, S., *Spinifex and Hessian*, Perth, 1936.

Hutchison, D. E. (ed.), *Aboriginal Progress: A New Era?*, Perth, 1969.

Inglis, J., 'One Hundred Years of Point Macleay, South Australia', *Mankind*, 5 (12), November 1962.

Loos, N. A., *Invasion and Resistance*, Canberra, 1982.

Markus, A., *From the Barrel of a Gun*, Melbourne, 1974.

May, D., *From Bush to Station*, Townsville, 1983.

McBride, I. (ed.), *Records of Time Past*, Canberra, 1978.

McMahon, A., 'Tasmanian Aboriginal Women as Slaves', *THRA*, 23 (2), June 1976.

The Mapoon Story According to the Invaders, Sydney, 1975.

Mattingley, C. (ed.), *Survival in Our Land*, Adelaide, 1989.

Mulvaney, D. J., 'The Ascent of Man: Howitt as Anthropologist', in M. H. Walker, *Come Wind, Come Weather*, Melbourne, 1971, pp. 285–312.

Mulvaney, D. J. & J. Golson, *Aboriginal Man and Environment in Australia*, Canberra, 1971.

Mulvaney, D. J., *The Pre-history of Australia*, rev. edn, Ringwood, 1975.

Murray-Smith, S., 'Beyond the Pale: The Islander Communities of Bass Strait in the Nineteenth Century', *THRA*, 20 (4), December 1973.

Olbrei, E. (ed.), *Black Australians: The Prospects for Change*, Townsville, 1982.

Plomley N. J. B. (ed.), *Weep in Silence*, Hobart, 1987.

Pope, A., 'Aboriginal Adaption to Early Colonial Labour Markets',

Labour History, 54, May 1988.

Reid, G., *A Nest of Hornets: The Massacre of the Fraser Family at Hornet Bank Station, Central Queensland, 1857*, Melbourne, 1982.

Reynolds, H., 'Jimmy Governor and Jimmie Blacksmith', *Australian Literary Studies*, 9 (1), May 1979.

Reynolds, H., 'The Unrecorded Battlefields of Queensland', *Race Relations in North Queensland*, Townsville, 1978.

Roughsey, D., *Moon and Rainbow*, Sydney, 1971.

Rowley, C. D., 'Aborigines and Other Australians', *Oceania*, 32 (4), 1962.

Rowley, C. D., *The Destruction of Aboriginal Society*, Melbourne, 1972.

Rowley, C. D., *The Remote Aborigines*, Melbourne, 1972.

Rowley, C. D., *Outcasts in White Australia*, Melbourne, 1972.

Ryan, L., 'The Struggle for Recognition: Part Aborigines in Tasmania in the Nineteenth Century', *Aboriginal History*, 1 (1), 1977.

Skinner, L. E., *Police of the Pastoral Frontier*, St Lucia, 1975.

Spencer, B., *Native Tribes of the Northern Territory of Australia*, London, 1914.

Spencer, B., *Wanderings in Wild Australia*, 2 vols, London, 1928.

Spencer, B. & F. J. Gillen, *Across Australia*, London, 1912.

Spencer, B. & F. J. Gillen, *The Arunta*, London, 1922.

Spencer, B. & F. J. Gillen, *The Native Tribes of Central Australia*, Dover edn, New York, 1968.

Stanner, W. E. H., *After the Dreaming*, Sydney, 1969.

Thorpe, O., *First Catholic Mission to the Australian Aborigines*, Sydney, 1949.

Threadgill, B., *South Australian Land Exploration, 1856–1880*, Adelaide, 1922.

Tindale, N. B., 'A Survey of the Half-Caste Problem in South Australia', *RGSSA*, 42, 1940–41.

Tipping M. (ed.), *Ludwig Becker*, Melbourne, 1979.

Wade-Broun, N., *Memoirs of a Queensland Pioneer*, Sandgate, 1944.

Walker, M. M., *Come Wind, Come Weather*, Melbourne, 1971.

Watson, D., *Caledonia Australis: Scottish Highlanders on the Frontiers Australia*, Sydney, 1984.

Wegner, J., 'The Aborigines of the Etheridge Shire' in H. Reynolds (ed.), *Race Relations in North Queensland*, Townsville, 1979.

Willey, K., *Boss Driver*, Adelaide, 1971.

Woolmington, J., *Aborigines in Colonial Society, 1788–1850*, Melbourne, 1973.

Wright, J., *The Cry for the Dead*, Melbourne, 1981.

Yarwood, A. T. & M. J. Knowling, *Race Relations in Australia*, North Ryde, 1982.

INDEX